Leonard M[...]

Dec 24 1942

OLD CIVILIZATIONS
OF THE NEW WORLD

Old Civilizations
of the
New World

BY A. HYATT VERRILL

Author of *Lost Treasure, Great Conquerors*
of South and Central America, etc.

THE NEW HOME LIBRARY
NEW YORK

THE NEW HOME LIBRARY EDITION PUBLISHED SEPTEMBER, 1942

THE NEW HOME LIBRARY, 14 West Forty-ninth Street
New York, N. Y.

CL
PRINTED IN THE UNITED STATES OF AMERICA

PREFACE

THE story of man in America, the mystery of his origin in the New World, the history of the rise and fall of remarkable cultures and civilizations older than those of Egypt, form a fascinating tale. Unfortunately, it is a tale little known to the average man or woman. Much has been written and published on the subject, but generally it has been neither interesting nor available to the layman. Most of the works have been of a strictly scientific or technical character; usually each volume, monograph or pamphlet has been devoted exclusively to some certain race, ruin or other phase of the matter, and the ordinary mortal who might seek to acquire even a superficial knowledge of prehistoric civilizations and aboriginal races in America would be compelled to peruse innumerable tomes, pamphlets and reports. Even then it is doubtful if he would learn a great deal, for only the professional ethnologist, archeologist or anthropologist can grasp the meanings of works filled with purely scientific terms.

A few books of a popular character dealing with certain localities or races have appeared, as for example Prescott's *Conquest of Peru,* but unfortunately in most of these the actual facts are largely hidden under an overburden of romance and legend.

As far as I am aware, and I believe I possess a

rather complete knowledge in this respect, no book
hitherto has treated of the entire subject of early
man in America, the prehistoric civilizations and
their remains, in a wholly popular manner. To do
this has been my aim in writing the present volume.
The purpose of the book is to give an accurate, un-
biased and unvarnished account of what we actually
know of the origin of man in America, his development, his early cultures and his civilizations; his arts,
sciences, customs, religions, governments, engineering feats, and, in fact, everything of human interest,
together with the causes of his downfall and the condition of his present-day descendants.

Obviously it would be impossible to cover fully
or even to mention every fact, detail or phase of such
a voluminous subject, or to describe all the races, with
their divisions and subdivisions, who approached anything that might be considered a culture or a civilized
state in America. Even were it possible, to do so
would result in a great amount of repetition and
would only prove confusing to the reader.

I have therefore confined myself to the principal
races and civilizations, and have attempted to present
a comprehensive and easily understood survey of the
subject. Wherever possible I have avoided using
technical or scientific terms. At times, however, this
has proved impossible, for in many cases there are
no recognized names or terms which can be applied,
aside from those coined and employed by specialists
in the fields of ethnology and archeology.

Also, I have refrained from expressing definite
opinions concerning many questions upon which
scientists do not agree, except in a few cases wherein

my own observations and discoveries entitle me to
my own theories and conclusions.

Otherwise, wherever or whenever a matter has not
unanimously been agreed on, I have given the known
facts, have outlined the various theories or suppositions advanced and held by the most prominent authorities on the subjects, and have left it to my
readers to accept whichever theory they prefer.

In many cases one is as good as another, and if
no one can positively state that a thing is so, neither
can any one definitely declare that it is *not* so.

Much of the material embodied in the book is the
result of my own work, investigations and observations made during many years of field work in
ethnology and archeology for the Museum of the
American Indian, Heye Foundation, of New York
City. Much has been secured from various authorities and from practically all available works on the
subject; more than eight hundred books, monographs,
maps, pamphlets, documents, reports, letters, codices
and histories in Europe and the United States have
been read and studied. A great deal of information
and many facts also have been secured through a
study of the collections in the Museum of the
American Indian, the American Museum of Natural
History; the National Museum at Washington; the
Larco-Herera Museum at Lima; the Museo Nacional of Peru; the Museo Nacional at San José, Costa
Rica; the British Museum; the Museum of the
University of Cuzco, Peru; the Museo Nacional at
La Paz, Bolivia; and many others, in addition to
numerous private collections in South and Central
America, in Europe and in the United States.

Without the free and hearty cooperation of many scientific friends and acquaintances, the preparation of this book would have been impossible, and I wish to take this opportunity of expressing my thanks and appreciation to all those who so kindly have aided me but who are so numerous that it is impossible to mention them by name.

A. HYATT VERRILL

CONTENTS

Theories of man's origin in America. Old and New World mammals. New and Old World domestic birds and animals. Birds of the Eastern and Western Hemispheres. Conclusions we can and cannot draw from these. Similarity of vegetation in Old and New World. Cultivated plants. Insects, reptiles, fish, etc. Common origin. Diffusion. Independent origin. Land connections. Is man indigenous to America? The question of anthropoid apes. Creation or evolution. Theories of man's migration to America. Age of man in America. Geographical alterations. Arguments in rebuttal. Intercourse between America and the Pacific islands. Variation in types and races. Isolated developments. Unique cultures. Ancient myths. Unsupported theories. An involved question. Superiority of American arts.

When culture began. Beginning of cultural influence. Evolution of culture. Duplication and its reasons. Tribal cultures. Common features. Environment, etc. Effects of locality, etc. Nomads and sedentary races. Varying conditions of life. Physical development. Influences not proof of relationships. Trading. Examples of observed influences. Changes in habits. Nomadic tribes' limitation. Geographical and other conditions. Wide variation in American races who developed civilizations. Attainments and characters. Development through necessity. Cave-dwellers to Pueblos. Extent of Pueblo development. Why ancient American civilizations were developed. A question of temperament. Imagination and art. Esthetic progress. Religions and their effects.

CONTENTS—*Continued*

CONTENTS—*Continued*

CONTENTS—*Continued*

CONTENTS—*Continued*

OLD CIVILIZATIONS
OF THE NEW WORLD

OLD CIVILIZATIONS OF THE NEW WORLD

CHAPTER I

THE ORIGIN OF MAN IN AMERICA

No ONE can conclusively state who were the first human beings to inhabit America. Neither can any one say whence or when these first men came; nor indeed whether they came at all or originated here.

Innumerable theories have been advanced to account for the presence of the so-called aboriginal Americans, or, as they are more commonly called, Indians, in the New World. Many of these theories appear to have excellent arguments to support them, but if we study them with an open mind, we will find almost if not fully as many arguments in rebuttal. Thus, the marsupials are confined to America and Australia and we might reasonably assume that this fact goes far toward proving some prehistoric connection between the two continents. Likewise, as the only living species of tapirs are those of South America and Malaysia we might assume some ancient direct connection between these two countries. On the other hand, we might argue that as camels, elephants, rhinoceri and hippopotami are found only in Africa and Asia, we have proof that there was no connection between those continents and America. But we must remember that while there are no living representatives of these creatures in the New World, there were many species inhabiting America in pre-historic days, as is proved by their fossil remains. The presence of any group of animals in widely separated areas merely proves that, for some un-known reasons, certain individuals or species of one group escaped the utter extinction suffered by other groups. Also, in many cases, evolution, due to environment or other causes, so changed the descendants of the original groups that they are scarcely recognizable. Thus the llamas, alpacas, vicuñas and guanacos are all camels, although dif-ferent from ordinary camels in outward appear-ance. Neither must we overlook the fact that there are far more forms common to America, Asia and Europe than to Africa or Australia and America. Our bison and the European bison are closely related. We have the caribou which to the ordinary observer is indistinguishable from the reindeer of Asia and Europe. The American moose and the Old World elk are very much alike, and there are few European or Asiatic mammals or birds that are not represented by closely related species in America. But it is a significant fact that, with few exceptions, all these are distinct species with characteristics which must have required countless ages for development. This proves beyond denial that any direct terrestrial bridge which may have existed between the New and the Old Worlds must have existed in the most remote times, and as far as we know long before man's presence.

We have still further proof of this in the birds. Thus the humming-birds are confined solely to America, as are the toucans, trogans and many other

birds, while the hornbills, birds-of-paradise, hoopoes
and other families are restricted to the Old World.
This is more surprising inasmuch as birds migrate
and wander for far greater distances than do mammals, and are not by nature obliged to follow land
routes. No one can explain why such birds as humming-birds should be confined to one of the hemispheres, whereas parrots, although they do not
possess such powers of flight as the humming-birds,
are found all over the world. So when we begin to
seek proof of man's migrations or origin by studying
the mammalian or bird fauna of various countries we
come face to face with facts which are if anything
more inexplicable than the riddle we are attempting
to solve.

The same is more or less true of the flora. While
many closely related species of plants occur on the
American continent and in Asia or Europe, there are
fully as many which are confined to one of these continents and which have no representatives, as species,
genera or even orders, in the others. The same is
true to greater or lesser extent of the insects, mollus-
ca, reptiles, fish and lowest forms of invertebrates.
Each hemisphere has certain species peculiar to itself
but closely allied to those of the other hemisphere, and
both have forms which have no counterparts elsewhere. The question therefore is: can we assume
that all had a common origin, that all were carried far
and wide in ancient times and gradually became differentiated through environment and other causes, or
can we assume that like conditions begot like results
and that evolution in the animal and plant world proceeded more or less similarly throughout the world?

If we accept the former theory, we can accept the theory that man also migrated to America from some part of the Old World; but if we believe the latter supposition, then we can equally well maintain that human beings also were evolved or created and developed quite independently in the New World as well as in the old. In all probability there is truth in both theories, for only in that way can we account for the similarity of some forms of life and the entire absence of others.

Unquestionably, at one time in the history of the world, there were either direct land connections or a series of islands between the two hemispheres. Whether or not these existed after human beings had appeared on earth, or whether they connected America and Oceania, America and Africa or America and Europe and Asia no one can state definitely. Probably there were migrations of human beings from one hemisphere to another. In fact, we have almost positive proof of that fact. But that does not prove that man may not have originated in America as well as anywhere else. Those who pooh-pooh the suggestion that man was evolved or created in the New World point to the fact that no anthropoid apes, either modern or fossil, have been found in America. But that is not proof that such remains may not exist, nor that, for some reason unknown, such remains existed but were not preserved as fossils, nor that the area such apes may have inhabited long ago may not have vanished below the sea. That anthropoid apes do not occur in America and that their fossil remains have not been discovered here no more prove that such creatures did not exist nor that man did not evolve here than the fact that marsupials are confined to Australia and America proves a direct connection between these two continents. And for those who have no faith in the theory of evolution, there is of course no reason why man should not have been created in one place as well as in another, or for that matter in a dozen or more localities independently.

On the other hand, if we consider the theories of man having migrated to America from oversea, we run against innumerable facts which both prove and disprove the suppositions. In my boyhood days it was a generally accepted conclusion that the American Indians, from the Arctic to Cape Horn and from the Atlantic to the Pacific, were all descendants of Asiatics who, at some former period, crossed over from one continent to the other via Bering Strait. But there were many arguments against this theory and many stumbling-blocks for those who held to it. Then a theory was advanced wherein it was maintained that many if not all of the Indian races' ancestors had reached America from northern Europe via Greenland. Others have claimed that Atlantis was no myth but a reality, and that the aborigines of America are descended from the inhabitants of that lost continent. Some authorities have satisfied themselves that the South Sea Islands, or some long-submerged archipelago in the South Pacific, were the localities whence the first men and women migrated to the New World; others argue in favor of some long-vanished mid-Pacific continent; still others claim that the Indians belong to the lost tribes of Israel; while some persons have brought forth plausible arguments to prove that the forebears of the red men were the hardy Norse Vikings. A vast amount of breath, and a veritable sea of ink have been wasted, life-long friendships have been sacrificed and countless fortunes have been spent over this one question, but without definite results.

After all, why should any one try to prove that all the aborigines of America had a common origin? Is there any more valid or plausible reason for assuming that all the American tribes are attributable to the same race or stock than to assume that all European or Asiatic races are descendants of one parent stock? Even if we admit that man originated in Asia, we must acknowledge the fact that the European races are the result of migrations, interminglings and conquests of many stocks from Asia, Africa and elsewhere.

No anthropologist, ethnologist or archeologist would dare to claim that the Norwegians are variants of the Slavs, nor that the Teutonic races are merely aberrant forms of the Gallic races. Why then should any one have the temerity to declare, and endeavor to prove, that all the so-called American Indians are descendants of migrants from any one locality, be it Asia, Europe or Oceania? Actually we know little regarding the origin of man in America, and it is not at all impossible that our descendants, centuries hence, will be as much in the dark as ourselves.

But we do know many more facts about the history, or at least the presence of early Americans than we did a few years ago. In the first place, we have to set back man's presence in America by a small matter of thousands of years. Not so long ago, any one who dared suggest that human beings dwelt in America prior to the glacial period, or that man roamed our mountains, plains and forests more than twenty thousand years ago, would have been shouted down as an iconoclast and a fool. But to-day we have positive proof that man not only inhabited North America during the Pleistocene period, previous to the Glacial period, but that Pleistocene man in the New World was the equal if not the superior of man in the Old World at the same time. In various localities, notably in gravel deposits at Frederick, Oklahoma and Raton, New Mexico, human artifacts have been found associated with the skeletons of known Pleistocene-period animals. Among these were mastodons, camels, ground-sloths, glyptodons, horses, elephants. Here, underneath the fossils, were found excellently made flint arrow- and spear-heads and other artifacts, so placed that there can be no question that they were deposited before the long-dead animals found their last resting-places in the gravels. Perhaps, if we had only one instance to go by, we might question this. But similar relics have been found among the fossil bones of Pleistocene animals in at least fifty localities in North America. And in more than one instance, as at Colorado, Texas, the flint weapons had obviously killed the creatures, some being within the skeletons and others embedded in the bones.

As these fossil mammals are typical of the first Glacial or Aftonian stage of the Pleistocene period, which is roughly estimated to have been more than five hundred thousand years ago, the men who made the stone weapons, and used them for killing bison and other huge animals, must have been well along on the road to culture before the famed Cro-Magnon and Neanderthal men of Europe first learned to throw a stone or wield a club.

Just what these immeasurably ancient Americans were like we cannot say, for up to the present time we have found no skeletons nor skulls dating from that time. But, judging from their weapons, which were not the crude, roughly hewn, hardly recognizable weapons of ape-men, they were highly intelligent and specialized human beings. Since, indisputably, they were in America at a time when only the lowest types of human beings, if any, inhabited Europe and Northern Asia, the natural query is: whence did they come?

There is no definite answer to that question. The adherents to the theory that man originated on this continent point proudly to this fact and claim it tends to prove their contention: man didn't come—he was here. Their adversaries reply, like the Irishman, by asking another question. If, say they, man originated on the American continent, why have we never found remains of ape-like men or anthropoid apes who, so scientists aver, were ancestors of man as we know him? And if man originated in America, why should the oldest and most primitive *skeletal* remains be found in the Old World?

These questions are not, however, such unanswerable riddles as they might seem. In the first place, far less anthropological research work has been carried on in America than in Europe, Asia or Africa. Europe and Asia especially have been fairly well searched for human remains for many years; they have been densely populated for a much longer period than any part of America, and in Europe there is

scarcely a square mile that has not been examined
and studied. Yet every little while some bone or
skull or other remnant of ancient man is unearthed
in such densely peopled and systematically searched
localities as England, France or Germany. Hence
the mere fact that the remains of low types of ape-
like humans have not been found in America is no
proof that they do not exist, nor that they may not
be found to-morrow or next week. The same is true
of the remains of the anthropoid apes; while the fact
that there are no living representatives of these apes
in America is no more of an argument against man
having originated here, than their absence from
Europe and continental Asia is proof that man did
not originate in those countries.

Unquestionably, half a million years or more ago,
the oceans and the continents were quite differently
formed and disposed than at the present time. For
all we know, there may have been fairly easy bridges
of islands or even solid land across the Pacific or
Atlantic. It is possible that the ape ancestors of mankind, assuming there were such, may have had their
homes upon lands which have long since been sub-
merged, and certain species—such as the orangs, gib-
bons, chimpanzees and gorillas—may have migrated
to Asia and Africa and hence escaped extermination,
even though none migrated to America. Or again,
if, for the sake of argument, we assume that man
evolved from apes in America and that such apes
survived prior to the Glacial period, the glaciers might
utterly have destroyed the apes, while the human beings, possessing greater intelligence and an ability to
travel afoot, might have survived by migrating south-

ward as the encroaching ice-cap moved southward from the Arctic regions. At any rate, there is only negative evidence that man did not originate in America, while we know that he was here and was a mighty hunter in the land before his compeers inhabited northern Europe.

There are just as many arguments for and against nearly every other theory of man's presence in the New World. In favor of the Bering Strait theory is the fact that many Indian tribes have physical characteristics similar to those of northern Asiatic races; that even to-day there is more or less of a migration between northeastern Asia and the extreme tip of northwestern Alaska, and that distinctively Asiatic dialects are spoken by many Alaskan and northwestern American tribes. But against this theory we have an equal or even greater array of arguments. In the first place, the facial appearance or external physical characters of a man or a race may be greatly influenced or altered by environment. Men who live on open sunny plains and deserts, or in lands where there is much snow, acquire squinting eyes or even slightly oblique eyes and high cheek-bones, just as mountaineers develop strong legs, deep chests and powerful backs, while tribes which travel largely by canoes develop broad chests, powerful shoulders and arms and become weak or under-developed in their lower limbs. Moreover, only a small percentage of all Indians of North, Central and South America possess the Mongol features. In the second place, the Asiatic dialects disappear completely as soon as we go far from the northwestern coast tribes, whereas, were all tribes descendants of Mongolian races, we would expect to find traces of the Mongol dialects among most if not all American tribes, no matter how far their ancestors might have wandered. Then there is the fact that if all American tribes are descendants of northern Asiatic migrants, the original migration must have taken place countless ages ago. Besides, it would require an enormous lapse of time for a handful of wanderers to multiply and spread from the Arctic Circle to Cape Horn and from ocean to ocean and gradually to develop the diversity of tribes, dialects, customs and religions which have existed for centuries among the aborigines of America. Yet the sponsors of this theory would have us believe that the theoretical migration took place at a time when the Mongol migrants were well along in arts, crafts and other attainments. If we accept this, then how can we account for the fact that the crudest of crude implements are found in graves in southern Chile, thousands of miles from Bering Strait? Finally, we have the fact that previous to the arrival of Columbus no domestic quadrupeds or birds of the Old World, and no cultivated plants of Europe or Asia, were known to the Indians, and that no domesticated animals and no cultivated plants peculiar to America were known in Asia or Europe.

There are almost as many and very similar arguments for and against the Greenland, the Atlantis, the west African or the southern European origin of American races, and, in lesser degree perhaps, the same holds true of the theory that man migrated to America from Oceania or from some long-vanished Pacific archipelago.

In the latter case, however, the arguments and

proofs in favor of the theory would appear rather
more numerous than those in rebuttal. In fact, about
the only valid or apparently valid arguments against
this theory are the claims that it would have been impossible for a large number of people to have crossed
the Pacific in primitive craft, and that if all the Indians are descendants of Oceanic races, traces of their
dialects would appear throughout the American continents. As a matter of fact, it would not be at all
difficult for any large canoe or catamaran to cross
from Polynesia to South America even at the present
time, and if such a migration ever took place thousands of years ago the chances are that at that time
there were many islands or archipelagoes which have
since disappeared. It has been fairly well established
that Easter Island is merely the remnant of an
archipelago that existed in comparatively recent times,
and it is not at all impossible nor improbable that the
submergence of this or some other archipelago or
island was the primary reason for its inhabitants migrating oversea to America. In fact, with the prevailing winds and currents of the Pacific, about the
only course that could have been followed under such
conditions would have been toward America. Also,
there is the undeniable fact that among nearly all the
tribes of western South America we find words—not
one or two but scores—which are strikingly like and
in many cases identical with words of the same meanings in Oceanian dialects. In some of their arts,
habits and religious beliefs there is a great similarity
between the natives of Oceania and the tribes of
western South America, while many of these South
American tribes are astonishingly like the natives of

the Pacific Islands in features, color and other respects. Finally, we have the strange bearded Indians or Sirionos of Bolivia, an isolated, primitive race with slightly wavy, fine hair, great bushy beards, typically Oceanian features, who bear no faintest resemblance to any other known Indian tribe.

Moreover, we know positively that there was some communication between the inhabitants of our Pacific coast and the inhabitants of mid-Pacific islands in prehistoric times. In excavating prehistoric graves on the Californian coast, members of an expedition of the Museum of the American Indian, Heye Foundation, obtained adzes, and ax-heads of Pacific island workmanship and composed of stone found only on those islands.

Also, among the thousands of artifacts recovered from the remains of the exceedingly ancient Coclé civilization in Panama, I found a number which can be explained only on the theory that the people who dwelt there were in more or less direct communication with the Orient.

Hence, it would rather seem that the trans-Pacific theory has more to support it than the others. But let me repeat, why is it necessary to assume that any one of these various theories is the only correct explanation of man's presence in America? Is it not reasonable to assume that human beings may have crossed from Asia via Bering Strait; that others reached the New World by way of Greenland; that still others came from Atlantis or southern Europe, and that tribes also crossed from Oceania or mid-Pacific archipelagoes? And is it impossible that these migrants may have found indigenous men already in

America? The intermingling of all these varied races might well have resulted in the wide diversity of types and tribes in America, and it would account for the fact that, here and there, throughout the length and breadth of the western hemisphere, we find individuals and tribes who seem types of far distant tribes and races; as well as words, artifacts and customs similar to, or identical with, like things of tribes separated by thousands of miles, and apparently in no way related.

Whatever the solution to the problem, despite the fact that the history of the American Indian is shrouded in mystery, we know that when the first Europeans set foot on the western hemisphere the country was inhabited by countless distinct and diverse tribes. Indeed, the variation of races, customs and dialects was far greater in the New World than in the Old. In California alone, more than one hundred distinct languages or dialects were spoken by the Indians within an area of a few square miles, a greater number for the same amount of territory than in any other portion of the world. The condition of the natives at the time of the European invasion varied as greatly as their tongues and characters. Some were primitive naked savages; some were nomads; some hunters; some agriculturalists. Some dwelt in the flimsiest shelters of brush and bark; others had large, well-built, wooden houses; some had dwellings of stone; others built their homes of adobe, and some used skins of beasts. All had advanced far above the ape-like type, and used well-made weapons, tools and implements. The majority were in the Stone age, but many had learned to smelt metals and used bronze or copper, gold and silver. Many had reached a high state of culture and had attained great artistic skill, while a number had developed advanced civilizations and in some ways had accomplished feats which had never been excelled, if equaled, by any other race in the history of the world.

It is in the attainments of these civilized American races that we find some of the strongest evidence against any theory of migrations from any known existent land.   Among these are the remarkable written or recorded language of the Mayas, the architecture of the pre-Incas, the ceramics of the Nascas, the calendar of the Toltec-Aztecs, the culture of the Chimus, etc.   Nowhere, in all the world, was there anything remotely resembling many of these things, and stranger still, and even more inexplicable, is the fact that many of these appear to have sprung into full bloom, so to speak, overnight.   It is for all the world as though some supergenius had invented or evolved an idea and perfected it in a day.   There are not, so far as is known, any remains of preliminary steps or beginnings to show a gradual evolution or building up, nor any evidence to lead us to assume that the results were the culmination of slow improvement through many centuries.

The Mayan writing is one of the most marvelous achievements of any race and is known only in its most highly perfected form, yet it must necessarily have required thousands of years for development. But it has no counterpart, nothing remotely resembling it, in the entire world. The Aztec calendar is another example. The Cyclopean architecture of the Andean highlands in no way resembles the architecture of any other known land or race, and, as far as we know, there is no intermediate type of architecture between these pre-Incan and the later Incan forms. Nowhere else on earth are there such structures as at Tiahuánaco in Bolivia, and nowhere are there remains showing an archaic or primitive type of such work. There are hundreds of similar examples of the same sort; of amazing feats and highly perfected mathematical, astronomical and scientific attainments which seem to have no beginning, but which, judging from what we know, appear to have been transplanted, fully developed, from some distant spot. No one, however, has ever been able to find the spot or spots whence they came.

If we assume that these races developed their cultures upon American soil and that they were of the same stock as the Indians, then why have no remains of such development been discovered? If the people came as migrants from elsewhere, with their arts and attainments already perfected, why has no one been able to locate their origin? And if we assume that these prehistoric races were indigenous to the New World, where were they hidden during the countless ages required to develop such astonishing cultural perfection from a primitive savage state?

To be sure, many persons have attempted to trace relationships between these prehistoric civilized Americans and various races of the Old World, basing their arguments on some certain features of architecture, portraiture or other matters. Thus the claim has been made that as pyramids are peculiar to ancient Egyptian and ancient American cultures there is some affinity between the two. Also that because the Mayas and Aztecs were pictured with heavy, hooked,

Semitic-like noses they were of a Semitic race, and that because the Aztecs' calendar-stone recorded the destruction of the world by a great flood, their ancestors must have been Israelites, or at least natives of the Biblical lands. In most of these cases similarities may be accounted for by far simpler explanations than racial relationships or migrations.

The pyramid is the easiest form of monument to build and is the only form of structure of large size which can be built without the use of staging, hoists and tremendous labor. Moreover, the American pyramids were totally different from those of the Egyptians in design, type, workmanship and every other respect, aside from general form.

Because the Aztecs recorded the destruction of the world by a great flood—and previously by a fire— does not prove that they were the lost tribes of Israel or had any knowledge of Genesis. Such things might be merely coincidences, or they might date back to myths and fables of such ancient origin that they were common to all races at the very dawn of human existence. I do not mean to declare positively that it is impossible that the ancestors of the Aztecs came from Asia Minor, nor that the story of Genesis, as recorded in our Bible, may not have been known to them. Genesis dates back to remote antiquity, and long before it was recorded on stone, clay tablets or in any other form, it had been handed down by word of mouth for untold centuries. It is not at all impossible that, once upon a time, dwellers in Biblical lands wandered away and that eventually some of their descendants reached America. As myths and fables, especially those of a religious nature, are

among the most persistently retained of all things,
it would be quite natural and in perfect accord with
scientific probabilities that tales similar to our Genesis
should still prevail among widely separated races. On
the other hand, primitive people are always subject to
floods, and in volcanic countries eruptions are a constant menace. A disastrous flood or an eruption
would unquestionably be embodied in the mythology
or history of a race, and, knowing no land but their
own, such people would assume that their restricted
habitat constituted the entire world. Very likely,
were we able to translate all the Mayan inscriptions,
we would find such records. There is scarcely an
Indian tribe, and none that I have visited, whose
legends do not contain stories of a flood or an eruption or both. Did we not possess a written language
and were we not in touch with the rest of the world,
our descendants, several thousand years hence, would
include in their verbal history (and probably in their
religion as well) highly colored versions of the
Mississippi flood or the St. Francis Dam disaster, and
we can readily understand that the inhabitants of the
Mississippi Valley, were they primitive people with
no knowledge of the rest of the world, might assume
that the flood which was so disastrous to them affected
the whole world equally. Then there is the question
of just how much of our Bible, and especially
Genesis, is mythical and how much allegorical. And
if we accept the calendar-stone's records as accurate
history in regard to the destruction of the earth by
fire and then by flood, then we must accept its record
of the world having once been destroyed by being
devoured by a jaguar. No doubt this impossibility

is purely allegorical, and hence there is no reason to doubt that the other records are equally allegorical.

Finally there is the argument supported by the Semitic-like noses of human beings depicted upon Mayan, Aztec and even pre-Incan sculptures and paintings. There seems to be a general belief that these people all had receding foreheads and enormous hooked noses because the majority of sculptured and painted figures show these facial characteristics. But we must not overlook the fact that the carvings and paintings also show human beings with the heads of beasts, with serpents' heads, with impossible limbs and digits, while the representations of well-known creatures and objects are so obviously conventionalized and exaggerated, for decorative or symbolic purposes, that no one for a moment would consider them accurate portrayals. Why then should we assume that the human features are any more true to life? Why should we take it for granted that the Mayas or Aztecs had enormous hooked noses and yet scoff at the idea that Mayan and Aztec jaguars had snakes' heads, or discredit the "Earth-Mother" being half-human and half-serpent when we find them so represented? Perhaps these races were notable for their noses and foreheads, possibly such features were peculiar to certain castes or families; or again perhaps they had a symbolic significance, or possibly the Aztecs and Mayas attributed such features to deities or gods and thought it flattering to portray ordinary mortals of renown with divine features. These races, as well as others, practised the artificial deformation of heads and thus produced the receding foreheads as shown. As this practise unquestionably had a

symbolic or religious significance it is not surprising
that the artificially shaped head should have been
represented so extensively. Indeed it may be that
the heads were molded to conform to the accepted
idea of what a deity's head should be, rather than the
other way about. Moreover, it is far easier to draw
or carve an expressive human face with a pronounced
nose than to represent a flat, straight or slightly
aquiline nose, and it serves to distinguish at a glance
between human and animal profiles even when complicated and confused by decorative details. As a
great portion of the Mayan and Aztecan carvings
were closely related to, if not part of, their written
records, it was most important that the human faces
should be recognized. Neither must we overlook the
fact that these races were past masters in the art of
depicting human expressions and emotions in profile
by means of a few lines, and without perspective or
shading. The beak-like nose lends itself admirably
to this type of art.

There is, in fact, nothing to prove that these races,
as a whole, normally possessed features of such striking peculiarities. Among the living Aimarás and
Quichuas of Peru and Bolivia, there are certain individuals with noses exactly like those shown on the
ancient sculptures. These are commonly known as
the "Inca noses," and the possessors claim direct
descent from the Incas and call themselves Incas.
Perhaps the Incas did have such beaks, but if so the
Spaniards failed to record the fact, and portraits
made in the days of the conquest do not show them.
Moreover, the few known lineal descendants of the
Incas have quite ordinary, Indian-type noses. But

it is easy to understand how, if the Quichuas should develop a new culture and should regard these big-nosed members of their tribe as royal, they would doubtless perpetuate them in their carvings. If we wish accurate knowledge of the predominating features of these ancient races we must depend more upon the effigy jars and the statues than upon ornamental and symbolic sculptures. In these we find that the ordinarily accepted type of Mayan and Aztec noses are far from universal or even common. Many of these portraits and statues represent human beings and deities with ordinary noses and features, although the same deities and persons in carvings, where in profile, have the huge noses and receding foreheads.

Furthermore, the effigy jars and statues, which are doubtless accurate portraits (aside from those which are obviously caricatures), show that the people of these races varied little from the present-day Indians in their facial characters. This is as might be expected, for the Mayas, the Aztecs and the Incans were not homogenous races of one blood. In all cases they were the result of conquest and confederation of many races and tribes by an intellectually superior people. No doubt these superior people, who formed the ruling classes,—the priests, etc.,—were of a distinct type from the bulk of the populations. It may be that they *were* migrants from oversea, and their noses may have distinguished them from the common herd. The Incas themselves were, we know from the records of the Spaniards, a much lighter-colored lot than their subjects, and possessed almost Caucasian features. Portraits made from life soon after and even during

the conquest prove this, and the same is true of the
aristocracy of the Aztecs. The Mayan civilization,
the Chimus, the Tiahuánacans and others having
ceased to exist at the time of the conquest, we have
no records as to the personal appearance of the ruling
classes of these races.

All of this goes to show that the deeper we delve
into the past history of the American races, and the
harder we try to explain the mystery of their presence
in the New World, the more involved and confusing
the whole matter becomes, and the less reason there
seems to be to support any one theory of their origin.

Leaving all questions of relationships with other
races aside, there is no doubt that these prehistoric
American races far excelled every other race of their
times in many ways. No such accurate calendar as
that of the Mayas was ever devised until the revised
Gregorian calendar was adopted. No such accurate
astronomical calculations were made by any other
people of their times as by the Aztecs and Mayas.
No other people invented such a remarkable form of
writing as the Mayas. No other race, not even people
of the present day, ever erected such walls and buildings as those of the pre-Incan races. No other race
ever carried out such Cyclopean works or such stupendous feats of stone-cutting as the Tiahuánacans.
No other race ever yet has woven—by hand or ma-
chine—textiles to equal those produced by the ancient
Peruvians. And the famed Roman roads and aqueducts seem scarcely more than child's play beside the
marvelous highways and other engineering wonders
of the Incans.

CHAPTER II

CULTURAL DEVELOPMENT AND INFLUENCE

MAN's culture, in its broadest sense, began when some prehistoric savage, slightly more intelligent than his fellows, picked up a stick and used it as a club. And cultural influence had its beginning when some other savage, seeing the crude club in use and realizing its advantages over bare hands, sought a stick for his own use. No doubt the first man to use a weapon took whatever was most convenient to his hand, and the chances are that he made use of it by accident rather than by design. But we may be almost certain that the second savage who availed himself of the other's example, went to no little trouble to secure a stick as much like the other in form, size, and even in color, as was possible.

Superstition is one of the most deeply seated and predominant characteristics of the human race, and the lower in the scale of intellect and culture the man, the more superstitious he will be. Because primitive man is extremely superstitious and sees a supernatural or magical power behind anything that is new to him or that he cannot understand, our second savage would have used what little brains he had to reason that it was the particular form or color of his fellow's club, and not its weight or strength, that made it an efficient weapon. Here was the beginning of cultural influence.

23

Once started along the lines of cultural development, primitive man advanced with rapid strides.
From a rude natural club selected at random to a
bludgeon carefully chosen was an easy step, and it
was almost as simple a step from the first rock used
as a pounder to well-made stone hammers and mauls.
Of course the evolution of stone implements and
weapons; the discovery and manufacture of bows,
arrows and spears; the development of fire-making;
the cooking of food, and the simplest attainments of
the most primitive savages, occupied an almost immeasurable period of time. But each step in the cultural ladder made the next simpler and opened the
way for innumerable other discoveries. It probably
took far longer for primitive man to discover how to
spin fiber into thread and make thread into rope than
it did for him to hit upon the scheme of weaving the
fiber into cloth. And it was probably a far greater
step, requiring much more time, from the first floating
log to the first crude dugout, than from the dugout
to a seaworthy craft.

During all the centuries, the thousands of years,
of evolution along cultural lines, the tendency of primitive man would be to copy or duplicate every utensil
and artifact made or used by another. If by chance a
hunter was unusually successful and used a spear with
a head of greenish stone, or if his bow was of a peculiar
form, of a certain wood or was even ornamented in a
certain way, his fellows would attribute his success to
such qualities and would strive to imitate them. Thus
gradually a general similarity of design, shape, type
and decorative motifs would result, and would be recognizable as the tribal culture. While the members of

one tribe might at times copy the utensils or the ornamental designs of another tribe when for any reason they considered them superior to their own, still as a general rule they would avoid doing so, particularly if the others were enemies. As a result, each tribe would be recognizable by its culture, while at the same time there might be strong evidences of one having influenced the other.

Aside from all this there would be the factors of environment; of climatic, meterological and geographical conditions. All of these exert a tremendous influence, probably even greater than we realize, upon cultural development, as do the botanical, zoological and many other conditions surrounding a tribe or race. People inhabiting a mountainous district will not only require certain types of utensils, implements and weapons which are adapted to mountain conditions, but will need those best adapted to the game, the climate and the other necessities of the particular mountain where they dwell. They will develop their culture, and even their personal peculiarities, in response to urges not felt by tribes in a lowland or a level district. Human beings who dwell in a cold climate must build up a culture which might be of little value in a tropical land. Desert tribes have their own problems which are quite distinct from those of races in a fertile area. In a forested territory, tribal cultures become very different from those whose homes are on open plains. In districts where game abounds primitive man finds it easier to gain a livelihood by hunting and fishing than by tilling the soil, and in order to do so he adopts a more or less nomadic life as he follows the game about and develops his hunting implements at the expense of domestic utensils. The agriculturalist, on the other hand, becomes a home-lover, and, having settled in the spot best suited to his needs, he remains there indefinitely, or as long as the soil will yield crops, and develops his culture along utilitarian and domestic lines.

Not only do these varying conditions of life and environment influence the manner of living, the habits, the customs, the artifacts and the dress of the tribes; they have as well a tremendous effect upon the religion, the physical development, the physiognomy, the skin color, the intellect, the imagination, the arts and the lore of a race.

Yet, even though every condition and every necessity may be distinct, an agricultural tribe may borrow or copy certain features of a nomadic hunting tribe or vice versa; a mountain tribe may find certain features of a plains or lowland tribe advantageous and may adopt them; a seacoast tribe may possess some object, utensil or decoration which an inland tribe imitates. Hence we may find most unexpected and inexplicable cultural influences cropping up in the most remote districts and among widely separated and widely different cultures.

Moreover, from the most remote times, primitive man has been a born trader. Objects prized as medicine, ornaments or for any other purpose, will be exchanged between neighboring tribes and, passing from tribe to tribe, may travel for incredible distances. Thus, objects of red pipestone, which occurs only in the vicinity of the Great Lakes, are found in ancient graves as far south as Chile. Dentalium shells from the Pacific were in use by the Indians of the Atlantic coast. Jade from Central America was used by the natives of Alaska, and quohog wampum from New England found its way to the Indians of the California coast. Aside from such natural objects, many man-made articles were traded and passed from hand to hand and from tribe to tribe over long distances. It is easy to understand how a certain type, form or ornamentation of a pot, utensil, weapon or other object, obtained by trade from some far distant race, might be copied, either wholly or in part, and might become typical of the local culture, although the influence of the original tribe who owned the object would be recognizable. Such influences, which do not show any proof whatsoever of actual tribal relationship or contact, are very common and are still in progress. While among the Guaymí Indians of Panama, I used a cotton hammock woven by the Arekuna Indians of the Brazil-Guiana border. The Guaymí women became greatly interested in this, to them, new weave, and in a few days they were busily making hammocks the exact duplicates of mine. Probably, at some future time, some ethnologist may publish a monograph devoted to the relationship of the Guaymís and Arekunas, and based on the similarity of their hammocks. In Peru, many of the rugs and blankets woven by the Andean Indians of Quichua stock are decorated with distinctively Navajo designs. A person unfamiliar with the history of these might jump to the conclusion that the Navajos and Quichuas were related or that they had once been in contact. The fact is that a mining man from New Mexico brought some Navajo rugs with him when he found employment at Cerro de Pasco. Wanting additional rugs of a similar pattern, he employed the native Indians to weave them, and the Quichuas, taking a fancy to the new motifs, adopted them and have used them ever since. Hence we should be chary of assuming that there is any relationship or contact between tribes merely because we find the artifacts or culture of the one influenced by the other. Far too often scientists regard such outside influences as of great importance.

Neither does it prove, because a tribe is nomadic, that it may not be related to or identical with a sedentary race or vice versa. Many of our nomadic plains Indians—such as the Sioux—were formerly agricultural and lived in established villages. The Navajos, who cultivate the soil and rear sheep and cattle, are near relations of the nomadic savage Apaches. Certain tribes of Carib stock are wanderers and have no settled homes, while others never move from their ancestral districts. Such variations may be due to personal characteristics, to accident, to the advent of some new factor in their lives, or to necessity.

As a general rule, nomadic and sedentary races are distinct, and it is the sedentary race that develops the highest culture and attains to a civilization. We may safely say that no truly nomadic American tribe ever reached a very high state of culture or established a civilization. By nomadic, I mean tribes which have no fixed habitations, but are constantly on the move, following the fish or game upon which they depend for food, clothing and innumerable other essentials. Many races which reached the highest state of culture and civilization were wanderers, or rather migrants; but their wanderings were forced upon them, and they were by nature, by heredity and by environment and development, sedentary people and not nomads.

I do not mean to state that nomadic, hunting tribes have not developed certain admirable arts and industries. On the contrary, many of our American nomads, such as the northern Sioux, the Apaches, the Cheyennes, the Arapahos and others have developed certain arts, such as buckskin- and bead-work, the fashioning of weapons, basketry and even pottery making, to a high degree. But by the very nature of their existence they have not, and never could, become obsessed with the idea of settling down, erecting permanent towns and establishing orderly, law-abiding communities until compelled to do so by the whites.

The matter of geographical, geological and meterological environment appears to have little if any relationship to this fact. Among the prehistoric and ancient American civilizations were those of mountain tribes, desert tribes, forest tribes, swamp tribes, highland tribes, lowland tribes, coastwise tribes, inland tribes; tribes inhabiting hot arid districts; tribes dwelling in steaming, rain-soaked, luxuriously verdant localities; tribes whose homes were among snow-capped peaks, and tribes who dwelt beside the sea. Neither was it a question of naturally warlike or peaceful natures. Some of the races whose civilizations were most remarkable were warlike, valiant, fighting people who carried on wars of conquest as far-reaching and as successful as those of Cæsar. Others, who were fully their equals in culture and civilization, were docile peaceful people who gave battle only in defense of their lives and homes. Some were

gentle and kindly, fond of innocent games and
amusements and passionately fond of music, while
others were almost inhumanly cruel, and gloried in
bloodshed, human sacrifices, suffering and even cannibalism.

But in every case they were people who possessed
a highly developed esthetic and artistic taste, a remarkable genius for organization, unlimited patience,
vivid imaginations, tremendous will power, an inborn
creative ability, and idealism in the extreme. These,
more than anything else, were the primary factors
which led certain races to attainments so far above
those of all other American tribes that it seems scarcely credible that they were of the same original race.

Probably the first distinct steps toward civilization
were the result of necessity. We know that in some
cases tribes have developed most unique habits, and
have gone far ahead of their neighbors and relations,
through the most fundamental instinct of man, that
of saving his own life. This was unquestionably the
case with the cliff-dwellers and the Pueblos of our
Southwest, races which reached a much higher stage
of culture than any other North American Indians,
and who, in some ways, approached closely to a civilized state. No doubt the ancestors of the cliff-
dwellers were the cave-dwellers, and it is highly probable that the descendants of the cliff-dwellers are the
modern Pueblos. The Pueblos are not, however, one
tribe or race, but belong to a number of distinct
stocks, each having its own culture, arts, dialect and
customs, but all living in much the same manner, and
all with a culture and with customs obviously the direct result of a common necessity and environment.

Possibly the first cave-dwellers used caverns for homes merely because they were the most convenient or perhaps the only available retreats. But they soon found that a cave, especially if in an inaccessible situation, is far more easily protected against foes and is a safer dwelling than a hut in the open. Being thus, by their mode of life, fairly free from molestation, and not being compelled to be forever fleeing from enemies or engaged in warfare, they had more time to devote to arts and industries and hence developed a high state of culture. From cave-dwellers, living in natural grottoes and caverns, to cliff-dwellers, living in stone homes under protecting overhanging cliffs, was a natural and easy step.

Had they not adopted this mode of life they undoubtedly would have been wiped out by their less cultured and more nomadic neighbors, or would have been compelled to revert to a nomadic life and savagery themselves, for even though the caves were excellent protection, they were limited in size and number, and, as the race increased, there would not have been enough caverns to accommodate them. Cliff-dwellings could be enlarged and added to, and possessed another advantage in that their inhabitants could maintain a watch on their enemies. Even as it was, the villages, far up on the precipitous mountainsides, did not always serve to protect the cliff-dwellers. Often they must have been taken by surprise, and many of their race must have fallen victims to the weapons of their wild enemies, for we find many of their skeletons with stone arrowheads embedded in the bones. Sometimes the wounded recovered, for the bones are healed about the weapons; others no doubt died slow and agonizing deaths, for the injured bones are still rough and splintered. As in nearly every case the position of the arrow-heads shows that they were shot from below and behind, it is obvious that the cliff-dwellers were firm believers in the old adage regarding the man who fights and runs away.

Being averse to fighting unless compelled to do so, dwelling in fairly safe and secure villages, the cliff-dwellers, like their ancestors of the natural caves, had a great deal of leisure to devote to the decorative arts, to inventing and formulating complicated religions and politics, to acquiring skill in weaving, basket-making, metal working, ceramics and other peaceful industries. They therefore greatly advanced their hereditary culture. Their ceramic ware was of a high quality and was most artistically formed and decorated. Their textiles were well made and showed great inventive and decorative ability. They made marvelous basketry, and were amazingly skilful in fashioning beads, ornaments and other objects of turquoise. The softer metals, such as silver and copper, were worked extensively. They executed far from mediocre sculptures and paintings on the rock walls of their homes. Yet they were far from being a civilized race.

From houses built of stones in crevices in the cliffs, it is almost as easy and natural a step to pueblos, as from natural caves to cliff-dwellings. The pueblo house or village is in fact merely an artificial cliff or cave-dwelling, possessing precisely the same defensive and protective advantages as either. By selecting a butte or mesa with precipitous sides rising well above the surrounding territory, and by erecting strong doorless houses thereon, and rendering these inaccessible when desired by withdrawing the ladders which gave access to the openings in the roofs, the Pueblo Indians vastly improved upon the homes of their cliff-dwelling predecessors' tactics. The position of the pueblo enabled its inhabitants to have a clear view in all directions for many miles; hence they could not easily be surprised by an enemy. In order to reach the village their foes would be forced to scale the sides of the butte or mesa, and could readily be held in check. And there was no chance of being assaulted from above, as in the case of cliff-dwellings. No fortress is absolutely impregnable, however, and the Pueblos were frequently raided and at times lost heavily in repelling attacks. That they were comparatively immune, however, from successful raids is proved by the fact that they continued to live, prosper and increase in the heart of a district peopled by such hereditary and savage enemies as the Apaches and Navajos.

But their very security prevented them from progressing further and attaining a true civilization. They were much the same in life and habits in the days of Coronado as they are to-day, aside from outside influences, and in all probability they had changed little if any during many centuries previous to the coming of the Spaniards. They had attained a certain degree of culture best suited to their requirements, they had reached a certain rung of the ladder leading to civilization, and there they remained.

Unquestionably many other ancient American races developed the nuclei of their cultures and their

civilizations along much the same lines as the Pueblos;
that is, through the necessity of self-protection. But,
unlike the Pueblos, they did not stop when they found
themselves fairly safe. Why some went so far ahead
of the others we cannot explain, just as we cannot
explain how or why any individual or any race out-
strips another in advancement. Very likely it is a
question of imagination and artistic temperament, all
else being equal.

In fact, it is largely the possession of an imaginative
artistic sense that differentiates man from the lower
animals. A sense of art implies imagination, and
none of the lower animals, as far as we have been able
to determine, possesses the slightest imagination.
But even the very lowest types of human beings have
imaginations. Necessity may drive a man, or even
an ape, to invent or discover something new. By a
process of simple reasoning, combined with instinct,
experience and experiment, primitive men, as well as
apes, dogs, horses and other beasts, may and often do
make epochal discoveries which prove of personal or
even communal benefit. Accident may have been responsible for the first fire kindled by man, and clothing may have been the natural result of trying to keep
warm by wrapping bark, skins or leaves about the
body. A man seeking shelter from a torrential
shower by cowering under the leaves of a tree might
well reason that he could use the same leaves to provide a shelter wherever he desired. A depression in
a clay bed may have contained water, and thus man
may have thought of using artificial hollows of clay
for receptacles; and a bit of the same clay, accident-
ally baked in his fire, may have taught him that

earthenware was better than sun-dried clay. But I can think of no accident, no natural event, no previous experience and no chain of reasoning that could have suggested the idea of art to early man. We have taught the higher anthropoid apes to behave quite like human beings in some ways. They have been trained to dress and to undress, to eat and drink, to smoke, to ride bicycles; to understand what is said to them; even to pronounce a few words. But no chimpanzee, orang or gorilla has ever been taught to draw a picture or to carve a stone or a bit of bone or wood.

It was when man first began to realize that he had an imagination that his true cultural development was assured. It was his ability to picture things in his mind's eye, and his desire to express himself that led him to draw his first crude pictures with a bit of charcoal or colored clay upon the walls of his cave. It was the same urge that made him scratch figures of animals and of his fellow men upon bits of bone and deer antlers, and it was the same striving toward the imaginary that taught him to sing, dance, produce music, to invent religions and to evolve ceremonials. As he progressed in other directions, as he acquired new industries, new vistas opened to him and his artistic sense developed as fast or faster than his manual attainments.

In the case of some races, imagination and art had their limits. Once the inner man was satisfied, once his life, his home and his family were safe, once he possessed a satisfactory home, tools, implements and weapons, his incentive to go further ceased and so did his artistic development. He was perfectly content

to confine his carving, his painting and his other artistic talents to decorating his utensils, his weapons,
his garments and his person. He could visualize
nothing beyond what he required for personal com-
fort and safety, and which he already possessed.
But in the case of other races, and other individuals,
irresistible longings and visions forever urged them
on. When these people discovered that they could
mold clay into any form, they devoted their talents
and their brains to expressing their imaginations in
the plastic material. When they discovered they
could chip stone and could carve and polish the hardest rocks, they realized the superior and enduring
character of the new medium and became sculptors.
And when they learned the use of metals they devoted
all their energies to developing this new art. Their
minds told them that clay houses were superior to
those of leaves and thatch; from clay to stone buildings was another step; and along with their better
living conditions and their desire further to improve
their lives these races developed mentally and physically as well as economically. They learned that in
unity there is strength. To carry out their ambitions
and their art they must have time and peace, and to
secure these they joined forces with their neighbors,
formed alliances and worked amicably together for
the benefit of all.

Being imaginative, and of course superstitious,
they developed complicated religions and mythologies, which became the chief inspirations for their
arts and their efforts. Just as their ancestors had
been pushed forward on the road to civilization
through the dire necessity of preserving their lives,

so the requirements of the religions they had evolved urged them on to still higher things. To placate the deities they had imagined or invented, to win the favor of their gods, to save themselves from dire results which were the creations of their own minds, they devoted their greatest efforts, their highest art to religious matters. As is the case with all civilized races, our own included, their utmost skill, their finest workmanship, their best talents were devoted to the erection of temples, monuments, idols and objects of a religious or sacred character. And in every case, despite what agnostics and cynics may say, the races which had the most ritualistic religions, the most extensive and complex mythologies and the deepest spiritual faiths, were the races which reached the highest development in arts, industries, organization, science and civilization.

The Egyptians, the Greeks, the Romans are outstanding examples of this incontrovertible fact in the Old World, and in the New World we have their counterparts in the Aztecs, the Mayas, the Incas and the pre-Incas. Probably no races in the history of the world possessed such a fanatical fervor for religion as these ancient Americans. Whatever the fundamentals of their beliefs, whether they were sunworshipers or otherwise, their religions were complex, involved and full of mysticism and symbolism. Their gods, demigods and spirits were innumerable and often had various forms and names. There were deities for nearly every act, deed, use, purpose, object, art, industry and desire, and there were temples, shrines, monuments, idols, offerings, sacrifices and ceremonials to each and all. Practically all the arts,

industries and customs were built up about the
religions. Religion being largely a matter of imagination, I still adhere to my earlier statement that
imagination was really the prime factor in their
civilizations.

CHAPTER III

PUZZLES AND PROBLEMS

ONE of the most fascinating features of the ancient civilizations of America is the mystery that shrouds them. At every turn, as we study these past civilizations, we come face to face with problems that appear to be impossible of solution. Innumerable theories, suppositions and surmises have been offered, and while many at first sight seem reasonable, yet when we examine and analyze them we find that there is scarcely one that fully meets the requirements. Considering the vast amount of work and study which has been devoted to the ancient American civilizations, it is simply amazing to find how little we actually know. We do not even know the origin of any one of the races which rose to such heights; we do not know positively to what race or stocks they belonged; we do not know when their civilizations or their cultures commenced, and, with one or two exceptions, we do not know when they ended or what brought about their downfall. We find ruins of magnificent palaces, splendid temples, great monuments, wonderful idols, ornate tombs; cemeteries containing thousands of burials, and evidences of a vast population, in a certain area. But there is no history, no tradition, nothing to show us who the people were or whence they came. And there is nothing to indicate the steps by which they reached their civilizations.

Another puzzling and still unexplained feature of the past civilizations of America is the fact that they were all developed in the tropical or semitropical portions of the hemisphere. It has been a fairly well accepted contention that the human race develops more intelligence and attains a higher type of civilization in northern than in southern districts. This would seem logical, for in cold climates man is faced with many difficulties which are wholly absent in warm climates. He must clothe himself to resist the cold, he must provide well-constructed dwellings in which to live, and he must labor almost continuously in order to provide food for himself and his family. He has every incentive to work, to develop mentally and physically, and to establish permanent homes, settlements, colonies and cities. With these tasks come organization, a social system, laws and governments. In the tropics, on the other hand, clothing is unnecessary; the flimsiest shelter will serve to keep off rain and sun; bountiful nature supplies food the year round, and human beings have a tendency to take life easily, to become lazy, to lose ambition and to degenerate.

One would therefore expect that, all other things being equal, the inhabitants of North America or of southern South America, would have reached a high state of culture and a civilization long before those of the tropical and subtropical areas of South and Central America. But for some reason which has never satisfactorily been explained no tribe nor race of North America, and no race of southern South America, attained to a true civilization in pre-Columbian days, whereas the highest civilizations in the hemisphere were developed in the hot tropical areas of Central America, in the subtropical Mexican highlands, and in the semitropical areas of South America.

Numerous theories have been advanced to account for this fact. One is that in the days when these civilizations were first established the districts were not tropical; that what are now temperate zones were then frigid, owing to the Glacial period, and that what are now tropics were then temperate. But the most ancient carvings, sculptures and paintings of these races represent human beings either nude or nearly so; they show birds, reptiles and quadrupeds of the tropics, and every known evidence leads to the conclusion that there have been very slight changes in the climate since the days when the civilizations first started.

Another theory is that in the American tropics man was not forced to devote his life to eking out a bare existence, and therefore had leisure to develop his mind, to occupy brains and hands with constructive work and to develop his artistic talents. But this is contrary to all accepted ideas of the effect of the tropics upon man, and is not borne out by present-day examples of races dwelling in the tropics.

Still another supposition is that the races which developed civilizations were driven southward and northward by hordes of savages, until they found comparative safety in the tropical jungles and subtropical mountains and deserts. But no one can offer a suggestion as to why there should not have been fully as many, if not more, savages in the tropics than in the north or south.

It has also been suggested that the civilized races of South and Central America were migrants, already possessed of a high state of culture or a semicivilization, who reached the shores of tropical America and that they never spread far from their original landing-places. Yet we have abundant proof that these races, or at least the masses, were of the same race as the other Indians, and if they arrived as migrants from oversea then they must have reached America long ages before they had developed any material cultures. It will therefore be seen that no theory put forth fully covers the matter.

Although, as I have said, no North American race ever reached a high or true civilization, still many tribes reached a high state of culture within the boundaries of the present United States, and several of these were well started on the road to civilization when, for one reason or another, their progress was checked. Omitting the most advanced of the various Indian tribes, many of which, such as the Iroquois, had established complex governments and had formed strong confederations approaching true commonwealths, we find such cultures as those of the mound-builders, the cliff-dwellers and the Pueblos. Here again are puzzles and problems we cannot solve. We do not know who the mound-builders were, nor are we any too certain of the identity of the cliff-dwellers, or of the Pueblos who are considered the descendants of the cliff-dwellers. No mounds similar to those of the mound-builders are known in any other portion of the world, and many of the artifacts found within the mounds are distinct from the work of any other known American race.

On the other hand, many of the utensils, vessels, etc., are very similar to those of well-known Indian tribes inhabiting the same or adjacent districts in pre-Columbian days, while the skeletons and skulls of the mound-builders show no strikingly marked peculiarities, and are generally conceded to be of the same race as the present-day Indians.

In many ways, however, the mound-builders attained to a far higher state of culture than any other North American race east of the Mississippi. They had advanced far beyond the Stone age. They had learned to work copper, and they fashioned excellent tools, weapons, helmets, ornaments and utensils of that metal. They made extensive use of fresh-water pearls, and they had developed the ceramic and textile arts to an admirable degree. But they made no large stone monuments or sculptures, built no elaborate stone structures, and could not by any stretch of the imagination be considered civilized people.

It has been claimed by some writers that they were an offshoot of or had been strongly influenced by the Mayas, but there is no real evidence to bear out this theory. Neither is there any proof that they were of Norse ancestry or had been influenced by the Vikings, as also has been suggested. Such theories, while romantic and interesting, come no nearer solving the mystery of these ancient people. We do not even know why the mounds were made, or what purpose they served. They may have been religious or ceremonial structures; they may have been primarily burial mounds, or they may have served as refuge places in times of floods. But the fact that they were built in well-defined forms, apparently of a symbolic character, would cause us to assume that they had some sacred or religious significance.

All we actually know of the mound-builders is that the mounds have existed for ages; that they were there when the first white men penetrated to the district; that the Indians of the vicinity had no history nor traditions as to the origin of the mounds or their makers, and that, as far as can be ascertained, the mound-builders appear to have vanished suddenly and mysteriously from the face of the earth.

Of course there must be some natural and probably simple explanation of these seemingly insoluble mysteries. Wars, pestilences, climatic conditions and geographical changes, as well as eruptions and floods, have been suggested. But wars and pestilences seldom wipe out a teeming wide-spread population at a single stroke, and such catastrophes as floods, earthquakes and volcanic upheavals leave well-recognized traces of their devastation.

Did we but possess any reliable recorded histories of the races we might find therein the explanation, or hints of the causes, which resulted in these wholesale disappearances. But recorded histories, even when they exist among the remains of the races, seldom consist of anything more than calendrical or religious matters. Of traditions and legends there are many; but as a rule these do not go back to the days of the old civilizations, and, when they do, it is often obvious that they have been built up or manufactured to fit conditions, and are no more than allegories. Possibly, at the time of the Spanish invasion, there were legends or traditions which contained a great deal of truly historical material, but as a rule when any such existed they were suppressed by the Christian priests as tending to keep alive the belief in the pagan gods and rites of the natives.

In Yucatan there were the so-called *Books of Chilám Balám* which were written subsequent to the conquest, and which constitute a sort of historical account of the Mayas; but they are largely based on the myths of the descendants of the Mayas, and their accuracy is very questionable. The *Popul Vuh* of Guatemala is another of these saga-like traditions of the Mayas of Guatemala. Much of it is obviously allegory and myth, but no doubt portions of the *Popul Vuh* contain a great deal of fact. The trouble is that no two of such legends agree. In fact, if we were to place much credence in these doubtful histories of the Mayas we would have to believe that not a single Mayan ruin or city antedates the thirteenth century. And we know positively, by the date-glyphs upon them, that innumerable Mayan structures of the highest type, and which were built when the empire was at its zenith, were erected in the fourth and fifth centuries or earlier. We must therefore regard all other details of these traditions and alleged histories of the Mayas with distrust, and the true story of the rise and downfall of the Mayan civilization remains as much a mystery as ever.

Much the same conditions surround the Aztecan civilization, although in this case we know too well the reason for its destruction. Moreover, the Aztecs were flourishing at the time of the Spanish conquest, so that we have accurate accounts of many features of their civilization which are unsolved mysteries in the cases of other races. In addition, the Aztecs had

their pictographic codices which recorded much of the
early history of the race and its migrations. But
these, or at least such of them as are preserved, are
rather indefinite and were probably drawn centuries
after the events pictured took place, and were worked
up from legends and traditions. Many Aztec, or
better, Nahua, legends appear historical at first
glance, but if we study them we find that, like those
of the Mayas, they differ materially, and that in
every case they are most suspiciously like fanciful
allegorical myths.

Even the accounts of the early Aztecs and their
predecessors, the Toltecs, as given in the works of
Ixtlilxochitl, a Mexican chronicler who wrote soon
after the conquest, are greatly at variance; but as he
undoubtedly merely recorded the existing traditions,
this is not surprising. According to one of his accounts the Toltecs reached a spot called Tlapallan
after voyaging southward from some unknown land.
A revolt of the chiefs against the Tlapallan king
forced them to flee in A. D. 439. After eight years
of wandering in the vicinity, they journeyed to
Tlapallantanzinco where they remained for three
years before commencing their subsequent wanderings which lasted for one hundred years. The other
account does not agree in regard to the dates nor the
localities, but states that the Toltecs left their homes
in the year 1-Tecpatl (A. D. 387), passed Xalisco
and landed at Huatulco whence they journeyed to
Tochtepec and then traveled overland to Tollantzinco, the entire journey occupying one hundred and
four years.

After this the accounts agree far more closely.

They state that the city of Tollan was founded A. D. 566 at the present site of Tula, the Toltecs having been guided to the spot by their great magician Hueymatzin (Great-hand). Six years were consumed in building the city which was known as the "Place of Fruits." Until the seventh year it was without a ruler. Then Chalchiuh-Tlatonac (Shining-precious-stone) was elected king. He reigned for fifty-two years, and the people progressed rapidly. His line continued until A. D. 994 when Huemac II ascended the throne. He ruled wisely for a time, but later his license and deceit caused a revolt.

Here the reasonable historical-like account suddenly changes to a highly fanciful and allegorical tale. It states that omens appeared in the heavens and that the magician, Toveyo, collected the people, and by the lure of his magic drum forced them to dance until he led them to the verge of a precipice where they fell over the brink and were transformed to stones in the cañon below. The sorcerer also destroyed a stone bridge so that thousands of persons fell into the river and were destroyed. Volcanoes and earthquakes were brought into play and innumerable supernatural occurrences took place (see Chapter IX), finally culminating in the disruption of the Toltecs. As so many of these traditions are obviously fanciful, or at least allegorical, it is pretty safe to assume that we cannot place any dependence upon any of them, the more so as the names of the alleged Toltec rulers are identical with those of Aztec deities, and as each king, by some coincidence, reigned precisely fifty-two years, the Aztecan cycle which equalized their calendrical and solar years.

We are therefore forced to admit that we really know nothing of the Aztecs' origin, their race or whether or not they were the descendants of the Toltecs. For that matter, it is rather doubtful if there ever was such a people as the Toltecs. The late Mr. Charles W. Mead, of the American Museum of Natural History, devoted a great deal of time to investigating the so-called Toltecs, and decided that the name was more geographical than racial.

Even less is known of the races of northern South America, which developed civilizations distinct from all others. We know practically nothing of the Chibchas of Colombia and still less of the Manabis of Ecuador, and we know almost as little of the Chimus, the Nascas, and the pre-Incas of Peru. In short, all we know about any of these races is that they left most marvelous remains as proof of their attainments.

Another mystery which no one can solve is the absence of any known traces of ancient cultured or civilized races in extensive areas where they might most reasonably be expected. Throughout Mexico and Central America, as far south as central Panama, ruins and remains of such races are extremely numerous. But from central Panama to Colombia the country appears absolutely barren of all signs of occupation by civilized or even highly cultured tribes. The few scattered remains that have been found here consist of crude pottery, equally crude stone implements, a few ornaments of gold, and a few rudely scratched or cut petroglyphs. If, as has been claimed, there was a northerly migration from South to Central America or a southerly migration in the opposite direction, or both, then there should be remains of these migrants in the area between central Panama and northern South America. Even if no such migrations ever occurred, it is a remarkable and inexplicable fact that the widest, most luxuriant and most attractive portion of the Isthmus remained uninhabited by highly cultured men when races north and south rose to such heights.

Perhaps the greatest mysteries of all are how the ancient civilized races of America performed their amazing feats and accomplished such astonishing works in metals and the hardest of stones. How they fashioned minute, chased gold beads—often built up of several pieces—no larger than the head of a pin; how they cut, polished, perforated and carved topaz, amethyst, garnet, agate, crystal and other precious stones; how they worked friable obsidian into thin polished rings; how they executed the most complex and beautiful sculptures in the most refractory of rocks; how they moved blocks of stone, weighing upward of two hundred tons, for miles across country and used them in their buildings; how they wove textiles far finer than is possible on any modern loom; how they cut long tunnels through mountains; how they invented the world's most remarkable numerical system; how they evolved a marvelous written language, and how they performed countless other feats which, with the known tools, implements and devices they had at their disposal, might almost seem to savor of the supernatural.

We cannot answer these riddles; as yet we have no reasonable theories to explain them, and all we can do is to accept the known facts, marvel and wonder.

CHAPTER IV

RELATIVE AGES OF AMERICAN CIVILIZATIONS

ONE of the greatest difficulties in solving the riddles of ancient American civilizations, is that we have no definite knowledge as to their relative ages. This is a much discussed matter upon which few recognized authorities agree. In the case of the ancient civilizations of Europe, Asia and Africa, it is not difficult to establish, with reasonable certainty, when they came into being, when they were in their heyday and when they fell or were destroyed. Experts can even state, to within a few years, when a certain king or Pharaoh was born, when he ascended the throne, how long he reigned, when he died and who his ancestors and descendants were.

Much of the material in the Bible is historical. The Greeks and Romans, despite their conquests and destructiveness were, fortunately, greatly interested in history, and in the lives, habits and customs of those whom they conquered or with whom they came in contact, and they left us a vast amount of priceless information. Most important of all is the fact that, with few exceptions, the people who were responsible for ancient civilizations in the Old World possessed written or recorded languages which can be tranlated and deciphered. The famous Rosetta stone gave the world the key to some of these, and others have been worked out independently.

But in the case of the ruins of the prehistoric temples, palaces and cities of the civilized races of ancient America it is a different matter. We have no truly historical records antedating the coming of the Spaniards; and the Dons, as well as the earlier discoverers of other nationalities, were far too much engrossed in killing off the natives, destroying their works, looting them of riches and ostensibly saving their souls, to bother much with recording their traditions, their histories or their more interesting peculiarities. Now and then some old priest or general had his interest aroused and wrote, usually from hearsay, regarding some outstanding features of the civilizations he was helping to wipe from the face of the earth. At rare intervals some unusually intelligent and far-sighted individual spent a great deal of time and took a bit of trouble to delve into the stories of the aborigines and wrote lucidly of what he had observed. But unfortunately most of these sincere and well-meaning writers were not trained scientists and possessed a very superficial knowledge of their subjects. They were inclined to accept everything they heard at face value, to form conclusions offhand, to judge matters in general by isolated examples, and to assume that matters which were every-day affairs to them were of no interest to others. And of course, in most cases, they were obliged to depend upon interpreters for securing information. As a result, in all the numerous accounts written by Europeans from the discovery of America until the complete conquest of the New World, there is little unquestionable material of great archeological or ethnological value.

Moreover, unlike the ancient races of the Old World, few of the ancient civilized races of America possessed written or otherwise recorded histories of their own. There were traditions, myths, legends and allegorical tales galore; but as far as is known neither the Aztecs, the Mayas nor the Incans had any definite knowledge as to the origin, the past history or the ancestry of their races. The Mayas, it is true, possessed a remarkable glyphed or written language in which certain events were recorded. The Aztecs used a very complete arrangement of symbols for dates and other records, and they had their pictographic codices which recorded their migrations in their past. But with their usual misdirected zeal, the Christian priests destroyed everything of a so-called pagan character they could lay their hands on, and among other things were most of these codices.

After years of patient study and investigations our specialists can now decipher most of the Mayan and Aztecan inscriptions and writings that are left to us. From these we know that many of the most important works of these races were carried out in the fourth and fifth centuries of our era. But that gives us little if any information as to the age of the civilizations, any more than the date upon one of our great buildings would aid some future archeologist—several thousand years hence—in determining the date of the landing of the Pilgrims or of the Declaration of Independence. And the most interesting, most mysterious and most puzzling of the various prehistoric civilizations of America left no intelligible glyphs, symbols or inscriptions to give us the faintest idea of their age or origin. We can therefore only guess at the relative antiquity of the early cultures and civilizations of the New World, and can only form opinions from the meager information we have, from a study of the ruins and remains, and from the fact that certain remains overlie others of greater antiquity.

At times, it is true, we can obtain some idea of their age by studying the decomposition of materials, such as stone; by the accumulation of alluvial and other soil, and by other matters of a similar nature. But often this method is far from reliable. A certain kind of rock may decompose far more rapidly in one locality than in another. Even when two objects of the same material are in the same area this may happen, for in one spot there may be or may have been more moisture than in another, or one of the stones may have been protected by soil, sand or a covering of some sort from erosion and climatic conditions whereas the other may have been exposed continuously. Or again, one of the objects, even if of the same material, may be far more ancient than the other although cut by the same race. The accumulation of soil and débris also varies greatly in various localities, at different seasons and at different times. Rains, droughts, fires, winds, the presence or absence of vegetation and a thousand other factors will greatly affect the rate of soil accumulation.

Human remains, when found, are even more unreliable as indications of the lapse of years. In such countries as Chile and Peru, bodies interred in the dry, rainless, nitrate-impregnated sand become dry or mummified and last, unaltered, indefinitely. Even textiles, feathers and woodwork are perfectly preserved, under the same conditions, for thousands of years. In dry caves, especially if buried in bat guano, mummies will also last forever, and to some extent the same holds true of bodies interred in well-constructed tombs. Even in damp warm climates, and when buried in the earth without a protective coffin or other receptacle, human skeletons will at times remain in a wonderfully perfect state of preservation for incredible periods, whereas, under what are apparently identical conditions, others may completely disappear in a few years. Within the underground tombs of a mound which I excavated recently in Scotland, human teeth, fragments of bones and several practically perfect vertebræ were found well preserved although the date of the burial is estimated at about 2000 B. C., and the earth was saturated with moisture. And yet, not far distant, graves of men killed in battle in the seventeenth century did not contain even a trace of human remains.

Unless we possess definite, established data as to the rate of the soil accumulation, the decomposition of certain rocks and of bones in a certain locality we have nothing by which to go. Even with this knowledge we cannot depend on estimates based on such data, for we have no means of knowing that the present rate is the same as it was a few hundred or a few thousand years ago. We know positively that climatic conditions in many localities have completely altered within the past few centuries, or even within the past few years. Areas now rainless, arid and desert-like, may have been well watered, fertile and covered with vegetation in the days when the ancient civilizations were flourishing, or the reverse may have been the case; and present-day wooded or cultivated areas may have been deserts. For all we can positively assert, the present tropical areas may have been temperate, or vice versa, and the surface of the earth may have risen or fallen for considerable distances.

Neither does the present-day condition of a ruined civilization mean very much in estimating elapsed time. We must take into consideration not only the climatic influences,—the wear and tear of the elements, the changes of climate,—but also the effects of vandalism, of treasure-seeking, of agriculture and of other changes due to human agencies. Many fine ruins, which otherwise would still be in splendid condition, have been almost utterly destroyed by man within the last few centuries. When the Spaniards removed the metal keys which held the stone slabs of Tiahuánaco in place, the buildings, which otherwise might have remained intact for the next thousand years, fell apart and became shapeless ruins. Countless thousands of tons of ancient edifices, monuments, idols and stonework have been broken up for railway ballast, for making concrete, for surfacing roads, and for constructing modern buildings. Many ancient buildings and even entire cities in South and Central America and in Mexico have been almost razed by collectors, treasure-hunters and out-and-out vandals. Still more have been ruthlessly destroyed in order to make room for modern structures, roads, railways or farms. In Peru a magnificent Incan burial-mound was recently cut through by a steam-shovel when a highway was being built between Lima and Callao, and countless valuable archeological objects were broken, ground to bits, buried under tons of material and forever lost to science. And it is now proposed that the remaining portion of this splendid mound be, removed in order to use it for filling an abandoned gravel-pit!

About Cuzco, Peru, the former Incan capital, the only remains of the Incan and pre-Incan civilizations left standing are those which the Dons found impossible or impractical to destroy, but by far the greater number were torn down or were utilized in building the Spaniards' houses and churches.

As I have said, one of the most remarkable features of many of the prehistoric American civilizations is the fact that, judged by our present knowledge, they appear to have had no beginning and no logical ending. Hence there is nothing with which to compare them when trying to place their age. There are no superimposed remains and no earlier, evolutionary or more primitive remains of the same races. Such abrupt beginnings and endings are the usual rather than the unusual thing. It is the case with our mound-builders, with the Coclés of Panama, with the Manabis of Ecuador, the Tiahuánacans of Bolivia, the pre-Incan civilizations of Peru, and even with the Mayas.

But when, as in certain localities in Mexico, Central and South America and elsewhere, we find the remains of one culture superimposed on one or more others, we can be assured that the lowest of the strata is the most ancient, even if we cannot guess their relative ages within several thousand years.

Also, we know that many of the prehistoric civilizations of America are of almost inconceivable age. At the very lowest estimate, we know that some of them go back for fully five thousand years, and we

can feel fairly certain that the youngest of the lot—
that of the Incas—was at least a thousand years old
when it was overthrown and destroyed by Pizarro.

Flourishing at the same time as this Incan Empire,
and also in Peru, was the Chimu civilization which
was much older; while antedating these and even at
the beginning of the Incan civilization, so long past
that there were no trustworthy traditions concerning
them, were the far more advanced and remarkable
pre-Incan civilizations. Probably that of the Tiahuánacans in Bolivia was the most ancient, but there
are reasons to think that even Tiahuánaco was of
more recent date than some of the cultures in Central
America.

There are several reasons for this assumption. The
Mayas in several respects had attained to a higher
state of civilization than any of the South American
races, which would indicate that their culture had
been in process of development for a longer period.
Also, geographically, meteorologically and geologi-
cally, Central America is far better adapted to the
development of a civilization than is Peru or Bolivia.
And if we admit that there was a northerly and southerly migration, as there probably was, or if the more
peaceful and cultured races were driven north or
south by more savage and nomadic tribes, then the
constricted area of Central America would have been
the logical spot in which they would have found refuge and a permanent home. On the other hand, if
we accept the theory that some of the original inhabitants of Middle and South America were of trans-
Pacific origin, then Central America would have been
the most promising locality in which to search for

their remains and for traces of the oldest cultures.
Arguing with this hypothesis as a basis, we can scarcely imagine migrants from the warm, verdured, well-
watered Pacific Islands, or from southern Asia,
settling down on the arid, desert west coast of South
America, or on the equally forbidding plains and
deserts of our own Southwest.

Assuming that Central America was thus the first
settled portion of America, or even of middle America, it is obvious that, as the population increased and
the limited area of this narrowest portion of the hemisphere became more or less congested, there would
have been migrations to the north and south, and that
these migrants, from a district wherein the races had
already made progress toward civilization, would
have carried the germs of their cultures to other lands,
where, under wholly different conditions and environment, totally distinct cultures and civilizations might
have been developed from the same stock.

Still another reason for believing that Central
America was the cradle of prehistoric civilizations is
the fact that in no other portion of the New World
were there so many distinct cultures within an equal
area. Throughout Central America, from Mexico
to Colombia, we find remains of innumerable ancient
races who had attained such advanced cultures that
they approached civilizations. Many of these extremely ancient peoples had developed remarkable
arts and industries. Their ceramics were of the highest quality; they executed marvelous stonework and
sculptures; they were experts in working gold, silver,
copper and other metals; they cut and carved the
most refractory of gem-stones, and in some of their

arts they have no superiors, if indeed equals, among modern civilized races.

Very little is known of these earlier cultured tribes of Central America and Panama. Judging by their remains, they were of several distinct races, with little if anything in common, for within a comparatively short distance the ceramics, sculptures and other objects obtained from one site will be wholly distinct from those of another. Yet, in a way, all show certain influences as if all had originated from a common nucleus or had been influenced by some other race.

For convenience archeologists have classified these various known cultures according to a more or less arbitrary system based largely upon localities. Thus we have the Nicoya culture, the Chiriqui culture, the Terriba culture and so on. They are, however, archeological puzzles, and we cannot even be sure that the present-day Indians of the districts are or are not their descendants. If so, then they have sadly degenerated and have lost most of the arts of their ancestors. But the chances are, that with a few exceptions, such as for example the Mayan races of northern Central America, the living Indians of these districts are the result of mixtures of the cultured races and the more savage tribes who, in all probability, were largely instrumental in destroying the cultures. These puzzling cultures have no real place in a work devoted to prehistoric civilizations, but they have a very important bearing on the origin of civilizations in America, for they prove that racial cultures had reached a higher and more diversified stage in Central America than in either South or North America at the same period. Hence, we can logically assume that true civilizations were first developed in Central America rather than in the areas to the north or south. Finally, and most important of all, as tending to prove that prehistoric civilizations in America were most ancient in Central America, is the fact that the oldest remains, as far as can be judged, of a culture which may be classed as a semi-civilization have been found within the boundaries of Panama.

This brings up the question as to just where we may draw the line between a culture and a true civilization. This is a difficult matter to decide. Broadly speaking, and from an ethnological point of view, every race and tribe that has learned to fashion any article or artifact has its culture. The more advanced the tribe, the greater its culture; but it is difficult to say just where a high culture ends and a true civilization begins. Every race that has developed a civilization of course has its culture; but that does not mean that a highly cultured race is necessarily a civilized race. Even the term civilization is indefinite. There are and always have been all grades of civilization, and there is no hard and fast standard as to just what requisites constitute a civilization.

It is not a question of art, for many savages have a highly developed sense of art and show great manual skill. It is not language, for some of the most barbarous tribes have the most highly developed languages, whereas highly civilized races may retain a very primitive form of language. Neither is it organization, for many tribes which can lay no claim to civilization are splendidly organized. Neither is it government, the erection of permanent buildings, a scientific knowledge, nor the invention of a written or recorded language or history. Were I asked to define the requirements essential to civilization, I should say that when a highly cultured race builds cities, establishes an organized form of government, enforces a code of laws, recognizes education, performs engineering feats, has a social organization and a religion, levies taxes, maintains an army, possesses a knowledge of science, is self-supporting and encourages arts and industries, it has reached a state which may be considered civilized.

The Aztecs, the Mayas and the Incas, as well as other races, fulfilled all these requirements and more, and yet, judged by our present-day standards, none of those races was civilized. But judged by the same standards, neither were the Egyptians, the Greeks, the Romans nor our own ancestors of the Middle Ages. And no doubt a few thousand years hence our descendants will look back upon the twentieth century and pity us for our primitive uncivilized state. Hence it will be understood that when I employ the term civilization, it is only in a relative sense, and as applied to all cultures which had risen appreciably above the primitive state.

According to the above definition, we cannot well include the mound-builders, the cliff-dwellers or the Pueblos among the ancient civilizations of America, although the former were probably the most ancient, highly cultured race in North America, while the Pueblos come very close to possessing a civilization.

Probably the oldest of the highly developed cultures or semicivilizations in Middle America was

that of the Coclés in Panama, while the earliest of
the true civilizations of Central America may have
been that of the Mayas or Toltecs.* There is considerable doubt as to which of these is the older, but
there is little question that the Aztec civilization was
the youngest of all, for the Mayan empire had
reached its zenith and had ceased to exist long before
the Aztecs attained their greatest height and power.

In the case of the prehistoric civilizations of South
America it is far more difficult to form an opinion
as to their relative ages. The Manabis of Ecuador
and the Chibchas of Colombia were unquestionably
very ancient; but we know so little in regard to the
former that it is impossible to say whether they should
be classed as civilized or merely cultured, and our
knowledge of the Chibchas is, if anything, even more
limited.

Of the better-known civilizations, it is generally
conceded that the Tiahuánacan is the oldest. Next
in point of age would be the pre-Incans, the Nascas
and the Chimus; but it is impossible to say positively
which of these antedated the others or whether or not
they were contemporaneous. But we may be quite
sure that the Incans were the most recent of all, and
that they occupied much the same place in South
America as the Aztecs held in Middle America.

---

*According to Joyce the Toltec culture was the result of Mayan influence
upon Mexican tribes.

CHAPTER V

BEFORE entering into a description of the various prehistoric civilizations of America, it may be well to take up certain features which were more or less common to all. Although the various prehistoric civilizations were all distinct in details and each is easily identified by its type, yet in some respects all were similar and unlike any others in the world.

While they showed the widest variations in details, in motifs, in conceptions, in workmanship and in character, nearly all of these ancient civilizations were remarkable for their stone sculptures and buildings. Not only did the artizans carve the hardest of rocks to a degree that would be a difficult task for a modern workman equipped with the finest and most elaborate tools of tempered steel, but, as far as we have been able to prove, it was all accomplished without the aid of any metal tools. No unquestionable implements of steel or iron have ever yet been found among the remains of these prehistoric civilizations, although of course that is merely negative evidence, for steel or iron soon vanish and leave no trace. And as we now know that the ancient Egyptians possessed fine iron implements, despite the fact that none had ever been discovered until King Tut's tomb was found, we may yet discover tools of steel in some prehistoric American tomb or ruin.

Innumerable copper or bronze tools and implements have been found, but not one of these is capable of cutting the softest stone, and the old belief that these people possessed a lost art of tempering bronze is purely mythical.

Not only did these prehistoric races execute the most amazing sculptures in hard stone, often in such materials as rock-crystal, agate, jasper, jade and obsidian, but they apparently did so with ease and rapidity. In some instances they seem, judging by appearances, to have cut and carved hard rocks for the mere pleasure of doing it, or to test their skill, much as a small boy uses his new jack-knife. In other cases the amount of rock cut away, the relief of the sculptured figures, and the mathematical and geometrical accuracy of carvings are such that only an extremely credulous person can believe the work could have been accomplished by the use of stone implements. There are single blocks of stone weighing many tons,—blocks fifteen feet in length, nine to ten feet in width and nearly three feet thick, elaborately sculptured and formed into monolithic gateways with portals cut with mathematical accuracy through the great mass of stone.

There are immense buildings, temples, pyramids and underground chambers of stonework, every square inch of the surfaces of which is completely covered with deeply cut, intricate carvings. There are stone stools, seats and metates (grinding-stones), idols and monuments ornamented with carved fretwork in most complicated designs; and there are human and other figures carved from transparent quartz, black friable obsidian and even gem-stones, so beautifully cut and polished that they would be a credit to any modern lapidary working with diamond-dust.

Fully as remarkable as the stone sculptures of these prehistoric people are the sizes of the stones they used in constructing their buildings, walls and fortresses. Though no two civilizations were alike in their architecture and technique, yet all built on a titanic scale and seemed to find it easier to quarry, move and use gigantic masses than to use more numerous and smaller blocks of material. Stones weighing several tons each are everywhere, and, in many instances, masses weighing from sixty to nearly two hundred tons each were quarried, accurately cut and faced, moved many miles and placed in position at considerable heights above the earth. Immensely high and thick walls were built of stones weighing more than twenty tons each, and so accurately cut and fitted, without the use of mortar or cement, that even to-day it is impossible to insert a knife blade between the blocks. If we were to judge these prehistoric workmen by their works we would be forced to the conclusion that they were herculean giants. But we know from the skeletons and skulls that they were men no larger, no stronger than ourselves; rather, if anything, a smaller and weaker race.

Another striking feature common to nearly all of these civilizations is the prevalence of certain forms and figures, which, although varying in details, treatment and conventionalization, are always easily recognized. One of these is the sun, which is not remarkable inasmuch as all of these races were, apparently, sun-worshipers. Others are the so-called plumed serpent, the figure of a hunchback, a squatted human figure, masked human faces, elephant-like figures, and others. Judging from the wide-spread use of these and the similarity of their salient features, it seems probable that all these diversified civilized races were or had been at some time in direct communication with one another or with some other unknown race from which the symbolic figures were borrowed.

In many of their industries, in their implements and utensils, in their weapons and even in their decorations and ornaments, there was often more or less similarity. All wove textiles of hair, wool or fibers; all used feathers extensively and showed great skill and art in weaving them into clothing, mantles, etc.; all were splendid wood-workers; all employed gold, silver and copper and performed wonders in working these metals. Nearly all held human sacrifices, although they varied in form, in occasion and in their significance. All were primarily agricultural. All had a most elaborate priesthood. All were immensely rich in gold, silver, precious stones and other treasures, although, as far as we know, the precious metals were never valued as we value them, but were esteemed for their beauty, their ductility and for purely ornamental purposes.

While by no means of a predatory character, all of these races maintained large standing armies, well armed, trained and drilled, and constructed forts and defenses which were truly remarkable. In many cases these buildings indicated a wonderful military knowledge, and were not only placed at the most strategic positions, but were designed with bastions, salients, moats and even loopholes, and were fully equal to European forts of the time of the conquest.

Nearly all these races had conquered and confederated many diversified tribes, and maintained their commonwealths, their rulers, their priests, their temples, their armies, their governments and their religions mainly through taxes and tribute collected over an enormous area. All showed a deep and profound knowledge of engineering, and carried out feats of bridge and aqueduct building, irrigation projects, road-making and transportation which would present serious problems to the best engineers now.

Most, if not all, possessed a knowledge of natural sciences and mathematics, well-worked-out calendars, sun-dials or other means of computing time, and some were well up in astronomy. All had many species of cultivated plants and had developed many distinct and superior varieties. They raised nearly all the known varieties of maize, beans, potatoes, squashes, pumpkins and melons; they had peanuts, cacao, bananas, pineapples and many other fruits and medicinal plants, and they had domesticated turkeys, ducks, geese, pheasants and other birds, as well as a number of quadrupeds, for so long that we cannot with certainty identify the original wild forms from which they were developed. In rainless areas all had established elaborate irrigation systems, and in districts where there was an excessive rainfall they had installed canals, trenches, drainage-systems, etc. In a general way their household implements and utensils were very similar, although each tribe or civilization had its distinctive forms, materials and types of ornamentation.

While certain forms of weapons were peculiar to one race or civilization, the majority of weapons were strikingly alike in character. All made use of bows and arrows, as well as blow-guns and darts. All used clubs of wood or of wood with stone heads. All used axes, mauls and hatchets of stone, stone-knives and daggers, and all used spears. It is probable that all made use of the spear-throwing-stick or atlatl, for it is found in remains from Mexico to Chile, as well as farther north. Although stone weapons and implements were the rule, yet all or nearly all of these people made use of bronze and copper weapons as well.

Certain types of weapons were, as I have said, confined to certain races or districts. Thus the Peruvian and Bolivian people used a peculiar form of mace or club with a star-shaped head of stone or bronze, sometimes made with the radial projections sharp and conical in form, at other times with one or more in the form of cutting, hatchet-like blades. These races also used slings (as do the living Indians of the district) and boomerang-like throwing-clubs. On the other hand, the Mexicans used a peculiar sword-like weapon with jagged obsidian teeth set along its edges. But as a rule the offensive weapons, and the implements of a peaceful character, were very similar and differed mainly in the materials used, the manner in which they were manufactured and in minor details.

Strangely enough, the quality of their weapons, tools and implements is no indication of their cultural status or the advancement these peoples had attained in arts and other matters. Those who had reached the greatest heights in other lines of industry and civilization often possessed the crudest weapons and tools.

If this applied to weapons alone, we might assume that as a race became more highly cultured, more powerful and more prosperous, the necessity for weapons decreased and all energies were devoted to arts and crafts of peace rather than to those of war. But we cannot account for it in this simple manner. In the first place, all of these prehistoric civilizations were surrounded and harassed by enemies, and they found disarmament and universal peace as visionary as they are among the nations of the world to-day. Even had there been no enemies to fear, they would have required weapons and fighting forces, for, as I have said, they were made up of many tribes conquered and confederated into a commonwealth which was, in every case as far as known, held together only by military power. Intertribal feuds and age-old enmities smoldered everywhere, and civil wars and revolutionary outbreaks were of frequent occurrence. In the second place, even had there been no necessity for devoting time and labor to efficient weapons, there would have been every reason for having the best of tools and implements. Yet, among the remains of some of these ancient civilizations which are literally astounding for their stone sculptures, their beautiful pottery and their textiles, we find no implements except those of a most primitive and apparently inefficient type. No living man, Indian or otherwise, could by any possibility duplicate the simplest of their stone carving by means of the stone implements we find in conjunction with them. It is not a question of skill, patience and time. It is a human impossibility.

On one occasion I selected several hundred assorted stone tools and implements obtained from the site of the Coclé temple, and, outlining a coarse simple scroll upon a fragment of soft stone which was a portion of an elaborately sculptured column, I set four of my Indians to work upon it with the prehistoric tools. Although the four were unusually intelligent and skilful men, and despite the fact that they worked and labored diligently for a week, and broke or wore out all of the stone implements, their united efforts failed to result in any noticeable carving or even in a recognizable pattern on the stone. Yet, at this same site, there were immense columns of basalt—some thirty feet in length by two feet or more square—accurately cut, tooled and carved; huge idols of quartzite and diorite sculptured with wonderful fidelity and detail; blocks of red jasper cut and polished and ornamented with deeply cut designs, leaving figures in high relief, and not a few sculptured figures in which several inches of hard stone had been cut completely away so as to leave open, fretwork-like designs. This is by no means a unique or an unusual case. The Manabi culture of Ecuador is remarkable for its immense carved stone seats or thrones, its sculptured slabs and monuments, and yet no tool or implement worthy of the name is known from the locality.

Indeed, even the stupendous works of the pre-Incas and the Tiahuánacans must have been accomplished by the crudest, most primitive of stone tools,—if we are to judge solely by what we find in the ruins. But, as I have already said, few intelligent persons with any imagination can believe this to be the case, and personally I feel certain that these people knew and used steel, or at least hardened iron—possibly meteoric iron. In fact, I cannot understand how it could have been possible for them *not* to have discovered iron. These races smelted and worked copper, gold, silver and even platinum. It is practically impossible to smelt copper or other metals without obtaining an iron "button," even though it be very small, and the presence of even a minute quantity of iron could not have escaped notice as it would have been so much harder than the other metals. Moreover, iron ore, of various kinds, is abundant in all the countries where these civilizations flourished, and it would seem inconceivable that people as intelligent, as skilful and as practical as were these races would not have learned to smelt the iron ores about them.

Various savage African tribes smelt and forge iron and produce excellent steel, and the Mayas, Aztecs, pre-Incans, Incans and Coclés were immeasurably above any of these African tribes in culture and intelligence.

But until steel or iron implements of unquestionably prehistoric origin are discovered in the ruins or among the remains of these prehistoric American civilizations, we can only wonder and surmise and confess that we do not know and cannot explain how such truly astounding feats were accomplished.

CHAPTER VI

THE POMPEII OF AMERICA

COULD we but know the stories of these past civilizations, we would no doubt find they had most tragic and most romantic histories. Unfortunately, their stories are usually buried with their long-dead people, and only now and then do we find evidences that enable us to guess as to their fate. Such is the case with the Coclé culture which I discovered in Panama in 1924.

Although I refer to it as a "culture," yet it is so far beyond other mere cultures in many ways that it may almost be considered a civilization. In many respects it is essentially different from all other known American cultures; in other respects, it shows remarkably striking similarities with such cultures and civilizations as the Nicoya, the Maya and the pre-Incan. Although nothing definite is known as to its history, its age, the race it represents or anything regarding it,—other than what we can surmise from the objects and artifacts uncovered and from a study of the remains,—yet there are good reasons for considering it the most ancient of known advanced cultures in Central or South America.

This assumption is based partly upon the decomposition which has taken place in much of the stone-work; partly upon the depth of the alluvial and other deposits which have accumulated since the culture ceased to exist, and partly upon the fact that many of the remains have been covered with volcanic ash from an adjacent volcano where geological evidence gives us a fairly adequate idea of the time which has elapsed since it was last in eruption. Leaving out the question of the decomposition of diorite and other rocks at this locality, a question not as yet determined, we have the best evidence of extreme antiquity in the alluvial and other deposits. From four to twelve feet of soil have accumulated since the abandonment of the site by the unknown cultured race which left us these mute remains. That alone bespeaks an enormous period of time, for while we have no definite data as to the annual rate of deposit in the locality we can form some idea of the ages that must have passed since the prehistoric people first worshiped and offered sacrifices before their idols at this spot. We know that the site has not been occupied or in use since the arrival of Europeans, and hence the thin superficial layer of mold that covers the uppermost potsherds and remains must represent the débris of at least four hundred years. Brush fires have probably destroyed a portion of the decaying vegetation which accumulated upon the surface, and some probably has been carried away by heavy rains. But even if we allow fifty per cent. destroyed annually in this way, the accumulation would not have exceeded two or three inches in a century. At this rate it would require four hundred years to deposit a foot of soil, and an accumulation of ten feet would indicate that some four thousand years have passed since the first monuments were erected. I say "first" for it is evident that the site was occupied and used through hundreds, probably thousands, of years, for in many spots there are remains buried twice the depth of others, while some are exposed at the surface of the earth. But in every case the accumulation of soil about them is several feet in depth.

The district where these remains were found, and where I carried on excavations for six months, is a level alluvial plain or llano lying between the Pacific Coast and the mountains, a district cut by many streams and rivers, broken by occasional knolls or small hills, and, with the exception of the river bottom-lands, sterile and wholly unfit for agriculture. It is therefore remarkable that a vast teeming population should have occupied this territory, especially as the prehistoric denizens of the area were obviously preeminently agricultural. The only explanation is that in the days when the prehistoric race dwelt here the country was fertile, and that the tufa and ashes from the volcano's eruption transformed it to a barren, almost desert land. There is every evidence to support this theory. Towering above the plains at the feet of the cordilleras is the volcano of Guacamayo. The broken-down crater is still raw and burned, the mountain still rumbles and emits steam and hot water from its fumeroles, and over a great portion of the llanos is a layer of volcanic ash which has not yet thoroughly decomposed to form soil. During the rainy season the entire district from sea-coast to foot-hills is transformed into a veritable swamp, the streams overflowing their banks and flooding the llanos, while during the dry months the plains become baked, the streams vanish or dwindle to mud-holes, the scanty vegetation withers, and the district becomes a parched desert country.

My statement that this area was once inhabited by a vast and teeming populace is based on several obvious facts: first, the immense number of burials, ceremonial monuments, village sites and mounds; second, the incredible number of potsherds, stone artifacts and other manufactured objects scattered over a wide area, and often forming deposits several feet in depth; third, the enormous size and great number of stone stelæ, monuments and idols which could have been moved and erected only by thousands of hands working in unison; finally, the remains of the culture have already been found over an area of approximately five hundred square miles. By this I do not mean that every square mile of the immense area is covered with remains, but over this entire area remains of the same prehistoric race occur, sometimes widely separated, at other times thickly covering hundreds of acres. Among the remains are kitchen-middens, refuse piles, village sites, burials, ceremonial or temple sites and mounds. In places, along some of the rivers, village sites extend for miles, and the strata of discarded stone artifacts and potsherds are from five to twenty feet thick. In other spots burials are so numerous that it is practically impossible to dig anywhere, over an area of many acres, without disclosing a grave.

Ceremonial monuments of stone are numerous, and there are hundreds of low rounded mounds full of pottery and stone implements, which were probably once surmounted by temples or buildings of some sort. By far the most extensive remains, the spot which so far has yielded the finest and most astonishing objects, and the nucleus of the whole culture, is a huge temple or ceremonial site which may well be called the "Temple of a Thousand Idols." The remains of this vast prehistoric place of worship cover a level area between two rivers, an area more than one hundred acres in extent, although only a small portion—about ten acres—has been cleared of jungle and partly excavated. This portion, however, appears to be the most important part of the whole, and was probably the central and most sacred part.

Although when first visited the site was overgrown with dense thorny brush and only the summits of stone columns were visible here and there, the clearing of the jungle and preliminary excavations soon revealed the arrangement and details of the place. Running north and south and east and west are rows of immense, hand-cut stone monuments or phallic columns placed in an almost geometrically perfect quadrangle. In the northern row there were thirty-one of these, spaced from eight to twelve feet apart and extending due east and west. One hundred feet east of these and one hundred feet south, were two immense basalt columns over fifteen feet in height and nearly thirty inches square, both of which had broken off and fallen to one side. One hundred and fifty feet south of these, and running due north and south, were twenty-seven columns. Two hundred and fifty feet south of these, and directly in line with them, were two more huge columns like those already mentioned. Three hundred feet west of these was a semi-circular row of smaller columns twenty-five in number. Three hundred feet north of these and three hundred and fifty feet from the first row of

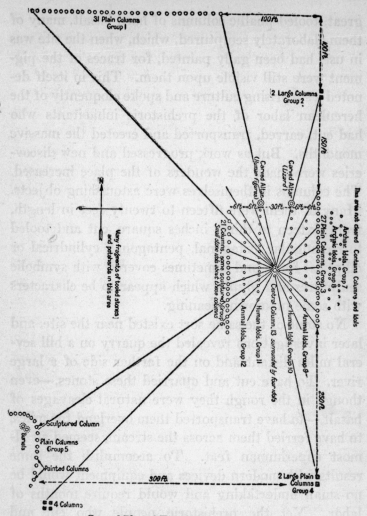

Ground Plan of Temple Site, Coclé, Panama.

thirty-one columns, were twenty-one others running north and south. Thus the three rows of stone monuments, with the two corner groups, formed a quadrangle approximately three hundred by seven hundred feet in area, an open court bounded by the great, tooled phallic columns of hard basalt, many of them elaborately sculptured, which, when the site was in use, had been gaily painted, for traces of the pigment were still visible upon them. This in itself denoted a surprising culture and spoke eloquently of the herculean labor of the prehistoric inhabitants who had cut, carved, transported and erected the massive monoliths. But as work progressed and new discoveries were made the wonders of the place increased. The columns in themselves were astonishing objects. Many of them were fifteen to twenty feet in length, from sixteen to thirty inches square, cut and tooled to rectangular, octagonal, pentagonal, cylindrical or elliptical form, and sometimes covered with symbolic sculptures and glyphs which appear to be characters with some unknown meaning.

No stone of the same sort existed near the site, and later investigations revealed the quarry on a hill several miles distant and on the farther side of a large river. To have cut and quarried these stones,—even though in the rough they were natural cleavages of basalt,—to have transported them overland for miles, to have ferried them across the stream, seemed an almost superhuman feat. To accomplish the same results with modern devices and equipment would be no small undertaking and would require months of labor. Yet the prehistoric people who cut and dragged the huge columns to this long-buried place of worship must have been limited to hand labor, to ropes and possibly rollers, to the crudest of tools. Even though thousands toiled and labored, years, decades, perhaps centuries, must have been required to transport the hundreds of monoliths, often weighing many tons, from the distant quarry to the temple. One marvels at the sublime faith, the sincerity, the belief in their deities that led these ancient people to this task and that kept them at it for month after month, year after year, until their temple was completed.

At times, too, their efforts must have seemed almost hopeless. Many of the finest columns were cracked or broken in transit and still lie where they were discarded by the wayside. And after the great stones were safely at their destination the work was only begun. Even the smaller columns were so heavy that eight or ten of my husky peons found it difficult to lift or move them, and we can scarcely conceive how or by what means the forgotten builders of the temple raised these immense monoliths to perpendicular positions and secured them firmly in place to form the straight rows of monuments that, in most cases, still stand.

Even more remarkable, more interesting, and indicative of even more inexplicable labor, are the innumerable stone images which were brought to light by the excavatory work. These, like the columns, were arranged in regular rows running north and south, and in all cases with the faces toward the east. East of the group of twenty-seven columns were two rows of these stone images. Six feet west of the same row of columns was a second line of idols, mainly of animal forms. Six feet west of these was a row of idols of human forms. Thirty feet west of these was still another row of human figures, and six feet west of these was another row of animal figures. It was evident that originally the idols had been evenly spaced about six feet apart, but through the ages many had fallen, others had sagged to one side or the other, many were broken and their fragments scatterd, while all which had been partly exposed above the surface of the earth had been broken off and eroded.

In the exact center of the area, and buried under fifteen feet of soil, was a great stone column nearly twenty feet in length, over two feet square, and most accurately cut and tooled. The lower portion still stood firmly perpendicular, but the upper portion had been broken in three places and the three sections were widely separated.

At the base of this central monolith were four stone figures—one a man, another a woman and child, another a jaguar and the fourth a bird—probably symbolic of the four cardinal points of the compass. Standing here by this central column with its stone idols, one quickly grasped the ground-plan of the entire site, for the idols and columns had been so placed and spaced as to form radiating lines with the central column as a nucleus, no doubt symbolizing the sun and its rays. At the base of this central monument, as well as at the bases of all the other columns, were large stones or boulders of semitransparent quartz or red or yellow jasper, artificially cut and polished and flattened on the upper side. Evidently these had served the dual purpose of sacrificial altars and supports for the columns or idols, for some were elaborately sculptured about the circumference and one was magnificently carved with a raised edge worked into the figure of a giant lizard or alligator. Moreover, on several were found remains of human skeletons—teeth and bits of calcined bone—among half-silicified charcoal.

Many of the idols or stone figures of this culture are marvelous examples of prehistoric stone carving. In size they vary from a few inches to seven feet in height, and among them are representations of human beings, birds, reptiles and practically every quadruped of the country. Some show men seated upon thrones formed of coiled serpents, upon chairs or stools held up by smaller human figures, or standing upon conventionalized animals. Several show the peculiar hunchback figure that I have mentioned as cropping up throughout Central and South America, and one shows a Siamese-twin figure connected back to back. On one a jaguar or puma is shown with its front paws resting on a wounded man, while another bears the figure of a jaguar holding a child in its jaws. One human figure is represented with one hand stroking a long chin-beard which is strikingly reminiscent of an Assyrian figure.

As a rule the human figures are shown with one hand upon the stomach and the other on the breast,—an attitude typical of Tiahuánaco figures,—but others have the hands resting upon the knees. Strangely enough, not a single carved or sculptured figure is represented with a vestige of clothing, the nearest approach to garments being a cord with an amulet shown about the neck of one of the largest and finest idols. But in every case the figures have carefully carved and elaborate head-dresses of a peculiar type. We may assume that the race used no garments, although the presence of spindle-weights indicates that they knew how to spin and probably how to weave.

In character of workmanship the idols vary greatly and show not only a perfect chain of development in the art of stone sculpture, but prove the tremendous lapse of time which must have passed between the beginning and the end of the temple. Those figures at the lowest level are crude, archaic and badly decomposed, while those nearest the surface are splendidly cut, elaborate in detail and are in perfect condition. In every case the figures or sculptured portions surmount pedestals or columns, either cylindrical or square, slightly tapered toward the base, and beautifully tooled.

The most astonishing of the idols is one bearing a figure which is so strikingly and obviously elephantine that it cannot be explained away by any of the ordinary theories of being a conventionalized or exaggerated tapir, ant-eater or macaw. Not only does this figure show a trunk, but in addition it has the big leaf-like ears and the forward-bending knees peculiar to the elephants. Moreover, it shows a load or burden strapped upon its back. It is inconceivable that any man could have imagined a creature with the flapping ears and peculiar hind knees of an elephant, or that any human being could have conventionalized a tapir to this extent. To my mind there is no doubt that the people who built this temple and reached such heights of culture in Panama in prehistoric times had either seen elephants, had domesticated some species of mastodon, or were in direct and frequent communication with the Orient and had heard descriptions of elephants from visitors from Asia. Until a better explanation is offered I see no other way of explaining the presence of this figure.

One of the most remarkable features of this ancient culture is the vast quantity of pottery that occurs everywhere. The burials are filled with it; closely packed masses several feet in thickness surround every column and idol, and over hundreds of acres it is impossible to lift a shovelful of earth without turning up potsherds. This accumulation of pottery shows, like the stone figures, the development of the culture and its great age. The lowest—from ten to twenty feet beneath the present surface of the earth—is of a crude, plain type, with little embellishment and usually decorated, if at all, with simple incised designs or rudely modeled ornaments in the forms of animal or human heads. Above this, and especially near the surface, the pottery is of a quality and beauty unexcelled in prehistoric American ceramic art. Indeed the beauty, the coloring, the motifs of this Coclé pottery are the most surprising features of the culture. One has but to glance at the specimens obtained to realize to what a high degree of perfection the ceramic art had been developed by these ancient people. Some pieces might have well come from Mexico, others are strikingly similar to examples from Ecuador, Peru and Bolivia, but by far the greater portion are wholly distinct in every way from anything hitherto known to archeologists.

Forms representing conventionalized birds, reptiles, quadrupeds and human beings are very common. Others are of the "portrait" type so abundant in Incan and pre-Incan pottery, and there are numerous figurines of birds, quadrupeds and human beings. In shape and size the vessels range all the way from tiny cups and bowls to large plates, pots and immense burial urns. Practically every known form is represented, and in addition there are several types peculiar to the culture. One is a square or rectangular form, another is a globular-bodied vessel with long, gracefully tapered neck like a carafe, while still a third is a teapot-like jar with spout and handle. With very few exceptions, the vessels have annular bases, and in every case (even the very largest ones two feet or more in diameter) all are so perfectly true that it seems impossible they could have been formed without the aid of a potter's wheel. In a number of instances the designs painted upon the pottery are most remarkable and apparently represent creatures of a prehistoric type. One in particular might well be intended for a pterodactyl or flying-lizard, and in some respects shows the characteristics of the famous "plumed serpent" of ancient Mexico. This plumed-serpent motif reappears frequently and in many forms, but as a rule the representations of animals are very accurately drawn and are easily recognizable. Regardless of the motif used or the central or predominant figure depicted, the pottery of this remarkable culture is distinguished by the use of a scroll of a peculiar and elaborate type. Sometimes the scroll itself appears as a decorative design, in other cases it is used in combination with other patterns, and often figures of men or animals are made up of scrolls cleverly wrought and combined to give the desired effect of a conventionalized figure.

But the outstanding features of the ceramics as a whole are the predominance of polychrome ware and the colors employed. Not only do the ordinary colors, such as black, white, brown, ocher and red appear

in endless combinations, but in addition, brilliant
blues, purples, soft lavender, pink, orange and other
shades. Green, however, was not used, and was probably a taboo or evil color, for green pigments are
common in the neighborhood.

Ornaments are scarce. A few clay ear-plugs, some
labrets or lip-pins of a polished black material, some
earthenware and stone beads were found, and I obtained one very beautiful nose-ring. This was a magnificent example of workmanship and was cut from
bloodstone with the two ends, where it clasped the
septum of the nose, finished with perfectly fitted gold
caps. Aside from these bits of the precious metal, no
gold was found, although in the graves of other prehistoric races of Panama gold ornaments are common.

Numerous stone metates were secured, but none
was of the ornate type abundant in other portions of
Panama and Central America, while the vast quantities of stone implements, weapons and other stone
utensils were of the crudest, most primitive type.
Comparing the wonderful pottery and splendid
stonework with the almost unrecognizable stone implements, one finds it difficult to believe that they
could have been produced by the same people. Most
of the stone implements are almost Chellean in type,
often merely chunks of stone slightly chipped or hammered into rude form, and the arrow- and spear-heads
are badly made, rough and crooked. Apparently,
however, the race was improving in the art of making
stone implements, for now and then axes, chisels, etc.,
were found which are fairly well shaped and have been
rubbed to a smooth surface. Still fewer were secured
which were beautifully made, but several bodkin-like

and chisel-like tools are remarkable examples of workmanship.

It seems almost preposterous to believe that a race which had developed stone sculpture to such a high degree should not equally have developed stone implements, if, according to accepted theory, the prehistoric artizans depended upon stone tools. To have thus cut and sculptured the huge stone blocks into the forms of human beings and animals such as those at the Coclé temple site, would have required a lifetime for each. Until other explanations and proofs are forthcoming we must believe that this was the case, or must confess that it is an unsolved mystery.

Unfortunately, the greater portion of all the pottery found had been intentionally broken—"killed" or sacrificed, as is the custom of many living tribes during ceremonial or religious rites or when interring the dead. Although, as I have said, potsherds, stone implements and broken stone utensils are scattered over a wide area, they are particularly abundant at the temple site and especially about the columns and idols. In many cases the earthenware vessels have apertures made by stones thrown at them; frequently the stones are found in the midst of the shattered vessels, and practically all the columns and idols bear smears of color made by the clay vessels thrown against them.

In many spots the fragments of pottery and broken metates and implements are so densely packed and so numerous that they form fully eighty per cent. of the soil deposit, and so firmly have they become cemented together by induration that they form a brick-like mass six to ten feet in depth. The same is true of the

burials. Evidently it was the custom of these people
to place their dead in a huge urn in a clay-lined grave
and to cremate the body by means of a fire within
the grave which not only burned the body but also
baked the walls and floor of the grave to a brick-like
hardness. Obviously, also, the friends and mourners
stood about and made offerings by casting their finest
pottery and utensils into the fire, for in nearly every
case the remains of the huge burial urns are surrounded by charcoal, and are completely buried amid
fragments of pottery vessels and stone utensils and
implements.

Apparently, however, secondary burials were at
times made, possibly these being reserved for certain
persons or certain purposes. In the rear of the semi-
circular row of columns southwest of the temple, two
such secondary burials were uncovered. The skeletons had practically disappeared, but impressions of
the bones left in the packed clay, and a few fragments
of teeth, revealed the arrangement. The bones had
been placed in small neat piles with the skulls facing
the east. One burial was on a legless metate, the
other on a flat-topped stone, and each was surrounded
by a number of miniature vessels, stone implements,
etc. Near these, traces of a third burial were found
mingled with charcoal upon a flattened quartz boul-
der at the base of a stone column bearing an incised
figure of a man with a feather head-dress, which
might indicate that the burial was that of a king, chief
or priest.

Although this temple site was no doubt the most
important place of ceremonials and worship of the
people, yet it is evident that ceremonials and sacri-

fices, as well as offerings of utensils, etc., were not confined to this one spot. At many places over the area once occupied by this prehistoric race there are similar but smaller rows of stone monuments with their characteristic altars, a few idols and the same accumulation of sacrificed or "killed" utensils on a smaller scale. In other words, the main temple corresponded to a great cathedral and the smaller sites were the equivalents of our village churches and chapels.

It would be vastly interesting to know just how these people lived, what were their customs, habits, beliefs; what sort of dwellings they used, and what was their personal appearance. We can determine very little about such matters, although we can form fairly accurate opinions regarding them. We can safely assume that they were nude, that they were not given to much personal adornment, and that they were intensely religious and very industrious. Undoubtedly they were agricultural and peace-loving, for there are few weapons of warfare or the chase among the remains. But the presence of fish-net sinkers, a few spear- and arrow-heads, an occasional animal or fish bone and numerous perforated chama shells prove that they hunted and fished to some extent.

They knew how to spin cotton, and it is clear that they made use of thread, cord and rope, for all these are represented in carvings or ceramics, while several of the pottery vessels have handles of rope form. Moreover, these were not merely twisted to represent rope, but were actually made up of three strands laid exactly like modern rope.

Probably they had hammocks, and as no remains of stone dwellings have been found we can feel reasonably sure that they dwelt in wooden or cane houses with thatched roofs which were far better adapted to the climate and country than stone houses would have been.

From the arrangement of the temple we can feel sure they were sun-worshipers, and from the number and character of the idols or effigies we can feel equally positive that they held many creatures sacred, that they revered certain human beings, that they had many deities, and that they believed in the plumed-serpent god. The fact that they "killed" or sacrificed their pottery would indicate that they believed that in this manner they prevented evil spirits from entering or abiding in them. Something of the same general character is practised by the Guaymí Indians of northern Panama to-day. During their ceremonials these Indians have numbers of small clay images representing animal and human forms and imaginary beings. These are not idols, but serve as proxies for such individuals as cannot be present in person, for "good-spirit-creatures," and for kindly-disposed deities. At the close of the ceremony these are broken or "sacrificed" and cast into a sacred fire to prevent evil spirits taking possession of the effigies. (See Chapter X.)

If we substitute a stone column or a stone idol for the sacred fire (although probably sacred fires and possibly sacrifices were in progress at the bases of the columns at the time) we can readily understand why the prehistoric denizens of Coclé destroyed pottery, implements and other objects during ceremonials.

Or it may have been that the people considered the
sacrifice of valued possessions fully as efficacious as
the sacrifice of human beings or animals. No doubt
food was also sacrificed at the same time, for sea-
shells, fish and animal bones are abundant among the
broken pottery. As the temple or ceremonial place
was unquestionably used for many centuries it is not
surprising that such vast masses of the sacrificed pottery should have accumulated about the sacred idols
and columns.

As to the personal appearance of these unknown
people, we can scarcely do more than guess, although,
judging from the fidelity with which they depicted
other forms, we have no reason to think that their
drawings and sculptures of human beings were not
fully as accurate. If such were the case, then we can
easily picture their physical appearance. Judged
from this standpoint, they were tall, well formed,
muscular. Their heads were of the round type, rather
broad, with artificially flattened craniums in some
cases, and with features that are unlike those
of any known American race. Nowhere do we find
the heavy beak-like nose of the Aztec and Mayan
carvings. Nowhere are there the strongly aquiline
noses of the Incan and pre-Incan races. Nowhere the
oblique eyes of the Mongolian. The nose depicted is
always well bridged, straight or slightly aquiline, and
the nostrils are narrow. The eyes are full and
straight, the lips rather full and thick, the chin is receding, and the eyes are set far apart. Whether
they were light- or dark-skinned we cannot say, but
we may feel sure that they wore their hair long,
braided or twisted into a sort of queue at the back,

and either braided into elaborate form upon the head or else covered with a cap-like, close-fitting and highly ornamental head-dress.

Why, it may well be asked, did the inhabitants of these villages and the worshipers at the temple disappear? What drove off or wiped out the teeming population so completely that no descendants have been left, that no traditions or records have remained to tell us who they were or whence they came? What was the catastrophe that destroyed the race and its advanced culture? Unlike the majority of similar questions which confront us when studying the remains of prehistoric American civilizations, and which are still unexplained mysteries, the answer in this case is simple. Only by the theory of a severe, a most terrible series of earthquakes and an accompanying volcanic eruption can we account for the condition of the ruins and remains. Nothing but an earthquake could have tossed the immense stone columns and images about. By no other means could these have been broken and the pieces thrown so far in various directions. In many cases the largest stone monuments are snapped squarely off, the bases remaining firmly fixed and upright, while the upper portions are thrown to one side and frequently end for end, or with the middle portion farther from the base than the top.

In many instances, too, the largest idols are found turned end for end, with the base of the pedestal uppermost, while others have been broken and the heads of the figures are found fully one hundred feet from the bodies. Still more eloquent of terrific earth movements is the fact that the strata of hard tenacious clay or "bed-soil" on which the idols and columns were set has been lifted and moved so that in places it presents a wave-like surface.

Moreover, in many places, a thin layer of volcanic ash covers the remains at the burial and village sites, and in one spot I obtained several entire vessels and many potsherds from beneath a layer of ash more than nine feet in thickness. This had obviously been hot when deposited, for it had been burned firmly on to the pottery.

Hence we can feel more than reasonably certain that the destruction of the culture was the result of an eruption of Guacamayo volcano which, as I have said, is barely six miles from the temple site. Such an eruption must have been accompanied by tremendous earth tremors and upheavals which probably did more damage than the falling ashes and red-hot mud. It is not difficult to imagine the terrorized people, who escaped from the first of the catastrophe, rushing madly from their razed homes to their temple. We can picture them striving to placate their gods by wholesale sacrifices, by the mad destruction of their most prized possessions at the feet of their idols. We can visualize their utter despair as the tremors shook the earth, the ground rose and fell, and the sacred monuments and images were broken and thrown down.*

---

*It is a rather remarkable fact, that the Aztecs' legend or myth of the Toltecs contains an account of a violent volcanic eruption near the city of Tollan which caused the Tollan rulers to order wholesale sacrifices in order to placate the gods. Although similar eruptions have no doubt occurred and have destroyed prehistoric settlements in many places, the ancient Nahua legend and the actual occurrence at Coclé are remarkably similar. It is not beyond the bounds of possibility or reason that the story was based on the eruption at Coclé. At all events it proves that a devastating eruption would have brought about the wholesale sacrifices which we know occurred at the Coclé site.

Possibly every member of the race was destroyed by the blasting heat, the poisonous gases and the blinding dust emitted by the volcano. But the chances are that many escaped, for at the temple site there are no indications that ashes or dust fell on that spot. Undoubtedly, also, those who may have survived, finding their gods powerless to help them, took refuge in flight. No doubt they had canoes upon the near-by rivers, and some probably pushed off in these while others may have fled by foot to north or south. Scattered far and wide, they may have reverted to primitive savagery and have completely forgotten their past culture and their identity as they mingled with other races.

But, on the other hand, they may have carried their culture with them, and in other lands and among other races they may have increased and prospered and built up new cultures and even civilizations which, though distinct in many ways, yet showed the influence of the arts and culture of Coclé. There are various valid and logical reasons for suspecting this, and, in other chapters, I shall mention them in detail.

CHAPTER VII

THE MAYAS

Of all the early American civilizations, the Mayan is probably the best known to the majority of people. This is largely due to the attention which has been given to the Mayan ruins, the immense amount of research work which has been devoted to the Mayas, and the extensive collections of Mayan specimens in the various museums. In many ways, too, the romance, the mystery and the spectacular features of the Mayan civilization appeal strongly to the imagination. Despite all this, the average person really knows little about the Mayas and their works and lives.

Although the Mayas are known to have occupied a vast area of country, an area of over fifty thousand square miles, yet practically all scientific research work has been confined to a very limited area in Yucatan, Guatemala and Honduras. Moreover, the greater portion of our studies has been devoted to the more spectacular features of this ancient civilization; to the temples, the palaces, the monuments and massive stonework. Although this has resulted in the accumulation of a vast amount of material upon the Mayan culture, it has given us very little information regarding the daily life of the people, their customs, habits and social condition. What we actually know of the Mayas is comparable perhaps to what archeologists, several thousands years hence, might learn of our lives and customs by excavating the ruins of our cathedrals, churches, capitols and public buildings and by studying our monuments and statues. No doubt most of the Mayas were poor

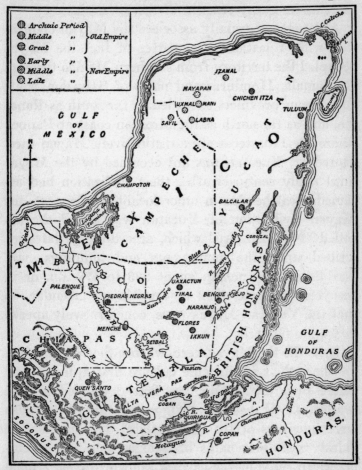

Figure 1—Map of Southern Mexico and Central America, showing the Principal Maya States.

in worldly goods and possessed little in the way of archeological treasures. In all probability they lived under much the same conditions as the semicivilized

Indians of the same countries to-day, and, scientifi-
cally speaking, the study of the large, impressive
works of the race are far more important than re-
searches in scanty remains of the lower classes.

Although we usually associate the Mayan civilization with Yucatan, as a matter of fact the Mayas
occupied the territory from southern Mexico through
Guatemala, Honduras and parts of Salvador, while
outposts or provinces extended as far south as Panama, and as far north as the Mexican coast at Pánuco
where the Huastecas are a distinctively Mayan race.
Moreover, Yucatan was not occupied by the Mayas
until many centuries after their civilization had attained great heights in other localities. In fact, the
Mayan civilization of Yucatan was all of the so-
called "New Empire" which, according to dates inscribed upon the monuments and buildings, was
established in Yucatan about 333 to 472 A.D. or in
the years 3760 to 3902 of the Mayan calendar, so
that the Yucatan Mayas were, comparatively speaking, quite modern.

Just who the Mayas were, whence they came, when
or where their remarkable culture first appeared, or
where their civilization was first developed are all
mysteries. It has been suggested that the Mayas
were survivors of the semimythical Toltecs, but the
oldest existing remains of Mexico show no resemblance to those of the earliest known Mayas. Some
authorities have suggested that the nucleus of the
Mayan civilization was in Chiapas, owing to many
similarities between the Zapotecan and Mayan cultures, but it is fairly well established that the former
borrowed from both the Mayas and Aztecs, and we

know that the Mayas were conquered and greatly influenced by the Aztecs long before the arrival of the Spaniards. In all probability the birthplace of Mayan culture was somewhere in Guatemala, for here we find the earliest known distinctively Mayan remains, as well as the most widely disseminated and varied Mayan dialects. In Guatemala alone there are more than twenty-four Mayan dialects spoken, the principal ones being the Quiché, Kakchiquel, Zutugil, Coxohchol and Pipil.

We also know, from their inscribed dates, how long the Mayan chronology had been established, but we cannot tell how long the race may have been civilized before the calendrical system was invented or the written language evolved. Moreover, there are many great gaps in the known or recorded history of the Mayas. Thus, although we know approximately the date at which the New Empire entered Yucatan, we know nothing definite regarding the Mayas' doings or what became of them in Yucatan during the interval of several centuries which elapsed between that date and the founding of the holy city of the Plumed Serpent (Chichen-Itza). But if recent discoveries are borne out, and if the date glyphs found have been correctly interpreted, it would seem that the Mayas' New Empire was first established in southern Yucatan in the district of Bacalar (Mayan Bakhalal), the first place mentioned in the Mayan records known as the *Books of Chilám Balám*. These give the date of the discovery of the spot as 472 A.D.; but Doctor Gann has found remarkable ruins in the same district which go back for more than a century before that date, or to about 333 A.D., and

which show indisputable evidences of a prolonged
period of occupation by a large population.

Long before the coming of Cortez, the Mayan
Empire or "Empire of Xibalba" had ceased to exist
as an entity, and the Mayan civilization was at an
end. The surviving Mayas were scattered, and the
people were divided into numerous tribal or feudal
states. They had little definite knowledge of their
ancestors, and the Aztecs had little more than myths
regarding the race they had once conquered, who had
left such stupendous, imperishable works buried in
the jungles of Yucatan and Central America.

But with the passing of years, and the slow, pains-
taking studies of innumerable scientists, something
has been learned of the Mayas' past history. We
know, from decipherable inscriptions and from the
remains, that the Mayas reached great heights during
their first or Old Empire; that they attained even
greater heights during their New Empire; that they
were conquered or at least brought under the domin-
ance and the influence of the Mexicans, and that during the later periods of their existence, the Mayas'
arts, beliefs, customs and mythology showed the
Aztec or Nahua influences very strongly. Hence
the purest Mayan works are those which existed
prior to the Aztec conquest.

We also know that the Mayas were distinct from
the Mexicans or any other known American tribe,
although unquestionably Indians. In their buildings, monuments, arts, religion and other respects
they differed somewhat from any known prehistoric
race, although certain details and features of this
culture were strikingly like those of a still more

ancient culture in old Panama.   (See Chapter VI.)

But in no other part of America do we find the same types of architecture, the same or similar monuments, or, what is of greater importance, the same or even a remotely similar written, perhaps I might better say sculptured, language.

As was the case with the Aztec and the Incan Empires, the Mayan Empire, or "Kingdom of the Great Snake," was a federation of many tribes rather loosely held together and with many semiindependent centers. Each city or town was an aggregation of houses and buildings clustering about a nucleus consisting of the magnificent temples and palaces, much as the towns of feudal Europe were built about the local castles.   The lavish, ornate and truly remarkable architecture was confined entirely to buildings devoted to religious or royal purposes and not a single example of a Mayan domestic building or ordinary house is known.   In all probability the masses dwelt in flimsy thatched huts of wood, cane or possibly adobe which have long since disappeared. The people, like the Aztecs, were sharply divided into the laboring and the aristocratic classes.   And, like the Mexicans, the poorer classes were scarcely more than slaves while the upper class and nobility lived in luxury, opulence and splendor.

Undoubtedly the Nahua invasion completely altered much of the life, many of the customs and arts, and even the religion of the Mayas, and it probably disrupted the empire.   The remnants separated into city-states, like those of Italy after the fall of Rome. It was probably at this time that the Guatemalan and more northerly Mayas separated.   There is no real proof that the Mayas ever formed another wide-spread empire, but there is evidence to show that each city-state had its own king and that feudal wars and quarrels were frequent, although all were more or less subject to the priest-kings of Mayapan. These priest-kings claimed direct descent from the Plumed Serpent (Kukulcan) and were largely instrumental in raising the New Empire to its high state. On the other hand, those who founded Chichen-Itza were not priests, but belonged to the warrior caste and were known as Itzaes. There is a great deal of

The Plumed Serpent (Kukulcan) from a sculpture in the "Temple of the Foliated Cross" at Palenque.

mystery surrounding the early dynasty of the Mayas and the number of their kings is unknown, but we may be fairly certain that the Quiché monarchs were supreme in Guatemala, that, during the various civil wars of the Mayas, Nahua mercenaries were employed, and that these Mexican soldiers of fortune introduced many arts, customs and words of their own race.

Like the Aztecs, the Mayas recorded events by codices, three of which are preserved. These are the *Codex Peresianus* in Paris; the *Dresden Codex* and the *Troano Codex* in Madrid. All of these deal principally with mythology, but they have never been fully translated. Unlike the Aztecan codices with their pictographic records, these of the Mayas were in characters like the inscriptions upon the monuments and buildings.

The mythology of the Mayas was if anything more involved and complicated than that of the Aztecs, and they had borrowed almost, if not quite, as many deities from the Nahuas as the Nahuas had borrowed from them. As a result, there was a multiplicity of gods, and while some are always easily recognizable, others are so variable that it is uncertain whether their various representations are of one or several deities. As no one has ever yet definitely determined the identity of some of these they are known to scientists by letters only. But there are certain distinct, important and well-known deities regarding whom we have quite detailed information.

Most prominent of all perhaps was the sun-god known as Kinichahau, (Lord of the Face of the Sun) in Yucatan, and as Kinich Kakmo (Fire-bird or Sun-bird) and identified with the red macaw or Arara (Fire-bird). As the Mayas were indirectly sun-worshipers, the sun-god held a very important place in their mythology. In nearly all the Mayan myths the origin of the race is solar, like that of the Incas, and since the sun rises in the east all of the Mayas' mythical hero-gods, who were supposed to have brought culture and civilization, were credited with coming from the east.

The Plumed Serpent, known to the Mayas as Kukulcan,* and in Guatemala as Gucumatz, was fully as important a deity to the Mayas as to the Aztecs, and the Mayan myths regarding him are

---

*Kukul meaning the Quetzál bird and Kan a serpent.

similar to those of the Nahuas. But his attributes differed considerably from those of the Mexican Plumed Serpent. Among the Mayas he was more of a thunder-god or god-of-the-sky, and although the holy city of Chichen-Itza was dedicated to him, and some of the most magnificent temples of the Mayas

The Plumed Serpent (Kukulcan) from a carving on a wooden lintel at Tikal.

were those of the Plumed Serpent, he was by no means their greatest divinity.

Probably that honor should go to Hunabku, the invisible and supreme god who was recognized by all the Mayan tribes (although they had their own special deities), and who was regarded as the unity of all gods and held much the same place in the Mayan religion as our Almighty holds in the Christian and Jewish faiths.

The moon-god was also a most important deity and was known as Itzama (Father of gods and men). He typified decay and the rebirth of life in nature, and was the deity of the west. His name was taken from his own legendary words to mankind: *"Itz en caan, itz en muyal"* (I am the dew of heaven, I am the dew of the clouds).

Chac-Mool, identical with the Aztecan Tlaloc was the Maya rain-god or water-god, and at the spring florescence young and beautiful girls were sacrificed to Chac-Mool by being cast into the sacred well at Chichen-Itza. This was one of the few human sacrifices if not the only one practised by the Mayas, whose religion, far less cruel and bloodthirsty than that of the Aztecs, called for self-sacrifice by bloodletting rather than the death of victims. Chac-Mool, although usually represented as a recumbent figure with flexed knees and with hands on his stomach, is also shown in paintings and carvings with a long tapir-like snout or nose, supposed to be symbolic of a spout for pouring water. In addition to being the rain-god he was the deity of the east.

Ekchuah, the black-god, was the special deity of merchants and cacao planters, while Ixch'el was the goddess of medicine.

The bat-god, Zotzilaha-Chimalman, who was supposed to dwell in a gruesome bat-cave, was the Mayas' god of darkness and was a sinister figure in their mythology. Throughout Mayan mythology and legends there is the ever-present conflict between light and dark, the sun-god Kinichahau opposing Zotzilaha-Chimalman. Many authorities believe that the entire Mayan mythology and religion were evolved from this eternal conflict between day and night or life and death. Strangely enough, the Mayas differed markedly from the Aztecs in that they had a great dread of death, whereas the Aztecs rather courted it than otherwise.

In addition to their true gods, the Mayas had four semideities or genii known as *bacabs* who were symbolical of the four points of the compass. Their symbol colors were yellow, white, black and red, and they were named respectively Kan, Muluc, Ix and

Cauac. In the Mayan mythology they supported the four quarters of the sky or heaven.

Finally we have the weird, uncertain gods of the codices which have been designated by letters.

Figure 2—Mayan Gods.

A-Death God.
B-Rain and Thunder God.
C-God of North Star.
D-Itzamma the all-powerful sky God.

E-Maize God.
F-War God.
G-Sun God.
K-Wind God.

The god *A* is a human figure with exposed backbone and a fleshless skull bearing the snail symbol as a sign of birth. He also wears crossed bones, and the glyph accompanying him shows a corpse head with closed eyes, a skull and a sacrificial knife. He is the symbol of the day, Cimi (Death), and presides over the home of the dead (west) or the setting sun.

God *B* has a tapir's nose. He is the most commonly recurring of all, and is shown walking on water and carrying torches, and is supposed to be a god of farming; but perhaps is identical with Chac-Mool.

God *C* is the god of the pole-star, and is shown surrounded by symbols of the various planets.

God *D* is a moon-god; an aged man with shrunken cheeks, wrinkled forehead, and having the symbol of night. His glyph is surrounded by stars and bears the numeral 20 showing the moon's duration.

God *E* is a maize-god with an ear of corn as his head-dress, and is probably the same as Ghanan or Yum Kaax (Lord of the Harvest).

God *F* is probably identical with the Aztec god Xipe, the deity of sacrifices, for his face and body are covered with black lines to indicate wounds.

God *G* is the sun-god or the sun, with the sun-glyph Kin, while god *H* is an unknown serpent-god.

I is a water-goddess; a wrinkled, shriveled old woman with claw feet, and a snake on her head, and is holding water-jars. She is probably a Mayan conception of the Aztec Chalchihuitlicue, and symbolizes floods and destruction, as she is often accompanied by a death symbol.

God *K* has an ornamented nose almost like a proboscis, and the numerous representations of his features on carvings led to the belief that the Mayas had an elephant-headed god. He is thought to be a form of Chac-Mool and is regarded as a storm-god.

L is an aged black man with toothless gums, perhaps a form of Ekchuah.

M is also a black god, but he has red lips and carries a roped package upon his head. He is supposed to be the god of travelers.

N is supposed to be the demon-god, Uayayab, who presided over the five "unlucky" days at the end of the year. He is known as "He by whom the year is poisoned."

O is an old woman goddess engaged in spinning, and is undoubtedly the goddess of domestic work, and perhaps of married women.

God *P* is a frog-god with a blue background representing water. He is at times shown sowing seeds or farming, and is probably a god of agriculture.

The Rear Head of the Earth-monster.

Many of these Mayan deities had more of a symbolic than religious character, and each week was under the auspices of a particular deity.

Like that of the Aztecs and the Incans, the Mayan calendar was based originally upon the lunar year, but it underwent many changes and alterations during its development. It first started with an arbitrary count of two hundred and sixty days, but was modified to bring it into accord with the solar year. This resulted in a series of three hundred and sixty day periods, to which were added five "unlucky days," thus bringing the computation to within one day of the true solar year. But the underlying original count of two hundred and sixty days still remained unchanged. In calculating Mayan chronology two main points must always be borne in mind. First,

that the unit of all time calculation was the single
day. Second, that the Mayas in reckoning time recorded only complete days. The basic element of
two hundred and sixty days in the Mayan calendrical
system was divided into periods of twenty days, just
as we observe a series of seven days in our weeks,
and just as we have a name for each of the week
days, so the Mayas had names for their twenty week
days. These were as follows:

1	Imix	8	Lamat	15	Men
2	Ik	9	Muluc	16	Cib
3	Akbal	10	Oc	17	Caban
4	Kan	11	Chuen	18	Eznab
5	Chicchan	12	Eb	19	Cauac
6	Cimi	13	Ben	20	Ahau
7	Manik	14	Ix		

(In pronouncing Mayan names *c* has the sound
of *k; x* is like *sh; i* and *a* are broad; *u* like *oo; ch*
like *ch.*)

Any single day indicated by its sign or symbol
fixed its position in the period of twenty days, just
as we fix Wednesday or Thursday in our week count.
But with these day names the Mayas combined numbers running from one to thirteen, so that the count
ran: 1 Imix, 2 Ik, 3 Akbal, 4 Kan, etc., to 13 Ben
when it became 1 Ix, 2 Men, etc. Hence, since twenty
and thirteen have no common factor higher than one,
two hundred and sixty days (twenty times thirteen)
must elapse before the day 1 Imix (or others) reappeared in a time-count. This was known as the
"round" and was very important, being used as a divine or ritual calendar for divination purposes, and it
ran in a constantly recurrent cycle through the whole

Mayan date system. Eighteen of the "months" of
twenty days followed by the five "unlucky days"
formed the Mayas' year of three hundred and sixty
days (eighteen months of twenty days). These
months were known by the following names:

1	Pop	7	Yaxkin	13	Mac
2	Uo	8	Mol	14	Kankin
3	Zip	9	Chen	15	Muan
4	Zotz	10	Yax	16	Pax
5	Tzec	11	Zac	17	Kayab
6	Xul	12	Ceh	18	Cumhu

Five Unlucky days or Uayeb

These names, together with numerals, in addition
to the day name and numeral, were used to fix a day's
position in the year. Thus a date such as 4 Ahau,
8 Cumhu would correspond to our Wednesday,
January thirteenth, the name Wednesday fixing the
position of the day in the week of seven days, just
as 4 Ahau fixes that day in the two-hundred-and-six-
ty-day period, while the thirteenth of January fixes
the day's position in our solar year just as 8 Cumhu
fixes that day's position in the Mayan solar year.
But the two systems differ materially in the systems
of numbering the month days. Ours runs from one to
thirty (or thirty-one) but each Maya month, being
but twenty days in length, had its days numbered
from naught to nineteen, a fact that must always be
remembered when studying Mayan chronologies, for
the Mayas measured only passed or elapsed time.
Such a date as 0 Cumhu indicated that the month
Kayab was over, but that the first day of Cumhu had
not been completed. It was much like reckoning
time by a clock and saying ten thirty, etc., thus expressing the last hour and the minutes of the new

hour, or as a man, once his twenty-first birthday is past, is in his twenty-second year but gives his age as twenty-one.

Since the day signs ran in a continual circle of twenty, and as there were twenty days in each month, each month of the year began with the same day sign and each day sign occupied the same position in each month. If it had not been for the five "unlucky days" at the end of each year, the positions of the day signs would have been constant year in and year out. But the addition of these five days caused each day sign to shift five places backward each successive year. Hence each year (and each month in the year) began with a day sign five days later than the preceding year. And since twenty is divisible by five four times, it follows that only four day signs could ever occur as initial days in the Mayan year, and that each day sign could only occupy four positions in a month. These were as follows:

Positions: 0.5.10.15
Ik
Manik
Eb
Caban

Positions: 2.7.12.17
Kan
Muluc
Ix
Cauac

Positions: 1.6.11.16
Akbal
Lamat
Ben
Eznab

Positions: 3.8.13.18
Chicchan
Oc
Men
Ahau

Positions: 4.9.14.19
Cimi
Chuen
Cib
Imix

Hence, in places where an inscription or date is doubtful, the choice is limited to four, or when a day sign is followed by a month date with a number that is impossible, it is safe to assume that a mistake was made by the sculptor.

Although the day signs returned to the same relative positions every fourth year it was not the case with their accompanying numerals. Thirteen divides three hundred and sixty-five with a remainder of one, so that each year began with a day sign one more than that of the previous year. Thus as New Year's Days, 1 Ik would be followed by 2 Manik, 3 Eb, 4 Caban, etc.

And as the highest common factor of four and thirteen is one, it follows that four times thirteen, or fifty-two years, must pass before the same day and numeral combination could recur in the same position in any one month. This period of fifty-two years or 18,980 days is known as the "Calendar Round," and where a day and month date, as 4 Ahau, 8 Cumhu, is given, the position of the day is determined within a period of fifty-two years only.

But in addition to this Calendar Round the Mayas had the "Long Count" based on a combination of the calendrical system and the numerical system. The Maya numerical system was perhaps the most noteworthy and remarkable mathematical achievement of any known race and has never been excelled even by Europeans. Unlike our system, which is decimal, that of the Mayas was vigesimal.

When we write such a number as 265, we know that the six has ten times the value of the five and that the two has ten times the value of the six. But in the Mayan system the figure six would have twenty times the value of the five and two would have twenty times the value of six. So the same number, 265, if written in the Mayan system, would mean five plus six times twenty plus two times twenty times twenty or 925 of our numbers. But when the Mayas used numerals for reckoning time the two would be considered as having but eighteen times the value of the six because a figure in the position of the two represented a number of periods of twenty times eighteen or three hundred and sixty days, and was therefore equal to the number of days in the eighteen months not counting the unlucky five days. Hence, when used for calendrical purposes, the combination of such numbers as two, six, five as a time count would indicate eight hundred and forty-five days. In the time count the unit was the single day and a complex numeral represented a sum of days grouped in periods corresponding to the numerical system. The name for a day was Kin or sun, and was expressed by a number occupying the position of our units. Twenty Kin made one Uinal or month indicated by a number occupying the position of our tens. Eighteen Uinals made a Tun or year of three hundred and sixty days with its numeral occupying the position of our hundreds. Twenty Tun made a Katun with its numeral in the position of our thousands, and twenty Katun made a Cycle or Baktun occupying the position of our tens of thousands.

Thus:

Kin   —1 day.
Uinal   —20 days.
Tun   —360 days. (18x20)
Katun   —7200 days. (20x18x20)
Baktun   —144,000 days. (20x20x18x20)

So that a Maya day count in a Mayan "Initial
Series" written in the terms of nine cycles or Baktuns, 14 Katun, 19 Tun, 8 Uinal, 0 Kin, usually
put down by archeologists as 9,14,19,8,0, would be
worked out as follows:

$$
\begin{array}{lr}
9\text{x}144{,}000 \ldots\ldots\ldots\ldots\ldots\ldots & 1{,}296{,}000 \\
14\text{x}7{,}200 \ldots\ldots\ldots\ldots\ldots\ldots & 100{,}800 \\
19\text{x}360 \ldots\ldots\ldots\ldots\ldots & 6{,}840 \\
8\text{x}20 \ldots\ldots\ldots\ldots\ldots & 160 \\
0\text{x}1 \ldots\ldots\ldots\ldots\ldots & 0 \\
\hline
& 1{,}403{,}800 \text{ days}
\end{array}
$$

or just a little less than 3,846 of our years. Such
a date appears on Stela A at Copan, Honduras.
This is a good example of the Maya Long Count,
and such a series was always followed by a day and
month sign with their numerals. Thus, in the inscription at Copan, the Long Count is followed by the
Calendar Round date 12 Ahau, 18 Cumhu. This is
a point of the greatest significance, for if the number
of days in the Long Count (1,403,800) is reckoned
backward from the date 12 Ahau, 18 Cumhu, the
Calendar Round date of 4 Ahau, 8 Cumhu results.
It is a most remarkable and interesting fact that
every known Calendar Round date preceded by an
Initial Series date is, by means of that series, brought
into direct relation with the mysterious 4 Ahau, 8
Cumhu. This proves that the Mayan calendrical sys-

tem was reckoned from some certain day (4 Ahau, 8 Cumhu) far back in the dim past, just as we reckon our time from the birth of Christ. But no date has yet been discovered among the Mayan inscriptions earlier than the second half of the ninth cycle, or more than three thousand four hundred and thirty years after that mystical 4 Ahau, 8 Cumhu which was apparently the starting-point for all Mayan historical chronology.

The Mayas' system enabled them to fix days within certain periods. If the numeral was appended the day was fixed within 260 days. If the month sign and its numeral were added it was fixed within 52 years. If the Tun sign was given it was fixed within 936 years. If the Katun sign appeared the date was fixed within 18,720 years, and if the Baktun or Cycle symbol was added the exact position of any day was fixed within a period of 374,400 years—a most astonishing mathematical achievement. But the Mayas went even farther than this, for at times a "Great Cycle" of twenty cycles or Baktuns or more than 7,500 years was used, while on a stela at Copan there is a date which apparently refers to a Great-Great-Cycle or twenty Great Cycles. Others appear on monuments at Palenque, while at Tikal is a date of nine terms or a Great-Great-Great Great Cycle or over 5,000,000 years!

To summarize: The date elements of the Mayas which are fixed beyond any question are:

1 The series of 20 day signs which, combined with the numbers 1 to 13, give the round of 260 days or Tonalmatl of the Aztecs.

2 The series of 18 month signs each of 20 days,

followed by a sign to indicate a period of 5 days. This is the 365-day year or Haab.

3 A period formed by combining 1 and 2 in which each day sign with its numeral is fixed as falling on a definite day in a definite month. This is the Calendar Round of 5 years of 365 days each.

4 The Long Count established by a partly vigesimal numerical system made by combining day and month dates in relation to the first day (4 Ahau, 8 Cumhu), the starting-point of Mayan chronology.

To correlate these various Mayan dates with our own dates is not by any means a simple matter, but for ordinary purposes the following table of correlated Mayan and Christian dates has been adopted.

Long Count	Katun	B.C.
9.0.0.0.0. .. 8 Ahau 13 Ceh...	8 Ahau	... 94
9.1.0.0.0. .. 6 Ahau 13 Yaxin.	6 Ahau	... 74
9.2.0.0.0. .. 4 Ahau 13 Uo....	4 Ahau	... 55
9.3.0.0.0. .. 2 Ahau 18 Moan..	2 Ahau	... 35
9.4.0.0.0. ..13 Ahau 18 Yax..	13 Ahau	... 15

A.D.

Long Count	Katun	A.D.
9.5.0.0.0. ..11 Ahau 18 Tzec..	11 Ahau	... 5
9.6.0.0.0. .. 9 Ahau 3 Uayeb.	9 Ahau	... 25
9.7.0.0.0. .. 7 Ahau 3 Kankin	7 Ahau	... 45
9.8.0.0.0. .. 5 Ahau 3 Chen..	5 Ahau	... 64
9.9.0.0.0. .. 3 Ahau 3 Zotz..	3 Ahau	... 84
9.10.0.0.0. .. 1 Ahau 8 Kayab.	8 Ahau	...104
9.11.0.0.0. ..12 Ahau 8 Ceh...	12 Ahau	...124
9.12.0.0.0. ..10 Ahau 8 Yaxin.	10 Ahau	...143
9.13.0.0.0. .. 8 Ahau 8 Uo...	8 Ahau	...163
9.14.0.0.0. .. 6 Ahau 13 Moan.	6 Ahau	...183
9.15.0.0.0. .. 4 Ahau 13 Yax..	4 Ahau	...202
9.16.0.0.0. .. 2 Ahau 13 Tzec ..	2 Ahau	...222
9.17.0.0.0. ..13 Ahau 18 Cumhu	13 Ahau	...242

Long Count				Katun	A.D.
9.18.0.0.0. ..11	Ahau	18	Mac..	11 Ahau	...262
9.19.0.0.0. .. 9	Ahau	18	Mol..	9 Ahau	...281
10.0.0.0.0. .. 7	Ahau	18	Zip..	7 Ahau	...301
10.1.0.0.0. .. 5	Ahau	3	Kayab	5 Ahau	...321
10.2.0.0.0. .. 3	Ahau	3	Ceh..	3 Ahau	...340

In addition to all this certain "periods" have been
established which are useful in placing the relative
ages of Mayan works. In our years they are:

Old Empire
  Archaic Period—Earliest remains to A.D. 104
  Middle Period—A.D. 104 to 202
  Great Period—A.D. 202 to 340
New Empire—A.D. 340 and later.

Remarkable as were the calendrical and mathematical systems of the Mayas, even more astonishing
in many ways was their written or rather sculptured
language. Beyond any question it was the greatest
scientific achievement of any race ancient or modern,
and yet it was developed at a very remote date. Most
amazing of all is the fact that it would appear to have
sprung into use fully developed and perfected, for
no one has yet discovered an archaic or primitive
form of the writing, and the earliest known inscriptions are of exactly the same type and character as
those of the most recent dates when the Mayas had
reached their highest attainments along other lines.
Yet we know that it was impossible for such a complicated, involved and elaborate system of writing to
have been conceived or invented in its perfected
state. Whether or not the system was employed for

every-day use or by the people as a whole, we cannot say, for all known examples are of a more or less pictorial character and are associated with decorative paintings, carvings, sculptures, etc. Moreover, all known Mayan inscriptions are of the so-called hieratic type, or, in other words, they relate exclusively to ceremonial, religious or astronomical matters or to dates.

Among many races, writing was divided into two forms: one a more or less secret or mystical system for the use of rulers, priests and wise men when recording important ceremonial or religious events, or for the purposes of art, and known as hieratic. The other form was for every-day use by the common people and is known as demotic. Hence, as all known Mayan inscriptions are of the former type, the written records so far deciphered throw no light whatever upon the ordinary lives and affairs of the populace.

The fact that Mayan remains were covered with inscriptions has been known for centuries, ever since the conquest in fact, and for many years archeologists and others have been studying them and striving to translate the inscriptions. As a result, practically all the Mayan records, sculptured or painted upon their monuments and other remains, may be deciphered with fair accuracy, although frequently there is some doubt as to the correct reading, while in many cases the symbols have been so obliterated or injured by time, the elements and other causes as to render it impossible to secure a complete interpretation of their meanings. The first real progress in deciphering Mayan writings was made by Diego de Landa, Sec-

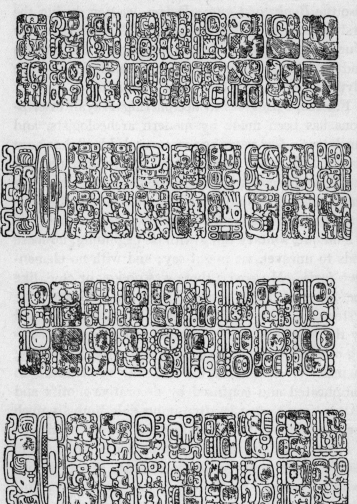

Figure 3.—Examples of Mayan Inscriptions. Sculptured Glyphs on Stela from Quirigua, Guatemala.

ond Bishop of Yucatan in 1524-79, who wrote a
Mayan history in which he explained the Maya calendrical system and the date symbols. There were
also the *Books of Chilám Balám,* written during the
first century after the conquest. These, written by
Yucatan Indians of Mayan ancestry, are chronicles
and histories of the race and throw much light on the
glyphs dealing with the Mayan calendar.

Far more progress in deciphering Mayan inscriptions has been made by modern archeologists, and
much that a few years ago was a sealed book has been
revealed. Largely, the great difficulty in deciphering
the Mayan records has been due to the fact that the
writing is of a hieroglyphic form and that there is
no related or similar system anywhere on earth. It
is a unique, solitary thing with no beginning, no loose
ends to unravel, we might say; and with no elemen-
tary form. Moreover, there was no key or clue, like
the famed Rosetta stone, by which a hint of the
system could be obtained. Also, the materials used
by the Mayas in their writings were formal, consisting of stone, wood, metal, shells and pottery. Finally,
to make it even more difficult, the records are so
complicated and confused by decorative motifs and
elaborations that it is often impossible to distinguish
the true writing from meaningless ornamentations.

It must be confessed that the results obtained by
deciphering the Maya inscriptions are disappointing
to the layman. So far, as I have said, every important inscription that has been read deals with
calendar dates or with comments upon and explanations of the data. Nowhere, among the thousands
of glyphs known, has one been found which tells us

Figure 4.

119

POP

UO

ZIP

ZOTZ

TZEC

XUL

YAXKIN

MOL

CHEN

YAX

ZAC

CEH

MAC

KANKIN

MUAN

PAX

KAYAB

CUMHU

UAYEB

Figure 5—Maya Month Signs.

120

anything of human interest, of the lives of the people, their rulers, their habits or even of their history. Possibly such matters were never recorded by writings of any sort. Possibly they were recorded on some perishable materials which have long since disappeared. Or possibly we may yet discover that what we now regard as meaningless ornamental and decorative work has a true significance and supplies the missing historical records.

It is not, however, surprising that dates and calendrical records predominate. The Mayas had reached a marvelous development in mathematics and astronomy, and had devised a calendar more accurate than any that existed prior to the modified Gregorian, and these matters all required most accurate and careful imperishable records. And as many of the monuments, and even buildings, bore a very direct relationship to calendrical events, it was only natural that they should bear glyphs recording dates and data.

The Maya glyphs are not, like the Egyptian and other hieroglyphs, placed in columns or rows of single symbols, but are grouped together and are combined in rounded or rectangular forms known as "cartouches," together with essential elements or constants carrying the meanings, but which vary greatly or may be largely obscured by decorations.

In every known inscription the cartouches are arranged in more or less parallel columns, and in each inscription the various cartouches are of equal size. They are read two columns at a time, from the upper left-hand column to the right and downward, ending with the lowest right-hand second column, Figure 3.

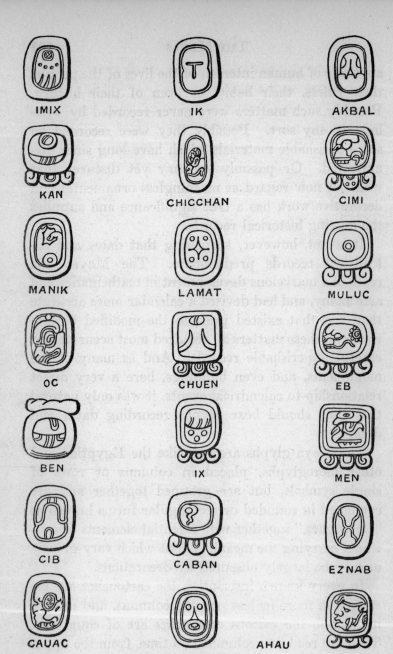

IMIX   IK   AKBAL

KAN   CHICCHAN   CIMI

MANIK   LAMAT   MULUC

OC   CHUEN   EB

BEN   IX   MEN

CIB   CABAN   EZNAB

CAUAC   AHAU

Figure 6—Maya Day Signs.

As a rule, the bar and dot numerical glyphs are the
simplest to decipher, Figure 4, a to e. Next are those
of the day and month names of simpler forms, such
as those shown in Figures 5 and 6. Date glyphs, however, are by no means easy to decipher, even when the
key to them is known. Three series of glyphs were
used in recording the Long Count periods, the third
system being a variety of the second. The first series

Figure 7—Maya Date Signs.

consists of normal signs as shown in Figure 7 right-
hand side. The second consists of face signs as in Figure 7 left-hand side. In the latter the Cycle sign is a
bird's head, often with a hand as the lower mandible.
The Katun is a bird's head often with a tusk or fang
in the corner of the mouth. The Tun is a grotesque
head usually with a skeleton lower jaw. The Uinal
is a head (probably of a frog) with a curl at the
angle of the jaw. The Kin or day sign is the head

Figure 8—Full-Figure Glyphs.

of the sun-god, sometimes with a tail, while the third series consists of full-figure glyphs with the heads only having significance, and corresponding with the second series described, Figure 8.

Three series of glyphs were used also in expressing numerals. These corresponded to the normal, face and figure glyphs of the period symbols. In the normal series five was expressed by a straight bar. Units below five or above one or more multiples of five were indicated by single dots. The highest number thus used was nineteen, owing to the use of the vigesimal system, and was shown by three bars and four dots. But as the Mayas regarded any vacant areas as inartistic, whenever the dots were few (as in Figures 4, a, b, c, d, e, etc.) they were usually supplemented by crosses, crescents or dots having no meanings, but serving merely as decorations. This often makes it very difficult to interpret numerical signs with certainty, especially where a carving is worn or injured. In addition to the dot and bar signs, the face signs were used to denote numerals as in Figure 4, but these varied a great deal. The heads used for numbers eleven to nineteen are similar in their main details to those for one to nine except that they have fleshless lower jaws. The symbol denoting ten is a head with a hand for the lower jaw, while the full-figure numerical symbols differ from the face numbers only in being elaborated by having complete bodies. Another very important glyph is that for Venus (Figure 9), for, like the Aztecs, the Mayas observed the periods elapsing between the appearances of Venus as the morning star, a period of almost exactly five hundred and eighty-four days, so that five of the planet's appearances coincided with eight years of three hundred and sixty-five days each. As the twenty day signs divide five hundred and eighty-four twenty-nine times with a remainder of four, every Venus period ended with a day sign four days later than the preceding one.   But as four divides

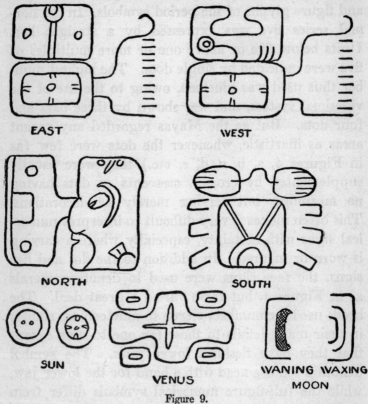

EAST

WEST

NORTH

SOUTH

SUN

VENUS

WANING WAXING
MOON

Figure 9.

twenty five times, only five signs could terminate the Venus periods.   Since the day symbols were accompanied by the numeral symbols from one to thirteen, and as thirteen divides five hundred and eighty-four with a remainder of twelve, the terminal day of each Venus period was distinguished by a number one less than the preceding. Consequently sixty-five Venus periods elapsed before the recurrence of the same day and number for an ending date. Thus the sixty-five Venus periods equaled two Calendar Rounds of fifty-two years each or one hundred and four years, and once in every one hundred and four years the Venus Count, Calendar Count and Year Count all coincided to a day, thus affording a perfect check upon year time. Still other glyphs indicate the various planets, such as the sun and the moon, Figure 9. Still others were used to denote points of the compass, Figure 9, and there were still other glyphs for colors, Figure 10.

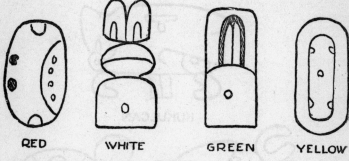

RED   WHITE   GREEN   YELLOW

Figure 10.

The various Mayan deities were also represented by conventional symbols or glyphs, as well as by carved likenesses. The glyph for Itzama the supreme god, Kukulcan's symbol, and the queer glyph representing Ahpuch, the god of death, are shown in Figure 11. All of these various glyphed symbols may be varied considerably, thus adding to the difficulty of deciphering Mayan inscriptions, and, quite frequently, two or more may be combined. Thus a head with a skeleton lower jaw, the symbol for ten, may have a crossed eye, the symbol for the head glyph of six, thereby indicating the number sixteen. But the head glyphs for eleven and twelve are not combinations of ten and one and ten and two as might be expected, but are shown by special forms of heads, Figure 4.

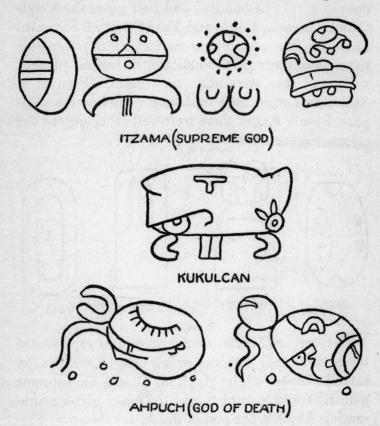

ITZAMA (SUPREME GOD)

KUKULCAN

AHPUCH (GOD OF DEATH)

Figure 11.

Up to the present time no symbols of a true alphabetical character have ever been discovered. Hence it is assumed that the symbols were all phonetic or at least ideographic in character. Thus in Figure 12A we have an ideograph for Kin, the sun or a day. Figure 12B is the symbol for Yax or green which was synonymous for early or first, and by combining these two symbols as in Figure 12C we have the glyph Yaxin, or first day or sun. The symbol for Ka or Cay, a fish (Figure 12D), conventionalized and combined with the symbol for Tun, a stone (Figure 12 E), results in the year symbol Figure 12F. Finally, to add to the difficulty of interpreting the inscrip-

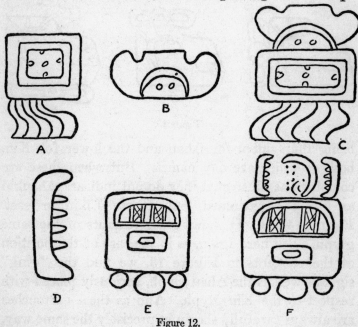

Figure 12.

tions, we often find a cartouche symbol, such as Figure 13A, associated with some element, as Figure 13 B, which may be affixed, prefixed, suffixed or superfixed as shown in Figure 13C, D, E, F, the position of the element having some significance which still remains undetermined. In the same way the varying of the relative positions of either elements or compounds composed of two or more symbols, each standing alone, no doubt had an important meaning, although we do not know what. Thus Figure 14A is the ordinary symbol for east, the upper cartouche

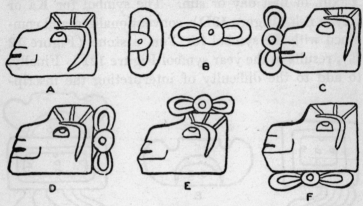

Figure 13.

being the symbol for Ahau and the lower for Kin, both of which are day names. But when these are combined as illustrated they do not indicate Ahaukin as might be assumed, but denote Likin or east. Figure 14B, C, D shows other variants of the same glyph. But here again, as in the case of the position of the elements in Figure 13, we find the "wing" sign, as well as the Ahau glyph, variously placed with respect to the Kin glyph. And as these cartouches are always carefully shown in precisely the same way, we can only assume that the positions and relationships of their various parts have great significance and probably give a wholly different meaning to the inscriptions.

Possibly, some day, all these puzzles may be solved and all the Mayan inscriptions may be translated be-

yond all guesswork. But at the present time, we can
do little more than determine the dates recorded upon
the monuments, buildings and other remains of the
remarkable people.

No doubt the immense, elaborately carved stelæ,
or stone monuments, which are so typical of the

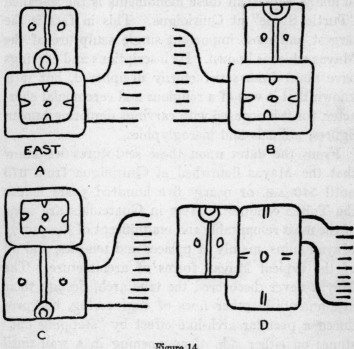

Figure 14.

Mayan culture, were primarily date records, for we
know that those at Quirioigua, Guatemala, were
erected at definite periods of five Tuns or years of
three hundred and sixty days. But it is fairly well established that these monuments were also of great religious or ceremonial significance. Many were of
enormous size, up to twenty-four feet in height above
the earth and four or five feet square, and covered,

over every square inch of their surface, with elaborate carvings. To carve these stupendous monoliths must have required fully five years, and in all probability much longer, so that each of the stelæ must have been designed, planned and started many years before it was destined to be erected. Even more remarkable in many ways than these monuments is the so-called "Turtle Stone" at Quirioigua. This in fact is the largest and most important single sculpture of the Mayas which is known. Its inscriptions and carvings have never been satisfactorily deciphered, but it is known that it was of a religious and ceremonial character, for it is covered with carvings depicting human figures, animals and hieroglyphics.

From the dates upon these sculptures we know that the Mayas flourished at Quirioigua from 373 until 540 A.D. or nearly five hundred years before the Toltec conquest. Here in Guatemala are some of the most remarkable and magnificent of the purely Mayan ruins, mainly of palaces and temples, and all of the typical Mayan forms of architecture. The Mayas never discovered the true arch, despite their attainments in other lines of engineering, but produced a peculiar arch-like effect by "stepping out" stones on either side of an opening in a wall until the two sides met. As this type of construction could not be carried out where the walls were widely separated, all Mayan buildings were exceedingly narrow, the widest arches being but sixteen feet. In many, the largest halls and rooms are only a few yards in width, and in several immense buildings at Bacalar, Yucatan, the chambers are only three feet in width. As it would manifestly be impossible for human beings of normal size to occupy or use such constricted quarters to any extent, we can only assume that they were devoted entirely to ceremonial uses.

Another striking feature of the Mayan buildings is that many of the walls slope outward or inward instead of being perpendicular. Frequently the walls are elaborately decorated with sculptures, as are the stairs, and in most cases they were originally painted in gay colors and had their interior wall surfaces magnificently frescoed. As a rule the roofs were surmounted by high, ornate and elaborate "combs" or superstructures. These were sometimes of carved wood, often of stone, and frequently of a cement-like composition or stucco. The extensive use of stucco, plaster and cement was a rather remarkable feature of the Mayan civilization. Such materials were used to some extent by other ancient American races; but the Mayas carried the use of stucco to the extreme. Not only did they employ it for covering stonework, and for floors, but they also molded or cast it into ornamental and decorative forms and carved it as well. Many of the cornices and the elaborate figures and sculptures which cover their buildings are of this material, although at first sight they appear to be genuine stonework. Oddly enough, too, the Mayas apparently learned to carve stone before they carved wood, for some of the stonework shows traces of an earlier development of art than the woodwork, the latter being carved and decorated in low relief precisely like that of the stonework.

No doubt a far greater amount of wood was used by the Mayas than is generally supposed, for even the most durable of wood disappears rapidly in the tropics, and it is only here and there, and at rare intervals, that remnants of Mayan woodwork are preserved. Usually these are in form of door lintels which have been protected from the weather by the adjacent masonry, and as a rule they are of sapote wood, the most imperishable of all tropical American hardwoods. As the Mayas were expert woodworkers it is highly probable that the majority of their buildings, as well as the dwellings of the common people, were of wood construction. Although there is much diversity in the details of Mayan buildings, yet they are always easily recognizable. In practically every case they were built upon artificial mounds or *kus*. Often the *kus* bore only an altar, a shrine or a monument, and as a rule the surfaces of the mounds were faced with stone or stucco covered with elaborate carvings and inscriptions.

Possibly the *kus* or mound foundation was designed to prevent the temples and other buildings from being flooded during the rainy season, but more probably its purpose was to add to the buildings' height and make them more impressive. Owing to the peculiar "stepping-in" method of building, the Mayas' edifices could not be made more than a single story in height. In many instances the builders overcame this difficulty in a very clever manner and erected buildings which gave the impression of having several stories. This was accomplished by erecting a building in the ordinary manner, and then increasing the height of the mound in the rear until it reached the roof level of the first building. A second edifice on this gave the effect of a superimposed story, and by again raising the mound a third or even more step-like buildings could be added to the whole. In many if not most cases, the mound or *kus* was higher than the building which surmounted it, while the elaborate "roof-comb" was as high again; the actual building being quite low and squat but appearing lofty and imposing when topped with its "comb" and standing upon the stone-faced mound which seemed a portion of the building itself. It is quite obvious that all the buildings were planned and designed by competent architects beforehand, and that the stones were all cut and carved before erection, although the finishing touches, the finer carvings, the painting and the stucco-work were added afterward.

While the Mayas never equaled the Peruvians in their engineering feats or the cyclopean dimensions of their architecture, yet no other American race, nor for that matter any race, ever approached them in the complexity, the extent and the beauty of their stone sculptures.

In every case the most striking feature of the Mayan architecture and monuments is the extremely elaborate carving and sculpture that adorn them. Everything, from the largest, most massive blocks of stone to the tiniest ornaments, was sculptured and glyphed, although the type of carving varied considerably in different localities. In the northern districts, bas-reliefs predominated, whereas in Honduras caryatides and human figures are the rule, and at Copan, once the Mayan metropolis, there are exaggerated bas-reliefs so deeply undercut that they appear like separate images not entirely cut away from their background of original rock.

The temple at Palenque in Chiapas is perhaps the finest example of prehistoric architecture

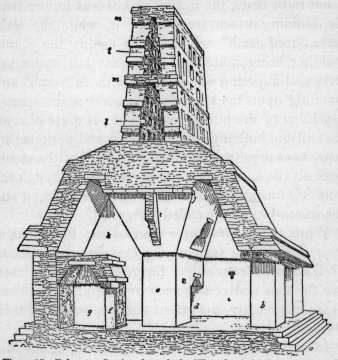

Figure 15—Palenque: Section through the "Temple of the Foliated Cross."

a. Stairway.
b. Pillar rested.
c. Vestibule.
d. Doorway to inner side chamber.
e. Doorway to inner main chamber.
f. Doorway to shrine.
g. Shrine.

h. Original position of mural tablet.
i. Masonry arch-brace.
j. Capstones of doorway arch.
k. Partition wall.
l. Steps for ascending roof-crest.
m. Middle floor and roof of roof-crest.

in the entire world, and yet this is but one of eighteen magnificent palaces or temples and twenty other enormous buildings in this mysterious, ancient city that was discovered by Calderón in 1774. A remarkable feature of Palenque is the subterranean apartments containing three stone altars or tables, which may have been used for sacrificial purposes, for Palenque was a holy or sacred city and its sculptures all represent priests or religious subjects with no warlike or regal carvings.

Chichen-Itza was another holy city dedicated to the Plumed Serpent or Kukulcan, and its "Temple of the Jaguars" surpasses any other known prehistoric structure in its beauty of design, its impressive carvings, its magnificent coloring and its wonderful frescoes. On either side of the main entrance is an immense snake-god with the body of a serpent and a serpent's head. These were painted in red, white and green, the sacred colors of Quetzál, as was the entire façade of the building, the roof of which was surmounted by an immense comb of magnificent open stonework. Among the innumerable bas-reliefs, which cover both the exterior and interior of the temple, are many figures of bearded men. It has been suggested that these represent priests of Kukulcan or the "Plumed-Serpent-god," who was always depicted with a beard, the supposition being that his priests either wore real beards or donned artificial ones. But is it not equally probable that these bearded figures represent those mysterious "bearded ones" who, according to Mayan, Aztecan and Incan legends, visited America ages before the coming of the Spaniards? There is a remarkable frequency of bearded gods and figures in both Mayan and Aztec sculptures and art, and at Itzamak the figure of Hunpictok (commander-in-chief of eight thousand flints) shows a mustached man where

it is carved on the stones of his palace.   In many
places, too, human beings are shown with remarkable
flat-topped heads, and it is a most interesting and
suggestive fact that most of the monolithic statues
or idols discovered at the Coclé temple site in Panama had precisely the same flat-topped craniums, and
that several had beards.   (Chapter VI.)

Among the many ruins of Mayan cities and buildings it is not unusual to find structures with such
small doors and chambers that they seem to have been
designed for the use of pigmies.   Such is the famous
"Dwarfs' House" at Uxmal.   This is built in two
portions, one on the summit of a pyramidal mound,
the other lower down, and both are far too small to
have been designed for normal human occupants.
This has led to the theory that a race of pigmies once
inhabited the district.   But as no other indications or
remains of a dwarf race have been found, it is far
more probable and reasonable to suppose that the
Uxmal Dwarfs' House, as well as similar structures
elsewhere, was intended for the use of either spirits
or supernatural beings.   At Uxmal there is also a
sacrificial pyramid so similar in design to the *teocalli*
of the Aztecs that in all probability it was of Aztec
origin, perhaps erected by Nahua mercenaries for
their own use or perhaps built at the time of the
Nahua conquest.

The great number and the magnificence of the
Mayan temples, and their innumerable idols and
monuments, prove beyond question that the Mayas
were an intensely religious people.   But apparently
their rites did not call for the wholesale and bloody
human sacrifices demanded by the Aztecs' gods.   The

statement that the Mayas never indulged in human sacrifice is without foundation, however. Possibly, indeed probably, sacrificial stones and human sacrifices upon them were introduced by the Nahuas, but certain ceremonials of their own demanded human victims. At the festival of the spring florescence, virgins were cast into the sacred well at Chichen-Itza as a sacrifice to the rain-god Chac-Mool, as I have already mentioned. Although to our civilized and modern minds the thought of hurling living maidens to a terrible death in a yawning black pit savors of unspeakable savagery and cold-blooded cruelty, it was not so regarded by the Mayas. No doubt the girls destined for the sacrifice felt immensely proud of being chosen by the priests for the purpose. It was the highest honor that could be bestowed upon a virgin, and the girls' faith, and their firm belief that they were winning eternal happiness and that their spirits would become the brides of the deity, made them willing martyrs. No doubt they vied with one another for the honor and were as keen in their competition as are modern girls in a beauty contest. And as those destined for sacrifice were selected because of their youthful beauty and purity, we may be quite sure that they were regarded with the most intense jealousy and envy by their less fortunate sisters.

At the time of this sacrifice, vast quantities of the most highly prized and valuable possessions of the people were cast into the well as offerings to the god. Within recent years the well has been entered and explored by archeologists in diving suits, and some of the most priceless specimens of Mayan art and handicraft have been recovered. Until this was done the story of the sacred well and its sacrificed maidens was regarded as more or less mythical, but beneath the black waters of the underground cavern were the human bones, the golden and jeweled ornaments, the weapons and artifacts, the countless objects which, from time immemorial, had been sacrificed to the rain-god.

Although fanatically religious, the Mayas, on the other hand, were an industrious, practical people. That they were industrious is obvious, for had they not been the most industrious of races they never could have performed such astonishing feats of engineering and of architecture, and could never have accomplished such a vast amount of sculpturing and yet supported themselves and their vast empire by agriculture. Neither did their industry run entirely to religious matters or to display. They were thoroughly alive to the importance of good roads, and built a veritable network of highways linking their cities with outlying districts. About their holy cities, splendid roads radiated into the country to enable pilgrims to visit the shrines, idols and temples with greater ease, and Chichen-Itza and other Mayan Meccas were connected by means of highroads with practically every town or center of importance in the empire. The practical side of their nature is also proved by the heights they attained in scientific matters. As I have said, they developed and perfected an astounding written language; they devised a most excellent calendar; they invented an arithmetical system superior to that of any other race, and their astronomical and mathematical knowl-

edge was extraordinary. Towers with narrow slits
served for their observatories, and by means of these,
and by the use of gigantic sun-dial-like arrangements
of great stone monoliths geometrically placed, and by
what must have been most complex mathematical
problems, they were able to calculate the movements
of the heavenly bodies, to foretell eclipses, to com-
pute the phases of the moon, the declination of the
sun, the time of the solstices, and in fact every astronomical event of any importance or consequence.
They also possessed an intimate knowledge of phys-
ics and of geometrical laws and theories, and they
were marvelously skilled draftsmen.

In the Museum of the American Indian, Heye
Foundation, in New York, there is a large Maya jar
of red pottery which is elaborately decorated with an
involved and complex design in low bas-relief. At
first sight this appears to be merely an ornamental,
modeled jar. But it is far from being this. Instead
of being modeled in the plastic clay this jar is sculptured, and the design, when closely examined, proves
to have been worked out with mathematical accuracy
from a plane drawing or pattern. It required the
utmost skill of the most expert modern draftsmen,
working with the finest and most highly perfected
instruments, to transfer the design upon the jar to a
plane; and yet this was a simple, an almost childish
matter compared to the problem which faced the
Maya artist who carved the jar. From a design or
pattern drawn or cut upon a plane surface he had to
work out his design in three dimensions upon a surface of two curves, a feat which few living artists or
designers could accomplish. And yet it was done so

perfectly and with such consummate skill that no-where, throughout the finished carving, can the slightest error or mistake be discovered.

In addition to all these attainments, the Mayas had developed many purely industrial arts. They wove beautiful textiles, they possessed wonderful dyes, they made pottery of the highest quality, they were expert metal workers, and they made paints and pigments of every color that were so enduring and fast that they have withstood the elements, the wear and tear of countless centuries, and are still as bright and fresh as the day they were laid on.

However, the Mayas did not devote all of their time to work. Like all the American races, they were passionately fond of sports, games and contests. That they considered recreations as highly important is proved by the fact that they went to great labor and expense to construct immense ball-courts. These were used for a game similar in many respects to the Basque game of pelota or jai alai. No doubt the Mayas were as enthusiastic over their ball games as Americans are over baseball. They probably had their favorites, their champions,—perhaps the counterparts of "big-league" teams. And they unquestionably gambled outrageously on the results of a game and regarded their famous players in the light of heroes, for humanity is much the same to-day as two thousand years ago, and there are no racial nor geographical boundaries when it comes to a question of sports.

CHAPTER VIII

THE DESCENDANTS OF THE MAYAS

At the time of the Spanish conquest, the Mayas, as I have described in the preceding chapter, had reverted to their original status of independent tribes. All spoke dialects of the Maya-Kiche tongue; but they differed materially in customs, habits and dress. Some still retained much of their ancestors' culture and some of their civilization, and the Mayan religion was almost universal, although often in garbled and perverted forms. The great cities of the Mayan Empire were deserted, many were completely lost and hidden in the rank jungle and forest growths of the tropics, and the existing Indians had little more than vague traditions and legends regarding their origin and their past. Yet they worshiped their old gods, using the ancient temples for their ceremonials wherein the *chiláms* or priests performed the rites.

They had not forgotten the ancient prophecy that at the end of the thirteenth age white men would arrive from over the sea and would subjugate the race, and they were no more surprised at the advent of the Spaniards than were the Aztecs or the Incas. In fact, they had been expecting them daily for years, and regarded them in the light of foreordained and semidivine visitors. They looked upon the Spaniards' horses as supernatural godlike creatures, and believed that the Dons controlled thunder and lightning which they used to destroy their enemies by means of their guns. This belief was not surprising, for in Mayan mythology, gods of thunder and lightning played very important parts and, according to the myths, often destroyed an enemy by a bolt of lightning. (See Chapter IX; Huitzilopochtli.) Even when they became quite familiar with the Spaniards and their steeds, and learned that the former were mortal, they still believed the horses divine.

Thus when Cortez was obliged to leave his unserviceable horse at Peten Itza, and the animal died while in the Indians' care, the terrified natives made an image or statue of the creature and called it Itzmin Chac (Thunder-and-lightning). It is quite possible, however, that in this case it was dread of Cortez rather than religious fervor which led the Indians to carve the stone horse, perhaps believing, in their simple minds, that the proxy of the steed would serve to hoodwink the Don into believing his horse still lived, and thus avert his anger. At any rate, the sculptured horse, Itzmin Chac, was as greatly venerated as any of the other deities, and was incorporated in the local mythology.

There is a vast amount of truth in the saying that "the old gods die hard." With few exceptions, the descendants of the ancient American races cling tenaciously to their immeasurably ancient religions and beliefs. Even to-day, many of the Indians of Central and South America secretly venerate or worship the gods of their forefathers. The Mayan tribes are no exception, although often the ancient Mayan deities and rites and the Christian rituals and saints are almost inextricably confused.

In the little church at Esquipultas, Guatemala, is the image of the "Black Christ," to which thousands of Indians journey annually from all parts of Central America, and even from Mexico and South America. The spot has become a shrine or Mecca for the Indians, and for hundreds, even thousands of miles, they travel to the obscure Guatemalan village carrying with them all their possessions in order to have them sanctified at the famous church. To all outward intents and purposes they are Christians making a pilgrimage to a Christian church in order to worship before a figure of Christ. No doubt many if not most of them actually are sincere in believing this to be the case. But, as a matter of fact, the underlying cause, the real urge that leads them to the spot is the ineradicable faith in their ancient gods and religion. The very fact that the image is black has a symbolic significance which can be traced directly to the ancient religions and mythologies (see Chapter X), and, delving deeper into the details of the annual pilgrimage and the shrine, we find evidences of the observance of the Mayan religion numerous. The Indians who care for the church and the image are of the Mayan priest clan or caste. Many of the ceremonies, rites and festivals of the pilgrims are obviously of ancient Mayan origin, and the little *santos* or images which the devout Indians bring to the church to be sanctified, and which serve as their own household gods, are figures of the ancient Indian deities. Moreover, among many of the Indians, the Black Christ is referred to in private as Ekchuah or as Hunabku (the former, the Mayan god of merchants, husbandmen and travelers; the latter, the

"God-father" or supreme deity of the Mayas), often prefixed with the Spanish *Cristo* (Christ), as Cristo Ekchuah or as Cristo Hunabku.

No doubt, in many other cases, much the same conditions prevail, and Doctor Gann reports finding the Santa Cruz Indians of certain sections of Yucatan worshiping in the ancient temples of their forefathers, and venerating and making offerings to the prehistoric idols of the Mayas. In some cases, he reports, the Indians combined Christian and pagan practises, burning blessed candles beside the idols, praying to a saint in the ancient ritual of the Mayas, or otherwise confusing and mingling their own religion with that forced upon them by their conquerors.

We can scarcely blame the Indians for such things. Their religion and their mythology are far more ancient than our own, they served their every need and purpose for countless ages before the coming of the white men; it was decreed in their ancient prophecies that the old gods would be restored in the end, and, after all, Christianity—introduced and forced upon them by fire and sword—has brought them little save poverty, semislavery, oppression and abuse.

In many parts of the territory once under Mayan dominion, the Indians have become industrious, civilized, law-abiding, and form a predominant portion of the population. But in other districts they have reverted to savagery, and are untamed, independent and implacably hostile. This is particularly true of many of the Indian tribes of the east coast of Yucatan, where the Indians of Santa Cruz de Bravo, Chunpom, Tulum, etc., are notorious for their ferocity, their wildness and their intense hatred of white men. Much of their hostility and savagery is unquestionably due directly to their experiences in the past, and to the cruelty, oppression and wrongs which have been their heritage from the days of the Mayan rulers to the present time.

But there is another and a far more romantic reason than this that underlies the valiant, unconquerable spirit of these Indians. Back in the year 1511 a certain adventurous Spaniard named Valdivia set sail from Darien for Hispañola, carrying with him a portion of the treasure secured by his fellow adventurer, Vasco Nuñez de Balboa. The ship, however, never reached its destination. When between the Central American coast and Jamaica, the vessel was wrecked upon the Las Vivoras reefs, and only twenty men escaped. In a small boat, without oars, sails, food or water, they drifted for two weeks at the will of wind and tides, and were cast ashore in a district known as Maia. Seven of the shipwrecked men had already succumbed to hunger and thirst, and we may be sure that the survivors regretted that they, too, had not died at sea when they realized the fate in store for them. Valdivia and four others were seized by the Indians and were immediately sacrificed and eaten, while the remaining captives were confined in cages to be fattened for later feasts.

Fortunately for themselves, they managed to escape and, fleeing through the bush, reached the country of Ah Kin Cutz, king of Xamancana, where they were made slaves. Eight years later, Cortez learned that two of these captive Spaniards still survived, and he succeeded in ransoming one, Geronimo de

Aguliar. But the other, a sailor named Gonzalo Guerrero, refused to accept deliverance. He had made his way to Chetumal, had risen to the rank of war-chief under Nachancan, the Chetumal king, had tattooed himself like the Indians, had married an Indian princess and had a promising family of three children. He had no desire to rejoin his countrymen or to deal with them. On the contrary, he had done all in his power to aid his adopted tribesmen in resisting the Spaniards, and he had instilled in them a fighting spirit, a military organization and a refinement of savagery which persist to this day, and which have been a large factor in enabling the Santa Cruz and Chetumal Indians to maintain successfully their independence.

In their arts and industries the Mayan tribes show the influences of the high culture of their ancestors. They weave beautiful textiles, make excellent pottery and produce wonderful metal work. As a rule, each village or tribe has its own distinctive types of weaving, of designs and of costumes; and while the various dialects, such as the Pipil, Quiché (Kiche) Zutugil, Kakchiquel, etc., differ somewhat, yet all are forms of the Mayan mother-tongue.

During their fiestas, usually held on holy days of the Catholic Church, these Indians perform very elaborate symbolic dances in which the old Mayan festivals, myths and hero-gods are strangely combined with historical incidents, Spanish characters and Christian saints. Arrayed in marvelous costumes representing the characters they assume, and with wonderfully and fearfully designed masks, the Indians perpetuate the events of the past. Dancers

representing Kukulcan and Cortez may be seen side
by side; there are Spanish soldiers, Mayan kings, hor-
rible-looking Mayan devils and gorgeously attired
viceroys. To the onlooker it all seems incongruous,
very confusing and very amusing; but to the Indians
it is a serious matter, and while it proves how misty
and garbled are their ideas of historical events and the
story of their race, yet it serves to keep alive their
ancient traditions.

By far the greater number of the descendants of
the Mayas are in the territory once under Mayan
dominion: in Honduras, Guatemala and Yucatan.
But as I have mentioned in Chapter VII the Mayas,
like the Aztecs, had numerous outlying and even far-
distant colonies or provinces. It is not surprising
that we should find much of the Mayan tongue, the
religion, even the arts and customs, surviving in the
land where once the Mayas held full sway. But
that any of these remote, isolated communities should
have survived and should have retained any traces
of Mayan origin is truly remarkable. For centuries
they have been cut off from all intercourse with other
members of their race; they have been surrounded by
tribes of distinct stock, and often by savages and
enemies, and they have dwelt in an environment and
under conditions which would tend to destroy or
eliminate all vestiges of their origin and their ancestral characters. Yet, as in the case of Aztec influence among the Guaymís (see Chapter X), these descendants of former Mayan outposts have preserved
some of their ancient characters to greater extent and
with less alterations than have the Indians' dwelling
within the Mayan area proper.

Far up on the Mexican coast, near the mouth of the Panuco River, is a small tribe called Huastecas, who retain a distinctly Mayan dialect and still possess Mayan characteristics. But they are by no means so remarkable as are the survivors of remote Mayan colonies to the south of the boundaries of Maya dominion.

Dwelling among the forest-covered mountains in the virtually unknown and unexplored district between Costa Rica and Panama are the few survivors of the Shayshán tribe. Five years ago, when I visited this tribe, it numbered less than fifty individuals, although the cacique or king informed me, and proved by his tally of knotted strings, that two years previous there had been more than two hundred and fifty. Influenza had been introduced by some stranger, or by some Indian who had visited the settlements, and the Shaysháns had been decimated by the disease against which they had no constitutional resistance. As practically every living member was at that time suffering from the effects, and as many were very ill, it is not improbable that to-day the tribe is extinct.

Like the Guaymís (Chapter X), the Shaysháns have no villages, but dwell in widely separated houses sheltering one or two related families, all under one chief or king who appoints deputies, usually of his own family or clan, to administer the affairs of the various districts and report to the king at stated intervals.

The houses are raised above the earth on posts, are floored with split palm wood, and have steeply pitched, low-eaved roofs of thatch. They are scru-

pulously clean, and the floors are usually carpeted
with sheets of bark-cloth. Carved wooden stools and
benches serve as seats, and the inmates sleep either
in pita-hemp hammocks or upon mats.

Although dwelling in a game country, the Shaysháns do little hunting. Neither are they true agriculturalists, but they depend largely upon wild
vegetables, nuts and fruits, together with bananas,
plantains, cacao and some maize which they raise. A
wild almond, a wild potato and the flower-buds and
fruit of the Piva-palm are their principal foods.

They are a light golden- or russet-brown, with
straight eyes, rather high but not prominent cheek-
bones, and with high-bridged, slightly aquiline noses.

They are excellent wood-carvers, make serviceable
but crude pottery, are experts at weaving the pita-
hemp fibers. Their weapons are powerful bows and
long arrows, as well as short blow-guns in which
they use clay pellets instead of darts as missiles.

Their religion is a modified sun-worship, but they
consider the sun-god, whom they call Kins'hou, as
of less importance than the being Ku'l'tan who is
supposed to be a personal or tribal deity, or Shaymc,
who is a divinity, or better a spirit, controlling the
rivers, floods and rains. Here we have a very striking proof of the survival of ancient Mayan ancestry.
Kins'hou is unquestionably an altered form of
Kinichahau, the Mayan sun-god; Ku'l'tan is obviously a version of Kukulcan, and Shaymc is in all
probability a modified form of Chac-Mool, the
Mayan rain- or water-god. Moreover, the name of
the tribe itself, Shayshán, means literally the "People
of Shaymc," or the "People of the Rain-God."

But there are even more positive and remarkable evidences of the Mayan ancestry of the Shaysháns. Over one-third of the words in their dialect are distinctly Mayan; practically all of their numerals are Mayan, and their names for various objects are almost identical with the names of similar objects in Guatemala or Yucatan.

Perhaps the most striking similarity of all is in the head-dress worn by the chiefs, and for ceremonial occasions. This consists of a fillet or band of braided pita-fiber or cotton to which is attached a group of feathers, in a sort of fan-shape arrangement, and which is worn above the forehead. It is in fact precisely like the head-dresses shown in old Spanish pictures of the Indians of Yucatan, and like those represented in the Mayan sculptures and paintings, but which are not, so far as is known, in use by any tribe other than these Shaysháns.

Still farther south, in central Panama, are the Coclé Indians, perhaps the descendants of the Mayas' most distant province in ancient times. Although to-day peaceful, industrious, civilized and in many, if not in all, ways the most worth-while civilized natives—red, black or white—of the Isthmus, in times past the Coclés were implacable enemies of the Spaniards, and maintained their independence for centuries, often defeating the pick of the Spanish soldiery.

To-day they number about fifteen thousand, and are the mainstay of their portion of the republic. They are excellent farmers; they raise horses and cattle; they are the principal rubber gatherers, and they manufacture many articles of rawhide, leather, horsehair and pita-hemp fiber, as well as excellent pottery, carved woodenware and splendid baskets.

They are the only Indians I have ever visited who have both dry- and wet-season houses. The former are open or partly walled dwellings of cane and thatch; the latter are of adobe or mud-plastered, wattled construction with thick walls and tiny windows high up under the overhanging thatched roofs.

Although thoroughly civilized, these Indians retain a number of their aboriginal arts and customs. They still have their caciques or chiefs, they still regard certain spots and caves as the abodes of spirits or perhaps deities, and once each year, on the Feast of Corpus Cristi, they hold an ancient dance. Dressed in weird costumes of painted bark-cloth, and with grotesque masks in the shapes of animals' heads, they exorcise the devils from everybody and everything within reach. Wielding long-handled whips with which they lash one another as well as onlookers and inanimate objects, they dance and rush about, yelling and chanting. Their appearance is certainly enough to frighten any self-respecting devil out of his wits; but the Indians take no chances and believe in flagellation to make matters more certain. Even then they are not entirely certain that the last devil has been driven off, and, to make assurance doubly sure, they troop into church and add the candles and prayers of the Christian religion to their own pagan rites.

An examination of the costumes worn in this devil-dance, and of the handicrafts of these Indians, reveals that the decorative designs and patterns are largely distinctively Mayan. Although the Coclés have no knowledge of their aboriginal religion and mythology, or at least claim they do not, still in their decorative paintings and carvings the symbols of the sun-god, of Kukulcan and of Chac-Mool, as well as those of various other Mayan deities or mythological characters, are often represented although in altered and conventionalized forms.

So long have these Indians been civilized and in contact with the Spanish-speaking Panamanians, that they have completely forgotten their own tongue. A few of the older men and women know some words of the Mayan dialect, and the meaning of the Indians' names for places and objects; but the majority have not the slightest knowledge of their ancestral dialect.

But the few words obtainable, as well as the names of localities and natural objects, are enough to prove the Mayan relationship of the Coclés. Thus the Coclé name for tree is *kuah* which is precisely the same as in the Maya tongue, and which gave Guatemala its name. The Spaniards, who had no *k* in their language, substituted a *g* in its place, and, altering *Kuah* to *Gua,* called the country Guatemala. There are many other evidences to indicate that the Coclés are of Maya stock, and while the chances are that they are the descendants of the members of a Mayan province or colony, there is another possible explanation.

It is not at all beyond the bounds of possibility that the original inhabitants of Coclé antedated the Mayas, and that the extremely ancient Coclé culture (see Chapter VI) was the nucleus from which the Mayan civilization was developed, or if not, that the inhabitants of the district, driven from their homes, wandered northward and carried certain of their arts and a part of their culture with them and that these greatly influenced the Mayan culture.   In that case many of the survivors may have remained in the neighboring districts and thus have been the ancestors of the existing Indians.   In that case it would not be at all surprising if both the Coclés and the Mayas had many features and even words in common.

CHAPTER IX

THE TOLTECS AND AZTECS

When the Spaniards under Cortez landed on the shores of Mexico, they found the country in possession of a highly cultured and civilized race whom they called Aztecs. Every one is familiar with this fact, but so much fiction, romance and misinformation has been told and written about the ancient Mexicans that there are many misconceptions. Many people are under the impression that all the inhabitants of Mexico, prior to the conquest, were civilized Aztecs. As a matter of fact, these people occupied and controlled only a comparatively small portion of the country, mainly the high plateaus and valleys, with their capital at what is now Mexico City, but which they called Tenochtitlan.

Aside from the Aztecs, there were countless diverse and distinct races and tribes in Mexico. Many were still savages, others were cultured, and some had a civilization of their own. Among these were the Zapotecs with their culture in southern Mexico, the Totonac culture about Vera Cruz, the Pipil culture on the western coast of Mexico and in Honduras, the Otomis about Guanajuato and Querétaro, the Mixtecas on the gulf coast, the Tlascalans who were enemies of the Aztecs and gladly aided Cortez, the Tecpanecs dwelling on the shore of Lake Tezcuco, the Huicholes in northern Mexico, and many others.

Many of these had been greatly influenced by the Aztecs; many had been conquered by them and were Aztec colonies, but in most cases each had its own dialect, its own arts and religious beliefs, its own attainments and culture, and many had their own rulers. For that matter, the Aztec Empire was a confederation of many tribes and cultures.

Strictly speaking, the term Aztec is a misnomer. Ethnologically the Aztecs (as well as many other Mexican tribes) were Nahuas speaking the Nahuatl language, and the Aztecs were only one of the numerous Nahua tribes. In their own dialect they called themselves the "People of Anahuac" and the entire empire became known as Aztec merely because the Aztecs rose from a small and obscure tribe to dominate and rule the others.

The term Toltec is also rather misleading. In the ancient Mexican legends and myths the earlier inhabitants of Mexico are spoken of as Toltecs and are described as a civilized race. It is very questionable, for reasons explained in Chapter III, if the Toltecs actually existed, and many authorities consider the name more geographical than racial. We know that some highly cultured race inhabited the Tollan district prior to the Aztecs, for ruins and remains of an earlier civilization are abundant there and elsewhere; but there is little if any evidence to prove that these are not of Aztec, or rather Nahua, origin. At any rate, if the Toltecs existed we do not know who they were, and the term Toltec is usually employed merely to distinguish the earlier culture of central Mexico from that of the later Aztecs.

We know very little about the Aztecs, or rather

the Nahuas, prior to their arrival in the Valley of Mexico. That they came from some distant locality in the north is clearly proved by their codices or written records, but unfortunately many of these are missing, having been destroyed by the fanatical Spanish priests. The name Aztec means "Crane People," and traditions and codices agree that their original home was a spot called Aztlan (the Place of Reeds) which some authorities have identified with California. Other spots mentioned in the codices and legends are Tlapallan (the Country of Bright Colors) and Chicomoztoc (the Seven Caves). The fact that the wanderers selected the marshy shores of a lake as the site for their capital would indicate that they came from a marshy country.

Fortunately for us, the Aztec Empire was still flourishing when the Europeans arrived on the scene, and hence, as in the case of the Incan Empire, we have a great deal more definite knowledge of their civilization than it is possible to obtain in regard to the Mayan and other civilizations which had vanished before the coming of the Spaniards.

But unfortunately, the Dons took far too little interest in the ethnological or archeological features of the natives. They were after gold and other treasure, and their campaign was one of wholesale destruction. Few of the leaders were more than illiterate adventurers, and the padres, who were the only men able to record scientific matters, were more interested in converting the natives to Christianity, or in destroying pagan gods and temples, than in studying their customs, beliefs and arts. To be sure, some of the priests and some of the laymen took a

keen interest in the races they were destroying.
Many of these men wrote voluminously of what they
observed and learned, and to them we owe an immense debt of gratitude, for their works, which are
still preserved, give us a better idea of the Aztec
civilization than would be possible by a study of
their remains alone. No doubt much more in the
way of documentary records was suppressed or destroyed than was preserved, for the Church was fearful of encouraging what it considered heathen and
blasphemous practises, or even of permitting records of such matters to exist. Several priceless
works of the early missionaries in Mexico were
sedulously hidden away and were not discovered until comparatively recently.

From what was recorded and preserved we have
learned a great deal about the social organization,
the government, the beliefs, the religion, the mathematics, the astronomy, the customs and even the
home life of the Aztecs, and we can readily decipher
their maps, codices and inscriptions. Still there is
a great deal of guesswork, for often contemporaneous writers failed to agree, and even more often they
forgot to mention the most important details, which
to them, no doubt, were such every-day and familiar
matters that they did not consider them worth recording. While countless specimens of Aztec hand-
work and art were saved and are still preserved, a
thousand times more were ruthlessly destroyed and
were forever lost to the world. Moreover, the
Spaniards, even the most educated, intelligent and
observant, were woefully handicapped when it came
to observing and recording matters dealing with the

natives. They were compelled to depend largely
upon hearsay and interpreters. Their tongues and
ears, accustomed to soft Castilian vowels, were not
adapted to speaking or hearing the peculiar sounds
and inflections of Indian dialects; their own spelling
was uncertain and far from uniform; and when setting down native names and words they found it
next to impossible to do so with the letters of their
own Spanish alphabet. The best they could do was
to spell the words phonetically, which was often impossible as no letters existed to express the proper
sounds. As a result, and also because names and
terms varied in different localities and dialects, a
vast amount of confusion occurred, so that to-day
we cannot always be certain whether different words
and names, such as names of deities and localities,
are synonymous or distinct.

In their civilization the Aztecs were inferior in
some respects to the Mayas, the Incas and other
American races. In their engineering feats they did
not approach the Peruvian races, nor had they perfected textiles, ceramics and some other arts to equal
those of the South American cultures. On the other
hand, they had reached greater heights in many arts
and attainments. Their feather-work was magnificent, and to supply the feathers necessary for ornaments and garments they maintained immense
aviaries of bright-plumaged birds whose feathers were
plucked at regular intervals. The rulers, priests and
officials wore clothing and mantles of feather-work
which aroused the wonder and admiration of the
Spaniards, and their feather mosaics upon shields and
other objects of hide, wood, etc., are among the most

remarkable known examples of American art. In
mosaic especially, the Aztecs surpassed all races of
the New World, and in some ways of the entire
world. Much of this was in turquoise. A wooden
shield covered with turquoise mosaic which is in the
Museum of the American Indian, Heye Foundation, in New York, is an astounding example of this
art. This shield, which is one of the few perfect
specimens extant, contains nearly fifteen thousand
pieces of turquoise laid on to form an elaborate ornamental design with human figures in the center. Innumerable objects were thus decorated with mosaic
work in turquoise, metal, mother-of-pearl, precious
and semiprecious stones, etc. It was used on wood,
shell, bone, metal and hide. Magnificent daggers
and knives of obsidian, mounted on beautifully
carved hilts of bone, had the entire surfaces of the
hilts covered with mosaic. Vessels and utensils of
all sizes were decorated in a similar manner. Stone
statues and idols were inlaid with mosaic, and even
human skulls were covered with mosaic.

In their carvings on shells, bones, wood and stone
the Aztecs exhibited a skill and refinement that has
never been excelled, and no material was too refractory for the Aztec artizans to carve and engrave. In
the American Museum of Natural History in New
York and in the British Museum are masses of
clear quartz crystal carved into the forms of human
skulls, human and animal heads and other shapes, as
perfectly modeled and cut, and as highly polished,
even in the smallest and deepest recesses, as though
done by the most skilled modern lapidist. Jade,
agate, topaz, sapphire, quartz, amethyst and prac-

tically every precious and semiprecious stone known to Mexico was carved, cut, polished and perforated with apparent ease by the Aztecs. Many of these gems are so small and the work upon them so minute that it seems impossible that it could have been done without the aid of a lens. But none of this work is as remarkable in some ways as the Aztec art in obsidian. Obsidian or volcanic glass is one of the hardest and most refractory of minerals. It is as brittle as glass and flakes with a touch. For forming edged tools and weapons, such as knives, spear- and arrowheads, etc., obsidian is almost ideal, and astonishingly beautiful weapons of the material were produced by many primitive American races. But the Aztecs, not content with producing weapons of the highest and most perfect workmanship, went even further and used obsidian for ornamental purposes, cutting and carving it as perfectly and readily as any other material. Many of these ornaments, such as earplugs, were cut so thin that they are almost as transparent as glass, and were polished on every surface. Large masses of obsidian were cut and polished for use as mirrors, and immense ceremonial objects were formed into complex shapes from the same material.

Among their weapons of obsidian were swords. These swords were peculiar to the Aztecs who, as far as is known, were the only pre-Columbian Americans to use them. The Aztec sword *(maquahuitl)* bore little resemblance to a sword as we know it. The blade was of wood, usually carved and often decorated with mosaic, and with both edges set with rectangular obsidian teeth placed close together like the teeth on a large saw. As metal was very scarce among the Aztecs little was used, and stone, especially obsidian, took its place for most purposes. Although they possessed silver, gold and copper, the latter metal was prized far more than the precious metals, and copper bells and other objects passed as money. In this respect the Aztecs were far behind the Incas and other American races who used copper or bronze for innumerable purposes, and who had acquired a remarkable skill in smelting, casting, hammering, welding, soldering and plating metals.

As far as is known, the Aztecs did not use metal weapons as extensively as did the Peruvians, but their stone and obsidian-tipped swords, spears and arrows were probably as effective as the metal weapons of their southern neighbors, until it came to fighting the Spaniards with their steel armor and firearms. Like the Peruvians and many other ancient American races, the Aztecs made use of the spear-throwing-stick, or atlatl, which still survives and is in daily use among the Guaymí Indians of Panama who, as described in Chapter VI, are of Aztec descent.

As the Aztecs were a warlike, or at least a militant, race, weapons and armament were of great importance to them, and some of their most perfect and beautiful examples of handicraft and art are to be found in their fighting gear. For protection they used padded or quilted cotton armor, armor of cane, and thick rawhide shields, as well as a form of helmet or casque. But they did not neglect the more peaceful arts. Their musical instruments were excellently designed and made, and, as in the case of nearly every object, both utilitarian and otherwise, they were highly ornamental, the drums made in animal or human forms, and the horns and flutes carved, inlaid and painted. Painting reached a high state among the Aztecs. Not only was it employed upon their beautiful ceramic ware, but true paintings were made upon parchment, cloth, etc. Elaborate maps were painted on these materials, and records, writings and codices were done in colors upon sheets of parchment, papyrus or cloth.

Along astronomical and mathematical lines the Aztecs and Mayas had advanced independently, and while both had developed an amazing knowledge of these sciences they differed materially in results. Thus the Aztecs' calendar, as well as their written or glyphed language, differed greatly from that of the Mayas. Broadly speaking, the Aztec writing was pictorial and symbolic. Even on their maps and codices, localities and events were recorded by means of pictures bearing some resemblance (although often so conventionalized as to be unrecognizable) to the objects they represented, rather than by arbitrary signs or elements of a phonetic character. But there is evidence that the Aztec scribes were rapidly developing a less cumbersome and more truly written language in which words were expressed by phonetic symbols. Thus in recording the names of persons and places they frequently used signs instead of the pictorial representations. Ixcoatl, for example, was represented by a small serpent *(coatl)* pierced by knives *(Iztli)*. Montezuma was indicated by a mouse-trap *(Montli)* an eagle *(quauhtli)* a lancet *(zo)* and a hand *(maitl),* the first syllable of each word giving the name "Mon-quau-zo-ma." But the system varied and had not been coordinated. At times an entire syllable would be expressed by an object whose name began with the syllable. At other times a single sound or letter would be represented by the same drawing, but the idea was to convey a thought by a sketch indicating the phonetic element.

The codices, moreover, were not intended to be read or interpreted by every one. As a rule they were learned by rote and were passed on by word of mouth from generation to generation, and in many cases knowledge of their exact meaning has been completely lost. Even after the Spanish conquest the Mexicans continued to record events by means of these painted codices, and on many of these the meanings of the symbols are elaborated and made lucid by means of notations in Spanish.

The same is true of the Aztec maps, and long after Mexico had come completely under Spanish rule and the natives had acquired a knowledge of Spanish, their maps were largely made with the typical Aztecan figures and symbols.

Did we possess a full series of the pre-Columbian codices we might be able to trace the entire history of the Aztecs and all their wanderings until they at last found a permanent resting-place in the Valley of Mexico. Several of these originals exist, and there are others which are very accurate facsimiles. These were made by Mexican artists who, from their memory and knowledge, reproduced the originals destroyed by the Dons. These copies were interpreted by the artists themselves and are therefore known as interpretive codices. Three are known: the first, the *Oxford Codex* in the Bodleian Library, is historical with a list of cities subject to Mexico; the second, the

Paris or *Tellerio-Remensis Codex,* records many facts about the settlement of the Nahua city-states; while the third, or *Vatican Codex,* is mostly of a mythological and calendrical character. Perhaps the most remarkable feature of this is the section representing the Aztec idea of the journey of the soul through the other world after death. The corpse, dressed for burial, is shown with the spirit issuing from the mouth. Ushered by an attendant in an ocelot skin, the soul, with a wooden collar about its neck indicating a prisoner, goes before Tezcatlipoca to be sentenced. Then the soul is tested for its right to enter the world of the dead, the realm of Mictlan, and is provided with a number of arrows or spears for self-protection. It passes two high peaks, which may topple upon it at any instant; a terrible serpent intercepts it; and if this is overcome it is faced by a huge alligator *(xochitonal).* Then it must cross eight successive deserts and mountains and be buffeted by a cyclone so fierce that it cuts the solid rock. Finally it encounters a demon *(izpuzteque),* and the fiend Nextepehua with clouds of ashes, until at length it wins the doors of the "Lord of Hell" where it is free to greet its spirit friends.

In some details the Aztec and Maya calendars are similar, although they are by no means identical, and it is evident that one either borrowed from the other or that both took their ideas from some common source. As the Mayan culture is far older than that of the Aztecs it is probable that the Mayas originated the system, but as the Zapotecan calendar embodies peculiarities of both, some authorities have held that it is the oldest. On the other hand it is far more probable that the Zapotecans borrowed from both the Mayas and Aztecs.

The Aztecs' year was of three hundred and sixty-five days without any correction or intercalary addition, and hence, in the course of time, their calendar lost most of its seasonal value or significance. Because of the omission of the extra hours in each solar year it became necessary for the priest constantly to alter the dates of festivals. The Nexiuhilpilitzli or "Binding of the Years" consisted of fifty-two years which ran in two cycles: one of fifty-two years of three hundred and sixty-five days, and the other of seventy-three groups of two hundred and sixty days each. The former was the course of the solar year divided into eighteen periods of twenty days or months with five unlucky *(nemontemi)* days over and above the others. These were not intercalated, but were included in the year and overflowed the yearly division of twenty days. The seventy-three groups of two hundred and sixty days were subdivided into smaller groups or "birth-cycles" of thirteen days. The twenty days were the basis of time reckoning *(cempohualli)* from the waxing to the waning of the moon. Every day in this period had its name or symbol, such as "snake," "wind," "reed," "house," etc.

Each *cempohualli* (twenty days) was divided into four five-day periods or weeks which were known by the symbol or name of the middle or third day in each. The day names ran on with no regard to the length of the year and the year itself was called by the name of the middle day of the week on which it began. As there were only twenty day names it is obvious that there were four: *(calli)* house, *(rochtli)* rabbit, *(acatl)* reed and *(tecpatl)* flint, which always re-curred in sequence because of the incidence of the Mexican solar year.

Four ordinary years made one "sun-year," and as no work was done on the "unlucky" days and the people lived in fear and trembling of the universe com-ing to an end during that period, the civil year permitted the day names to run continuously from year to year. The priests, however, kept their own reckoning or religious calendar, and always began their year with the first calendar date, regardless of the symbol or name dominating the civil year.

Thirteen years formed a *xiumalpilli* (bundle), and four of these, fifty-two, produced the complete Bind-ing of the Years. Hence each year had a double aspect: first as an individual period of time, and sec-ond as a part of the sun-year. These were so named and numbered that each year in the entire series of fifty-two years was differentiated.

As I have mentioned, a terrible fear came over the people as the end of each fifty-two-year cycle ap-proached, for they believed implicitly that at the close of some one of these cycles the world would end. To their minds, a foreordained time had expired as ap-pointed by divinity, and as no one, not even priests, could foresee which cycle would mark the end of the universe, the people always prepared themselves for the worst. For some time after each Binding of the Years the people prostrated themselves, offered sac-rifices and abandoned all tasks and occupations. As the first day of the new (fifty-third) year dawned, the people anxiously watched the Pleiades for the ex-pected omen of destruction or a new lease on life. If the constellation passed the zenith, time would continue, and immediately thereafter there was great rejoicing. Gods were placated by wholesale human sacrifices, fires being kindled by friction upon the breasts of the victims, and the hearts and bodies being consumed as the flames spread. The hearth fires, which had been allowed to go out, were rekindled from the sacred fires of the temples, and life was again resumed.

Originally the birth-cycle of two hundred and sixty days was a lunar cycle and bore the names of thirteen moons and formed a portion of the civil calendar; but later it had nothing in common with the civil calender, the lunar names were abandoned, it was used only for religious purposes, and the days were designated by numbers from one to thirteen. In this connection it is interesting to note the frequent recurrence of thirteen in calendrical, religious and other matters of the Aztecs and other ancient American races. Nearly all the prophecies were based on that number; it was considered a sacred and lucky number, and throughout Aztec, Mayan and Incan myths and legends we find it appearing with great frequency. No doubt the mysticism of thirteen arose from the original lunar year of thirteen moons, but it is rather strange that these early Americans regarded thirteen from the opposite point of view of all the European races.

In science the Aztecs were not far advanced, aside from their calendrical system and their architectural attainments. Mainly their science, so-called, consisted of astrology and divination, the priests claiming to be able to foretell the futures of newly born children and the progress of souls after death, by means of their calendars and the stars. They also made prophecies and practised divination by means of omens obtained from the flights of birds, the appearance of seeds and fruits, birds' feathers, bones and innumerable other objects.

Although they had developed a rather complete and remarkable form of pictographic written language, yet, if judged solely by their spoken language, the Aztecs would be regarded as low in their civilization. Their dialects were of the incorporative type, so common among the American aborigines, in which several related words are joined to form one long word. By merging the various words, or portions of them, and by slightly altering their forms and then joining them, the races produced single words of most inordinate length and involved meanings. This led to almost impossible sounds and still more impossible pronunciations. For example, the simple expression "nine years" was *qhiucnauhxihuitl,* as nearly as it can be written in letters of our alphabet. Faced with such words, it is a wonder that the Spaniards ever made any headway in the language, and, as Spence remarks: "The greatest glory of the Spanish priests was that they learned the language in the interests of the Christian faith."

In their social organization the Aztecs were peculiar. The government was an absolute monarchy in many ways and held sway over practically all of the modern states of Mexico, Vera Cruz and Guerrero. But within the empire were many city-states and small republics with local rulers who were practically independent.

The royal line was not hereditary, but the eldest surviving brother of the monarch ascended to the throne. In case there was no surviving brother the eldest nephew of the deceased king succeeded him. But like many customs, even in modern days, this rule was often ignored, and in case of the rightful heir being incompetent or otherwise undesirable, the ministers usually elected some outsider as a monarch because of his military ability, his knowledge of political and religious matters and his character. Whoever ascended the throne of the Aztecs was invariably a man of the highest culture, artistic refinement and aristocratic blood. The state council was composed of electors and other important individuals, and their duties were to look after the finances and other details of the government. Practically all military, civil, judicial and religious positions of any importance were held by members of the nobility. Every city and province had its local judges who exercised both civil and criminal jurisdiction, and whose opinions superseded that of the emperor. There were also lesser judges or magistrates who attended to petty cases, as well as police officials and a well-organized police force.

In the city-states and semiindependent republics a distinct feudal government existed, as for example at Cholula and Tollantzinco where the Alcolhuans had paramount control. In fact, Mexico in the times of the Aztec Empire was in many respects similar to medieval Europe where there were numerous feudal lords and barons, each supreme in his district, but all owing allegiance to the king. Also, as was the custom in medieval Europe, the Aztec priesthood had vast powers and complete control of education. Education was highly organized and was divided into primary and secondary grades, the boys being taught by the priests, and the girls by holy women or nuns. The secondary or *calmecac* education was devoted entirely to deciphering the codices, to astrology, divination, religion and the higher sciences. Despite the fact that the Aztec priesthood was a hierarchy with immense power, especially in matters of religion, the priests unquestionably used their power largely for the good of the people, instructing the Aztecs in their faith, and ever trying to instil the cardinal virtues. Even the Spanish padres admitted this, and Sahagun says that they "performed the duties plainly pointed out by their religion." The upkeep of the Church and priesthood depended upon land tenure with the revenue derived therefrom, together with a rule or law of "first fruits," the surplus being distributed among the poor.

The head or high priest was known as *Mexicatl Teohuatzin* or Mexican Lord of Divine Matters. He had a seat on the king's council and was second only to the monarch himself. Next to him was the high priest of Quetzálcoatl who led a secluded life and had authority only over his own caste. Under these two chief dignitaries of the church were the ordinary or secular priests who dressed in black and wore long hair covered with a mantilla-like cloth and who were known as *tlenamacac,* and the still lower or "little priests" *(lamacazton)* who were in effect lay-brothers or novices. It must not be thought that the Aztec priests led a life of ease, luxury and carnal pleasures by any means. Their life was rigorous and austere in the extreme, and was devoted mainly to fasting, penitence and prayer when not busy observing the exacting rituals of their faith. Even their nights were not devoid of labor, for they were required to rise frequently in order to give praise to their gods. Absolute cleanliness of persons and garments was rigorously enforced, and the priests were frequently compelled to draw their own blood or offer other forms of self-sacrifice.

The domestic life of the Aztecs was remarkable for the simplicity of the lives of the poorer classes and the voluptuous display of the aristocracy. The greater portion of the masses was forced to labor strenuously in the fields or at the various trades and arts, such as feather-work, metal working, building, quarrying, stone-cutting, jewelry- and weapon-making. Others were venders of fruits, vegetables and flowers. Still others were servants, street sweepers, porters, etc. On the other hand, the aristocracy led a life of laziness and luxury equal to that of ancient Rome. At their banquets, where the women sat at separate tables, they dined on venison, wild turkey, game, the most delectable fruits and vegetables, pastry and rich sauces served in vessels of solid gold and silver. The use of tobacco was universal, and for their national beverage they had the pulque or juice of the maguey plant, either unfermented or fermented. At certain times on ceremonial occasions, human flesh was eaten, but probably this was solely for religious reasons, for the Aztecs' religion enjoined the killing of slaves and captives and the consumption of their flesh in order to obtain unity with the deity in the flesh.

The religion was complicated, and the Aztec mythology contained a vast number of gods and goddesses with innumerable lesser deities and sacred heroes. In fact, the number of their gods was so great that scientists adopted the system of numbering them rather than attempting to classify all by name. Moreover, to add to the confusion, many of the deities bore two or more names and were gods or goddesses of two or more matters.

The rituals provided for a certain amount of cannibalism, for many human sacrifices, and for cold-blooded cruelty, while at the same time there were baptisms, confessions, consubstantiation, etc. In many ways the Aztec religion was superior to that of either the Greeks or Romans, and at the time of the Spanish conquest it was rapidly evolving into a worship of one supreme god. This was the air-god (Tezcatlipoca) also known as the "Fiery-Mirror," the Aztecan Jupiter, who carried a polished shield in which he was supposed to see all the actions and deeds of mankind.

The Aztecs believed in eternity as regards the soul, but with eons or epochs, each of which was dependent on the sun. At the close of every four "suns" or epochs, the world was supposed to meet with disaster; the exact nature of each being recorded and foretold.

To enumerate and describe even a small proportion of the Aztec deities would require a volume in itself, and it is possible to mention only a few of the more important and interesting of their gods and goddesses. As I have said, the Aztec religion at the time of the Spanish conquest was tending toward the worship of one supreme god; but the deity Tezcatlipoca, who was apparently destined to become *the* Divinity,

was by no means the most important god of the Aztecan mythology. This was Tonatiah, the "Sun-Chief"
or sun-god, the principal source of life, and known
also as "Teotl" or "God." He was also at times
called Ipalneomohuani or "He by who men live," and
he was the ever-present background of the worship of

AZTEC

NASCA

SUN GODS

all the Aztec deities. Human sacrifices were made
to him, and the hearts of sacrificial victims were always held up and offered to him first. It was the
sole business of many warriors to secure captives to
provide the daily sacrifices to this insatiable deity.

The man who secured the most prisoners for this sacrifice was regarded as the champion, and the warriors devoted to the god believed that they would remain in his service after death and would share his life. He is usually represented as licking up the blood of his victims, and his chief festival was celebrated by the symbolic sacrifice of all the other gods by attiring and painting the victims to represent the lesser deities. It is a most interesting and remarkable fact that this Aztec sun-god is usually represented with a projecting tongue, and with conventionalized jaguars in his hands or at the sides of his head, and that the chief deity of the Nascas of Peru was shown in precisely the same form, even to the protruding tongue. It would seem that this must have been more than a mere coincidence, and yet we have no evidence to lead us to think there was any relationship or connection between the Nascans and the ancient Mexicans.

Tezcatlipoca, the air-god, whom I have already mentioned, was also known as Nezahualpilli (Hungry Chief); Yaotzin (the Enemy); Telpochtli (the Youthful Warrior); Yoalli Ehecatl (Night Wind) and Moneneque (Claimer of Prayer). He was regarded as the life-giver and death-dealer, and was supposed to rush along the dark highways like a wind, seeking persons whose time had come. Stone benches for him to rest upon were provided by the thoughtfully considerate Aztecs, and were placed beside the roads screened by foliage. It was believed that if a person seized by this god should succeed in overcoming him he would be granted whatever he desired. This god was credited with being the originator of most of the Aztecs' arts, and the guide in developing their civilization. He is usually represented with a spear and a polished shield, and is often shown with a golden ear hanging from his hair and with several small golden tongues surrounding it, the whole being symbolical of the god's status of Claimer of Prayer.

Numerous human sacrifices were made to this god, during ceremonials, one of which was the *Toxcatl* held on the fifth month of each year. At this time a physically perfect youth, who had long been prepared for the rite, was sacrificed. The victim, selected from among the prisoners destined for sacrifice, assumed the name, garments and all the attributes of the deity and was regarded with reverence and awe by the people who believed him the earthly representative of their god. He was cared for with the utmost solicitude and was entertained in the homes and at the tables of the nobility during his year of preparation. During the day he rested, but at night he went forth on the highways with shield and javelin, resting upon the stone seats or rushing along the roads accompanied by attendants or pages. Later he was given four beautiful virgins as companions, and his last days were a round of continuous feasting and pleasure. Upon the day appointed for the sacrifice he bade his girl companions a fond farewell, was carried up the steps of the pyramid, and was sacrificed upon the altar.

Another important Aztec god was Huitzilopochtli, the war-god. According to Aztecan mythology this god was the son of a pious widow, Coatlicue, who afterward became a goddess herself. The myth relates that while she was praying on a mountain a

small bundle of bright-colored feathers fell from the
sky upon her. These she placed in her bosom intend-
ing to offer them to the sun-god, but in a short time
she discovered she was to become a mother. Learning this, her sons and her daughter Coyolxauhqui
decided to kill their mother in order to wipe out the
family disgrace. While they were attacking her, the
war-god was born, fully armed with shield and spear
of blue, with a head-dress of humming-bird feathers
and a feather leg-guard. He instantly destroyed his
brothers with a flash of lightning and beheaded his
sister. His name, Huitzilopochtli (Humming-bird
to the left), was bestowed upon him because of his
legendary leg-covering, and his mother, Coatlicue or
Coatlantona (Snake-skirt), was made the goddess of
the earth or Earth-Mother. She is represented as
a fearsome-looking being with a death's head, clawed
hands and feet, and with a skirt of braided rattle-
snakes, symbolic of lightning.

Chicomecoatl, the goddess of agriculture, is rep-
presented as a human face in the mouth of a rattlesnake. Her chief ceremonial was *Xalaquia* from
June twenty-eighth to July fourteenth, during which
period young virgin captives, painted red and yellow
to symbolize maize, performed intricate dances, for
which they had been especially trained. On the last
day of the festival these maidens were carried up to
the altar and sacrificed. During the time of the
Xalaquia, and until the death of the last victim, it
was unlawful for the people to use new corn in any
form.

The god of human sacrifice was Xipe (the Flayed
One), who is represented as attired in the skin of a

flayed human being. On his festivals of man-flaying
the victims were stripped of their skins which were
worn by the god's devotees for a period of twenty
days. At this time, also, the Aztec monarch assumed
the character of the god, wearing a crown and jacket
of spoonbill feathers, a skirt of overlapping green
feathers, and with hands and feet covered with the
skins of the extremities of the sacrificed victim. Although Xipe was always a red god he had three forms
or characters: the spoonbill, the blue cotinga and the
jaguar, symbols of earth, heaven and hell.

The rain-god, Tlaloc, was probably adopted from
the Mayan mythology and was identical in form and
attributes with the Maya Chac-Mool. In Aztecan
mythology he was the husband of Chalchihuitlicue,
(the Emerald Lady) and their numerous children
were the Tlalocs (Clouds). Many children and maidens were sacrificed to this god. If the victims wept
as they approached the sacrificial altar it was considered a good omen for a prosperous rainy season
to follow. Tlaloc's Emerald Lady wife was usually
represented or symbolized as a frog, and at the feast
of *Etzalqualiztli* (When they eat bean-food) priests
devoted to the god's cult plunged into the lake and
imitated the sounds and movements of frogs. Sacrifices to Tlaloc and his wife were made in the mountains at special altars and at artificial ponds where
there were extensive cemeteries devoted entirely to
the victims of the sacrifices. The volcanoes of Teo-
cuinani and Popocatepetl were considered the abodes
of the god and goddess, and on the former there was
a temple to the rain-god containing a green stone
image of Tlaloc who is always represented as resting

on his back with head raised, knees drawn up and hands holding a disk upon his stomach.

Probably the best known and most famous of the Aztecs' gods was the "Plumed Serpent" or Quetzál-coatl,* although he was by no means their most important deity. He was a far less cruel and blood-thirsty god than most of the Aztec deities, and, un-like them, he did not demand human sacrifices but preferred the blood of his devotees and worshipers shed by themselves. His priests, who were of a dis-tinct caste, were accustomed to pierce their tongues or ears to secure the blood which they smeared upon the mouths of the idols. There are many myths and legends connected with Quetzálcoatl, but all agree that he was a white stranger with a flowing beard. One myth states that he first appeared in the form of the *quetzál* or resplendent trogan, and that while in this form he was captured in the snare of a hunter, Hueymatzin, himself a hero-god. Owing to this, the *quetzál* became the sacred bird of the Aztecs and Mayas, and temples were devoted to its worship. Another legend relates that Quetzálcoatl arrived in a strange winged ship at the spot now known as Vera Cruz, and that he taught the Aztecs many arts, in-structed them in religion, and established their civili-zation.

Among other things he prophesied that long after his departure white strangers would arrive from over-sea and would overthrow the Aztec kings and enforce another religion, but that eventually he would return to reestablish the Aztecs and their faith. Whether or not there was any basis of truth in this myth, it is

---

*Quetzál, the resplendent trogan, and Coatl, a snake.

impossible to say. But it is a remarkable and indisputable fact, borne out by contemporaneous written records, that the Aztecs were not at all surprised when Cortez and his followers arrived at Vera Cruz, and that many of the natives mistook the conqueror for Quetzálcoatl. Moreover, the legend of white men visiting America, and later going back to the "Land of Sunrise" whence they would again return, was widely disseminated prior to the Spanish conquest. The Maya priest, Chilám Balám, prophesied that, at the end of the thirteenth age, white men would arrive in Yucatan; and the Peruvian Inca, Atahualpa, told Pizarro that his father, Huayna-Kapac had prophesied on his death-bed that, in the reign of the thirteenth Inca, white men would come from the sun and subjugate the Peruvians. Perhaps the most remarkable and inexplicable features of all these prophecies or legends are the recurrence of the mystical number thirteen in such widely separated localities as Yucatan and Peru, the fact that the Spaniards arrived at the time foretold, and the amazing similarity of the myths with our own story of Christ with its promise of His return. At any rate, the natives' implicit belief in these legends was a large factor in their comparatively easy conquest by the Europeans, for the Aztecs, like the Peruvians, felt that they could not escape their predestined fate.

The Aztec legend or prophecy went much further than the others, however, and foretold that eventually the old gods and old rule would be reestablished, although, as so often happens in the case of prophecies, the exact date of this renaissance was uncertain. But unquestionably much of the unrest in Mexico during the past few years is due to the fact that thousands of the Indians still have faith in their ancient tradition and, with few exceptions, the descendants of the Aztecs are still looking forward to their millennium and the reinstatement of their ancient gods. As is the case with the descendants of the Mayas, the Incans and others, the Mexican Indians have a deep-seated faith in their pagan deities, athough nominally Christians, and while some, such as the Huicholes of northern Mexico, have driven out the priests, have cast aside the Christian religion and have returned to the worship of their ancestral gods, the majority maintain a profound secrecy as to their true beliefs and devotions, and profess entire ignorance of the gods and ceremonies of their ancestors.

As Quetzálcoatl is always represented as a white man with a full beard and attired in a black robe bordered with white crosses, and as the Mayan Plumed Serpent god, Kukulcan, is also represented as a bearded man it seems quite probable that the myths were based upon the actual arrival of some European in ages past. Certain persons have claimed that the Plumed Serpent was a Viking, despite the facts that his legendary advent was centuries before the Norsemen reached the New World and that his representations are found among the most ancient American remains. The pious Spanish padres, on the other hand, identified Quetzálcoatl with St. Thomas and other apostles, and in their writings, pointed out the many similarities between the Aztec religion and their own. It has even been suggested that a divine being may have appeared to various races, including the ancient Americans, and taught them religion similar to Christianity, and that, during the following ages, the religion became perverted and distorted until unrecognizable.

Although the myths regarding Quetzálcoatl agree fairly well as to his arrival and his beneficent teachings, they vary greatly as to his departure. One says that he cast himself on to a funeral pyre and that his ashes flew up and were changed to birds while his heart became the morning star. According to this legend he vanished for four days, then wandered for eight days in the underworld, until the morning star appeared, when he was resurrected and went to Heaven as a god,—a story strikingly like our account of the Resurrection. Another version is that he became disgusted with the perversion of the Aztecs' faith and their devotion to worldly lusts and pleasures, and departed on a magic raft of entwined serpents. Still another relates that he was overcome by Tezcatlipoca, the god of night, who descended on a spider's web and offered Quetzálcoatl a draught supposedly to produce immortality, which in reality effected such an irresistible longing for home as to cause him to depart. Both in Mexico and among the Mayas, Quetzálcoatl was regarded as the god of dawn, as a god of light, of the sun, of thunder, of winds and of the cardinal points of the compass. Aside from his name of Quetzálcoatl he was known to the Aztecs as Ehecatl (the Air), Yolcuat (the Rattlesnake) Tohil (the Rumbler), Nanihehecatl (Lord of the Four Winds), Tlauizcalpantecutli (Lord of the Light of Dawn), etc. Symbolic of these attributes, are the whirls and wind symbols which usually surround him, his temples built in circular form, and the representation of his head as the second of the twenty day signs, Ehecatl or wind.

In making statues, figures or otherwise depicting their gods and goddesses, the Aztecs sometimes represented them as imaginary beings, as semihuman, as part human and part beast, or as ordinary men and women. Frequently several gods would be shown with identical features, forms, etc., and were only recognizable by certain ornaments, details of dress or even by distinctive colors. Thus, in the codices, the gods Tezcatlipoca and Huitzilopochtli are always easily identified, for the former is pictured with two black bands across the face: one below the mouth and the other beneath the eyes and separated by a blue band, while Huitzilopochtli is painted with similar bands of blue. On the codices, Otontecutli is distinguished by two black facial bands, while Xiuhtecutli has a band above the mouth and another above the eyes. The same system of identification marks was carried out on idols, masks and other representations, the colored bands being either painted or, more often, formed of mosaic set in recesses cut in the stone. This not only prevented any mistake being made as to which god was represented, but it made matters much simpler for the artists, sculptors and codex-makers. The latter in particular would have had great difficulty in drawing distinctive features for every deity and always duplicating them when painting the hundreds of small figures upon the codices. But by drawing the figures in conventional form, with no difference in features, and by designating each deity by his facial markings and symbols, the task became quite simple.

Most of the Aztec gods were repellent, cruel and bestially bloodthirsty deities; but they were not all of this character. There were Xochipili or the "Flower-god-child," the special deity of flowers, who was represented as a beautiful child adorned with blossoms; the "Obsidian Butterfly" or Itzpapalotl, and many others, as well as innumerable mythical beings who were not true gods but were more in the nature of symbols, as, for example, the *Xiuhcoatl* or "Turquoise-snakes," the symbols of fire and water. To the layman, and for that matter to many scientists, the Aztec mythology is very confusing and intricate, for the Aztecs had adopted bits of the mythologies of many Mexican races and of the Mayas, and had added them to their own. It is often impossible to say whether deities and forms of religion were of Aztecan or Mayan origin, for often the same gods and myths were common to both. On the other hand, certain gods and features of the religions were confined exclusively to one or the other race and unquestionably were of distinct origin.

In addition to worshiping their various gods, the Aztecs also worshiped the planet Venus, known to them as Citlalpol (the Great Star) and as Tlauizcalpantecutli (the Lord of Dawn) and identified with Quetzálcoatl who sometimes bore the same name, and whose heart was supposed to have appeared in the heavens as the morning star. The court of the temple to *quetzál* contained a column bearing the symbol of Venus; sacrifices were made to the planet each time it appeared; and as it rose the people were accustomed to stop up their chimneys so that no evil might enter with the light from the star.

Taken as a whole, the Aztec religion was probably the most cruel and sanguinary of any of the faiths of the ancient Americans. It called for countless human sacrifices in which the victims were killed by having their hearts torn from their living bodies by the high priests. But the widely accepted idea that the sacrificial victim was secured in place upon the altar by means of a stone yoke or collar about his neck, is probably quite erroneous. Such stone collars are not uncommon, it is true; but there is no evidence that they were employed for holding the victim upon the altar. In fact, all known evidence tends to prove that if these collars actually were used in connection with human sacrifices it was in a symbolic way only, the form of the collar representing the abode of death in the shape of the conventionalized open mouth of a mythical monster. Moreover, it was probably entirely unnecessary to secure the victims upon the altars, for they also believed in human sacrifices and felt that they were winning immortality and divine attributes by being sacrificed, and were usually far from unwilling victims. The men, as well as the women and children, destined for sacrificial purposes were either prisoners of war or captives taken from other tribes for the sole purpose of sacrifice.

One of the strangest customs of the Aztecs was their annual battle with the Tlascalans. Each year the warriors of the two races met on a prearranged spot, not to kill one another but solely to secure prisoners for sacrifice. Each warrior seized an opponent and endeavored to carry him off, and the battle became a mad struggle of groups pulling and tugging to bear away or rescue the combatants.

Once taken, the Tlascalan captives were placed in cages and carried triumphantly to Mexico. Here they had an opportunity, although a most slender and unfair chance, of winning their freedom. With one foot secured by means of a rope or chain to a huge slab of stone, the prisoner was given a tiny shield and a toy weapon and was attacked by a professional warrior with full fighting equipment. It was in fact a one-sided form of the ancient Roman gladiatorial combats. If the woefully handicapped captive succeeded in defeating six of his opponents in succession he was granted freedom, but the instant he was wounded he was doomed to sacrifice.

But because their religion was cruel and bloodthirsty we must not assume that the Aztecs were either a cruel or a sanguinary race. There is no evidence to show that they were by nature any more cruel or inhumane than other races. They were a dominating race, ambitious, natural-born conquerors, clever and shrewd traders, and merciless in exacting tribute from their conquered subjects. In all probability the Spanish rule, bad as it was, was mild compared to that of the Aztec kings. But in their every-day life they were good-natured, light-hearted, hospitable, fond of music and flowers and given to festivities of the most peaceful and beautiful character. Religion of course held a very high and important place with them, as it does with all primitive races, and a large part of their lives, a good portion of their art, a great deal of their work and most of their customs and ceremonies were closely connected with or were wholly devoted to religious matters. Even their folk-lore was principally of a religious

character or embodied gods and deities, and hence
it is practically impossible to differentiate between
actual tradition or history and purely allegorical
myths.

We cannot even be certain how much of their
codices is actually records or true history, and how
much is recorded myths. But we know that they
wandered for a long time before settling down, and
that during their migrations they must have acquired
many arts and industries from tribes with whom they
came in contact. Likewise, these other races undoubtedly were greatly influenced by the Aztecs.
Hence, over a vast area we find objects and remains,
as well as existing customs, which show Aztec or
rather Nahua influence or vice versa, even though
they are far beyond the boundaries of the Aztec
Empire as it existed at the time of the Spanish conquest. Moreover, there were traditions among the
Aztecs, which to some extent were borne out by the
codices, and some of which still persist, to the effect
that the race remained for long periods at various
localities prior to their arrival in the Valley of
Mexico, and that colonies were established in these
places with vast stores of treasure, supplies, arms,
etc., to be used in case of emergency or as required.
According to these tales these colonies or outposts
were reserve bases forming an almost complete line
of retreat, and were strongly fortified and hidden in
the secret fastnesses of the mountains. But as
centuries passed and no need of calling upon these
reserves arose, they became forgotten and the secrets
of their locations lost, so that when at last the empire
was attacked by the Spaniards the reserve forces and

treasures were unavailable. Possibly these traditions are purely imaginary tales or myths; but there are reasons to think that they had at least a basis of fact. Because no one has ever discovered any of these "lost cities" does not prove that they did not exist or that they may not exist at the present time. There are vast areas of practically unexplored mountain regions in Mexico, and still larger areas wherein a city or several cities might remain hidden and unknown. It was these tales, and the possibility of such cities existing, that inspired the late Thomas Janvier with the theme of his delightful and realistic book, *The Aztec Treasure House.*

At all events, it is well known that there are countless temples and places of ceremonials in Mexico which were never looted nor found by the Spaniards, and, during and after the conquest, bands of Aztecs sought refuge in the wilder portions of the mountains and continued to worship their ancient gods and to live their own lives safe from Christian interference.

From time to time reports are made of discoveries of most remarkable and priceless specimens of ancient Aztec objects in caves and secret hiding-places; but whether these were hidden by the Indians to prevent them from falling into the hands of the Dons, or whether they were left by refugees who survived and maintained their rites and customs after the conquest, we cannot say.

Even the history of the founding of Mexico City, or as the Aztecs called it, Tenochtitlan, is so interwoven with myth and legends that we cannot be certain of anything regarding it. According to one tradition the Aztecs were guided to the site by their chief, Huitzilopochtli who afterward was deified as the god of war. Upon reaching the spot, the Nahuas observed a huge eagle resting upon a cactus and holding a snake in its talons, and with its wings outspread to the sun. This was a good omen and the people drove piles in the mud of the lake and established the city. Another legend is to the effect that the Aztecs sought refuge on the west shore of the lake, and in the marsh discovered a sacrificial stone on which a prisoner of war, Prince Copal, had been sacrificed forty years previous. From a crack in the altar a Nepal cactus had sprung up, and upon this there perched an eagle. Considering this a propitious sign, the high priest dove into a pool and there met the water-god, Tlaloc, who gave permission to build the city. As Indians are greatly influenced by omens and signs it is not at all improbable that the city was founded because of an eagle perching on a cactus, and it is quite fitting that the national emblem of Mexico should be an eagle holding a serpent and resting on a cactus plant.

Whatever the truth may be as regards the establishment of the Aztec capital, it had grown to a most imposing city at the time of the arrival of Cortez. At that time it contained upward of sixty thousand houses and over three hundred thousand inhabitants, and was more than twelve miles in circumference. Several other towns of nearly equal size were on the near-by islands and shores, and "Greater Tenochtitlan" as it might have been called, had a population totaling several millions. The city was intersected by four broad avenues at right angles, running north, east, south and west. Numerous canals served as smaller thoroughfares, and the four main roads were extended across the lake on dikes. The houses of the lower classes were of adobe, and those of the well-to-do were of red stone. Usually they were but one story in height with large flat roofs covered with flowers of which the Aztecs were passionately fond. The houses were mainly coated with a white stucco or cement, and everywhere, towering far above the lesser buildings, were the pyramidal temples or *teocalli* (high places) of stone. These were built with broad winding stairs or platforms leading to the summits whereon was the shrine of the deity to whom the temple was dedicated and the sacrificial stone.

The largest of these *teocalli* was the temple built by king Ahuizotl and dedicated to the god of war, Huitzilopochtli. The enclosing walls of this temple measured nearly five thousand feet around, and were covered with carvings of festooned braided serpents called *Coetpantli* (Serpent-walls). Within the huge court the pyramid, three hundred feet square at the base and over three hundred feet in height, rose in six platforms of rubble covered with stone facing held together by cement and coated with gypsum. Three hundred and forty steps led to the summit where there were two triple-storied towers, each fifty-six feet in height, containing statues of the war-god and sacrificial stones of polished jasper. In this place the sacred fires were kept burning perpetually, and were tended by holy virgins. The Aztecs believed that the extinction of the sacred fires would bring an end to their power, and more than six hundred braziers of these sacred fires were maintained in Mexico

City alone. Clustered about this great pyramid of the war-god were more than forty smaller *teocalli,* as well as the "Pyramid of the Skulls" *(Tzompantli)* where the skulls of the victims of sacrifices were kept. Within this, the Spaniards counted more than one hundred and thirty-six thousand human skulls.

These *teocalli* or pyramidal temples were typical of the Aztecan culture and it is doubtful if any American race, if indeed any race on earth, ever erected more massive and imposing structures, although from an architectural and engineering point of view they were far less noteworthy than the buildings of other American races. The Aztecs never equaled the Mayas or the pre-Incas in their architecture and engineering, nor in perfection of stone-cutting and the size of the blocks of stone employed. But in their own way, their edifices were unexcelled if equaled anywhere. Moreover, the types and ornamentations varied greatly in different localities. In the north of Vera Cruz there are pyramids with roofed temples, and with massive roof-combs similar to those of the Mayas. At Teotihuacan and at Xochicalco there are most striking remains. The former, once the sacred city of the Nahuas, is famed for its temples of the sun and moon with its immense cemetery wherein the devout found their last resting-places, and in a way was very similar to the holy city of Pachacamac in Peru. The base of the Temple of the Sun is four hundred and twenty-six feet square, and the pyramid rises to a height of one hundred and thirty-seven feet, while the base of the moon temple is seven hundred and thirty-five feet square and its height is two hundred and three feet. Upon the summit of the Temple of the Sun was a huge stone image of the sun-god with his breast inlaid with a great star of solid gold. From the pyramid of the moon a path or road, known as the "Path of the Dead," led to the river through a vast burial-ground covering over nine square miles. Here have been found wonderful ceramics, terra-cotta figures, mosaic masks and other objects. Many of the buildings contain chambers over seven hundred feet square with walls eight feet in thickness, and with mosaic floors.

Near Yezcuco is Xochicalco (the Hill of Flowers) with beautifully sculptured blocks of porphyry more than twelve feet in length. At Tolan, water pipes were used, and there are also immense columns formed of two sections mortised and tenoned together. Perhaps the most remarkable ruins in Mexico are those at Mitla in Oaxaca, which some authorities consider Mayan rather than Aztecan. But they are distinct from all known Mayan buildings, and as the Aztec Hades was known as Mictlan we may feel reasonably sure that it should be considered Aztecan, or at least Nahuan. The lintel stones of the Mitla buildings are often eighteen feet in length, the walls are straight or perpendicular and are designed to support roofs, instead of converging as in Mayan architecture; and the "Hall of Columns" is a most striking spot with its rows of immense phallic monuments. But the most remarkable features of Mitla are the huge subterranean chambers or rooms. These are completely lined with stone with every square inch of the surfaces elaborately and magnificently carved with intricate symmetrical designs. Into these highly ornate underground rooms or vaults were cast the dead bodies of warriors and of sacrificial victims. And here the devout or fanatical members of the community were wont to practise a terrible form of self-sacrifice by being voluntarily thrown into the underground charnel-house to wander among the corpses until they died an awful lingering death of starvation and thirst.

In stone-cutting, as in their other arts and decorations, the Aztecs used geometrical designs and patterns extensively. But they also employed many animal, human and floral motifs, although not to such extent as did the Mayas. They had a wonderful eye for form, and a remarkable facility for catching the salient features of any object and for reproducing forms and obtaining effects by means of a few lines, and by exaggerating certain essential details or features. Proportion and perspective meant nothing to the Aztec artists and were practically nonexistent in their art. For this reason many of the Aztec paintings and carvings have a decidedly Japanese appearance, although invariably so typically Aztecan that they could not be mistaken for anything else.

The Aztec pottery was very beautiful and distinctive. Red, black and orange were the predominating colors used, but practically every known color and shade occur on their ceramic ware. Much of the pottery was painted, but more was decorated by means of pigments applied by clay stamps. Clay molds were also employed in order to duplicate utensils and figures, and much of their pottery had a true glaze.

As I have mentioned, there are numerous remains

of a very ancient and highly cultured race in Mexico, which unquestionably antedate the Aztec Empire. Whether these are the remains of a totally distinct race, such as the semimythical Toltecs, or whether they are the earlier or archaic forms of Aztec work has not definitely been established. But they exhibit many features in common with the Aztecan culture, and they grade almost insensibly into the later Aztec types. For this reason, and because the Aztecs, if we are to believe their own recorded history, arrived in Mexico at a comparatively recent date, we must assume either that the Nahuas wandered for many hundreds or perhaps thousands of years over the country, building cities and developing a culture and a civilization before they established Tenochtitlan, or else that their civilization was superimposed upon an earlier culture and was largely borrowed. In the former case the Aztec legend of the Toltecs was in all probability an allegorical mythical history of their own race, while if the latter theory is correct the story of the Toltecs was probably built up and invented by the Nahuas to explain the presence of the older civilization they found.

The Mexican chronicler Ixtlilxochitl, who wrote soon after the Spanish conquest, gives two versions of the Aztec legend of the Toltecs. In one the Toltecs are said to have reached Tlapallan (the Country of Bright Colors) near the sea after voyaging south from their original homes which they left in the year "1-Tecpatl" (A.D. 387). Having passed Xalisco and landed at Huatulco, they journeyed to Tochtepec and hence overland to Tollantzinco. The other legend differs mainly in that it tells of a revolt of the chiefs against the king of Tlapallan which forced them to flee or suffer banishment. This took place about A.D. 438, and after some eight years of wandering in the vicinity they migrated to a place called Tlapallantanzinco where they remained for three years before they commenced the century of wanderings. Both myths agree that the city of Tollan at the present site of Tula near the Valley of Mexico, was established about A.D. 566, and that the Toltecs were guided to this spot by the necromancer Hueymatzin (Great Hand). The place was called the "Place of Fruits" owing to its fertility, and six years were expended in building the city with its palaces and temples.

In the seventh year they elected a ruler called Chalchiuh-Tlatonac (Shining Precious Stone) who ruled for fifty-two years and under whose régime the people progressed rapidly. This first dynasty continued until about A.D. 994 when Huemac II ascended the throne. At first he ruled wisely and honestly, but later he developed licentiousness and dishonesty which eventually caused a revolution and omens foretelling some great calamity. Then the mystical sorcerer, Toveyo, appeared, and, beating his magic drum, drew the people to him. Forcing them to dance, he gradually led them to the verge of a precipice where they were dashed into the canyon below and were turned to stone. Toveyo also destroyed a stone bridge with his magic, so that thousands of people perished in the river, while, to add to the calamities of the unfortunate race, volcanoes burst into violent eruption.

In order to placate the outraged gods, the Tollan

rulers ordered wholesale sacrifices.* But when the first victim was placed upon the altar the horrified priest discovered that he possessed neither heart nor blood, while such a stench arose from the body that a pestilence followed and destroyed thousands. Huemac was also attacked by the Tlalocs or gods of rain, and after he had begged them to spare him, offering all his riches and rank in return, they departed after threatening six years of plagues. Droughts, floods, frosts, heat, toads and locusts followed, until nine-tenths of the population were destroyed.

By this time Huemac had reformed and tried to establish his illegitimate son, Acxitl, upon the throne. The Toltecs rebelled at this, but their leaders were bribed and Acxitl ruled well for a time. But he had inherited his father's character, so at last the people again revolted, and, led by Huehuetzin, attacked the city. The savage Chichimecs also beset the place and settled near. At last a council of wise men met at the sacred city of Teotihuacan. Here they were attacked by a giant who appeared in various weird forms, including that of a beautiful child, and who slew most of the men, declaring that the gods were disgusted and that all were doomed. Once again the city was attacked by Huehuetzin and the Chichimecs, until at last, after a three-year war, the survivors were forced to seek refuge in the marshes of Lake Tezcuco, and the empire came to an end.

Unquestionably, whether these legends refer to the

---

*This is astonishingly like what actually occurred in Panama when the prehistoric Coclé civilization was destroyed by an eruption, and wholesale sacrifices of pottery and valuables, as well as human sacrifices, were made. (See Chapter VI.)

earlier Nahuas or to a different and still earlier race, they are largely allegorical; but practically all American aborigines' traditions are filled with allegories, and it is extremely difficult if not impossible to sift the facts from the fiction. But we know that whatever may have been their former history, the Aztecs reached their highest attainments in many lines after they founded the City of Mexico or Tenochtitlan. And as they advanced in civilization and power and subjugated other races and brought them under Aztec dominion, they absorbed, borrowed and adapted various features and phases of the many cultures and religions. This resulted in a very complex mythology, a most involved religion, a remarkably varying culture and a most elaborate and fabulously rich and powerful court. The palace of the Montezuma, as the Aztec emperor was called, literally outshone that of Solomon, and the famous king of Israel in all his glory would have paled by comparison with the Aztecs' ruler. His garments were of the finest cotton most beautifully woven in intricate symbolic designs of many colors. His mantles were marvelous affairs formed of hundreds of thousands of tiny, iridescent feathers from humming-birds and trogans, and scintillated with all the prismatic brilliancy of the rainbow. Precious stones and massive golden jewelry adorned his arms, legs and breast. He carried a wonderful ceremonial shield of priceless feather mosaic. His obsidian-bladed dagger had a hilt of carved jade and turquoise inlay, and upon his head he wore a golden crown topped by the long, waving, iridescent green plumes of the sacred *quetzál*. Scarlet, white and green were the colors of this

sacred bird; scarlet, white and green were the royal
and ceremonial colors of the Aztecs, and to this day
red, white and green are the colors of the Mexican
flag.

Probably no other American race was so rich in
objects of art as the Aztecs at the time of the conquest. The Incas, it is true, possessed incalculable
sums in gold and silver utensils and ornaments; but
they had little else of intrinsic value,—aside from
precious stones or gems. But the Aztecs, although
not so rich in precious metals, possessed a great
amount of gold and silver in addition to vast quantities of precious and semiprecious stones, feather
mantles and robes beyond price, and mosaics of turquoise and other materials so beautiful and valuable
that even the rapacious Spaniards appreciated and
preserved them. And yet, to the Aztecs, copper was
of greater value than anything else, and rather crude,
practically worthless copper bells served as money!

No doubt it was largely the sheer beauty and value
of Aztec mosaic and other work that caused so
many objects of Aztec art to be preserved instead
of being broken up or melted down by the Dons.
Hence the museums of the world possess an unusual
and remarkable number of specimens of Aztec
weapons, ornaments, utensils, jewels, mosaics, etc.
Fortunately, too, the Mexican Government long ago
awoke to the scientific value and importance of all
articles pertaining to the ancient inhabitants of the
country, and the Museo Nacional in Mexico City is
a veritable treasure-house of Aztec and Maya specimens. But there are more in the various museums
of the world and in private collections. Very often

the owners of such objects have no idea of the scientific value or even the origin of the specimens, which have been handed down for generations, and consider them so much "junk." As a result, amazing "finds" are constantly being made in the shops of curio and antique dealers and pawnbrokers. No doubt many of these have most romantic and fascinating histories if we but knew them.

But none could have a more remarkable and interesting story than the famous Aztec calendar-stone. This remarkable piece of stone carving is in the form of an immense disk twelve feet in diameter and weighing over twenty tons. It was cut from a single block of black porphyry and was completed between the years 1487 and 1499 A.D., if the date upon it has been correctly interpreted. It was originally placed in the great temple at Mexico City, but was thrown down by the Spaniards under Cortez and was completely buried beneath the débris and ruins of the Aztecs' buildings. In 1560 it was rediscovered, but the bishop, fearing the influence of its presence upon the Indians, ordered it reinterred. For more than two centuries it remained buried and completely forgotten and lost to the world until in 1790, when, excavating in the Plaza Mayor, workmen once more brought the marvelous stone to light. It was then built into the façade of the Cathedral where it remained until 1885 when it was removed and placed in the Museo Nacional where it still remains.

Although ordinarily referred to as a calendar, this elaborately carved stone disk is in reality a calendar, an Aztec history of the world, a prophecy and a record of Aztec myths. The sculptured figures, which at first sight appear complicated, confusing and largely ornamental, consist in reality of symbols and glyphs arranged about the central figure of Tonatiah, the sun-god, with the symbol *Olin,* a day sign signifying an earthquake. The historical portion is divided into five suns or ages, four of the past and one of the present. The present age or period is dominated by the existing sun symbol: *Olin-Tonatiah,* because the earth (according to the Aztec prophecy) is destined to be destroyed by an earthquake. Arranged about the symbol *Olin* are the four past suns or cycles, each enclosed in a rectangle and designed to be read from right to left. The first of these symbols is *Ocelotl,* or the jaguar; the next *Ehecatl,* or the wind; the third *Quiahuitl,* or fire-rain, and the last *Atl,* or water.

The interpretation of these is that the first sun or age was destroyed by a jaguar, the second cycle or sun was destroyed by a hurricane, the third by a rain of fire, and the fourth by a flood. Each time, according to the symbols, one human couple escaped destruction and lived to repopulate the earth. At the top of the stone beneath the tails of two reptiles is the symbol for *"13-Acatl"* or reed, indicating that the present or fifth sun began or appeared in that year. Another symbol indicates that the present sun will end with the promised destructive earthquake on the day *"Olin-4."* This date symbol is followed by three hieroglyphs indicating the points of the compass. Next in order, outside the historical portion of the stone, are the twenty Aztec day signs or symbols, while surrounding all are two reptilian monsters meeting face to face and with their tails at the top of the stone. These are the Turquoise-snakes or *Xiuhcoatl* and are symbols of fire and water. In the mouth of each is a human head representing the fire-god, Xiuhtecutli, while on the sides of the stone are sculptured representations of the Obsidian Butterfly, Itzpapalotl.

To the Aztecs, no doubt, the inscriptions and carvings upon this highly important stone meant a great deal more than is conveyed by our interpretation of the symbols, for, as I have said, signs and symbols may reveal a long and detailed story to an Indian who understands them. A striking and well-known example of this is the sign-language of our western plains Indians. By means of a few rapid movements of the hands, a long and complete sentence or description may be conveyed. And in many places, and among many tribes of South American Indians, a few stones arranged in a certain order or a few apparently meaningless glyphs on a rock will give full details regarding trails, rapids, the location of villages and other important information. So we may feel fairly certain that the ancient Aztecs, when looking at their great calendar-stone, could read a full and detailed history of the past, and an equally complete account of the prophecy for the future.

In a way this applies also to their sculptures, paintings, idols, codices, etc. To-day, even with our rather full and intimate knowledge of the Aztecs, their language and their mythology, there are many matters which still puzzle us and about which we have no definite knowledge. For example, we cannot say definitely why various representations of a god or deity should vary in details of costume, decorations, etc., and we do not feel by any means certain that the correct interpretation has been given to many symbols and date signs. But undoubtedly every variation in the figures of gods and other objects, every dot, line and detail of a symbol, had its definite and important meaning.

CHAPTER X

WHERE MONTEZUMA STILL RULES

THOUSANDS of the descendants of the Aztecs still dwell in Mexico, and while some retain many of their ancient arts, crafts, languages and even their dress and home life, they are largely civilized, and are—outwardly at least—Christians. Even when they have their tribal or village chiefs, they are merely units in the Mexican republic. But by far the greater portion of the Mexican Indians whose ancestors were members of the Aztec Empire have completely forgotten their ancient customs and manner of life, even their tribal names in fact, and in every way are thorough Latin Americans. The bulk of the Indian population of Mexico belongs to the laboring or peon class, or are farmers, small tradesmen, vaqueros, artizans, etc. But many of the most prominent and wealthy Mexicans, many of Mexico's most noteworthy politicians, generals, statesmen, jurists, educators, artists, authors and scientists are of pure Indian blood, and can trace their ancestry back to the Aztecs. Even presidents of the republic have come from the ranks of the Indians, and Indian blood flows in the veins of the majority of the country's population. But nowhere in Mexico, as far as is known, are there Indians who still retain the religion, the customs and the traditions of the Aztecs, or who perpetuate the name of the Montezuma.

So complete was the conquest by the Spaniards, so tireless the priests in establishing missions, so ruthless and fanatical in destroying everything savoring of paganism, that within a comparatively short time after the conquest only the most remote, inaccessible and valiant tribes managed to maintain a semblance of independence and a portion of their own customs and habits. But the Aztec Empire had established far-distant colonies and provinces, some of which were as far south as Panama. Originally, no doubt, these outposts of the Empire were in more or less direct and constant communication with the headquarters in Mexico; but they were separated by hundreds of miles of wild country inhabited by savage, hostile tribes; they were frequently attacked, and many were completely wiped out, while others were cut off from the rest of their race, and in the course of years their existence, even their locations were forgotten. Left to their own devices, dependent upon themselves, forced constantly to battle with savage neighbors who surrounded them, the members of these colonies gradually lost much of their arts, civilization and religion, and reverted to a semibarbarous state. No doubt many of them became so greatly altered by environment and admixture with other races that all traces of Aztec ancestry were lost, and to all intents and purposes they became distinct tribes. But in one case at least, even to the present day, the language survived, many of the Aztec customs remained, and their ruler has always been known as Montezuma.

These people are the Guaymís of northwestern Panama, who dwell in the fastnesses of the high mountain plateaus, who have never been conquered,

and who have sedulously and successfully guarded
their territory and their race from the encroachment
of the whites. Few strangers have ever penetrated
beyond the borders of their territory, for the Guaymís have learned from the bitter experience of their
fellows and neighbors that the coming of the white
man spells the doom of the Indian. For over thirty
years they resisted the Spaniards, until at last the
Dons gave up, feeling the game was not worth the
candle, and left the Guaymís unconquered and independent. Their territory became recognized as an
Indian zone where the Guaymís were supreme, and
each succeeding government has officially recognized
the Guaymí country as a *"Zona de los Indigenos"* to
be left alone. How many of the tribe dwell within
this zone it is impossible to say, but at the time I
visited them I calculated, from information given me
by the various chiefs, that the tribe numbered more
than thirty thousand.

Physically and mentally they are far superior to
the other Central American tribes. They average
much taller than most tropical Indians, and are well
built and proportioned. Their color varies from an
ocher or russet to a light olive, many of the women
being no darker than a brunette white woman. The
eyes are straight, fairly large and are not infrequently brown or hazel. The hair is rather fine and is a
deep brown rather than black, and in the case of the
women is often decidedly tawny. The typical Guaymí face is rather oval, with broad forehead, high
but not very prominent cheek-bones, heavy rounded
chin, and a straight or slightly aquiline nose with
high well-developed bridge. Like many other tribes,

they file or rather chip the front teeth to points, and occasionally cut decorative notches in them.

They are primarily agriculturalists and cultivate cacao, upland rice, maize, sugar-cane, tobacco, coffee and many vegetables and fruits. They own many cattle and horses, and are typical "horse Indians," although when traversing the fearful mountain trails they prefer to trust to their own bare feet and, remarkably enough, usually travel by night. But they seem to possess the eyes of cats, and in the inky darkness they cross narrow hog-backs between yawning abysses and scale dizzying precipices as surely and fearlessly as though following a road in full daylight. They have no villages but dwell in single, or sometimes groups of two or three, houses many miles apart. Their houses are well built with walls of split logs and high, steeply pitched roofs of palm thatch, and are large, often sixty feet in length, twenty feet wide and thirty feet high. Each house is, in effect, a self-contained community of from ten to thirty or more individuals. Around the walls are a number of raised platforms, often partitioned off by palm-leaf mats. Each of these is occupied by a separate family, all the occupants of the building being, as a rule, related or of the same clan. The members of each family sleep, dress and keep their personal possessions in these separate apartments, but all share equally in the use of the main house and its furnishings, although usually each family has its own fire.

The furnishings of the house are simple but ample for all needs. Somewhere along one wall will be a long seat or bench, there are numerous carved wooden stools or rawhide chairs, and often there will be a rude but serviceable affair of split palm bark supported on posts which serves as a table. Occasionally there will be hammocks, but as a rule the Guaymís prefer to sleep upon mats or hides spread upon springy palm-wood platforms or on couches. Unlike the majority of Indians, especially those of Central and South America, the Guaymís are cleanly in habits and are quite alive to the importance of sanitation. The hard-packed earth floor of the house is swept several times a day; all provisions are kept on raised platforms or are hung upon rafters and posts; drinking water is stored in jars and calabashes which are kept covered and out of reach of dirt and dogs, and no live stock other than the dogs are allowed in the houses. Great care is taken to build the houses upon raised ground so situated that there is no chance of drainage reaching the near-by stream that supplies the drinking water, and no one is permitted to bathe or wash in this stream, a separate brook or river being used for such purposes. Even latrines are provided, and in their personal habits and dress the people are far more cleanly than the average white man.

The costume of the women consists of a loose wrapper-like garment reaching from neck to ankles, usually of brilliant color and often ornamented with drawn-work and with geometrical designs of appliquéd cloth in contrasting colors. The men's costume is more elaborate and is totally unlike that of any other known tribe of the present day. It consists of a loose blouse or smock of vivid green, orange, blue, yellow or red, elaborately tucked and with bosom, shoulders and sometimes sleeves ornamented with appliquéd designs, and trousers of homespun blue or white cotton with appliquéd patterns along the outer seams of the legs. The designs used on the garments, as well as on all other articles and utensils, are geometrical, and are distinctively Aztecan, frequently being exact replicas of the motifs used in the decorative carvings at Mitla and elsewhere in Mexico.

About their necks, the men wear close-fitting collars of magnificent beadwork; broad beadwork gorgets cover the upper part of the chest; there are necklets of teeth, seeds and claws, and frequently a short apron-like breech-cloth of bright-colored cotton, of woven fiber or even of beadwork is worn. Ordinarily both men and women wear hand-plaited palm-leaf hats, usually with a band of feathers about the crown. For ceremonial occasions, for dances and at various other times the men wear feather head-dresses consisting of a pita or cotton fillet to which are attached the plumes of various birds, the particular kind of feathers used depending upon the rank or official status of the wearer and the occasion. Thus ordinary members of the tribe may use owl, hawk, parrot, macaw, wild turkey, heron, eagle and many other feathers according to individual taste or the class of the function which they are to attend. But no one other than a dance-chief may use the plumes of the egret; medicine-chiefs are recognized by head-dresses of hair from the tail of the giant ant-bear; ranking chiefs are designated by one or two plumes of the *quetzál* in their feather crowns; and the regal head-dress of the high chief or Montezuma is entirely of the longest, most magnificent plumes of this sacred bird of the Aztecs. But as one individual is often a ranking chief, a dance-chief and a medicine-chief, or holds any two of these positions, he wears the crown indicative of the rank in which he is serving at the time. Although when about their houses or in good weather the men and women wear the garments described, when working or when traveling through the mountains in rainy weather they strip to breech-cloths and carry their more conventional apparel in waterproof coverings of homespun cotton coated with crude rubber.

Both men and women paint their faces but do not tattoo. As the facial paintings are not purely decorative, but are of a symbolic character, and as it is important that each design should always be the same, the Guaymís use carved wooden stamps for applying the colors. Only the Indians themselves know the full significance of all the facial paintings, for they are as numerous, as varied and as complicated as the glyphs upon an Aztec sculpture. But some of them are simple and easily recognized. Diagonal lines meeting at the bridge of the nose and extending across the cheeks beneath the eyes toward the corners of the lower jaw form the tribal mark. Just below these are the clan or family symbols; rank is indicated by markings upon the nose and chin; married and single persons are distinguished by forehead marks, and there are designs and colors to show whether the individual is to participate in a dance, a religious ceremony, a feast, a council, a marriage or a funeral, while other symbols indicate a courier on official business, a chief's deputy, a messenger, or even the particular district where the individual dwells.

In their social and governmental systems the Guaymís are unusual. Each household has its own head-man, although he is not always the patriarch of the family group, but may be regarded as the head of the family because of his intelligence, his ability or merely because he is a general favorite. The heads of the various houses are subject to sub-chiefs elected by them, and gather in council and consult with the latter on all local matters of importance. Each of these sub-chiefs may be in virtual control of a number of houses covering a wide area and all are subject to three ranking hereditary chiefs, each in charge of a definite section of the tribal territory. Finally there is the supreme chief or Montezuma who occupies the position of emperor or king and rules all. But only upon the rarest occasions or for some matter of paramount importance do the ranking chiefs call upon Montezuma for a decision or support, and comparatively few of the tribe have ever seen their king.

The Guaymí religion is basically a modified sun-worship, the belief being that the sun is the visible manifestation of a supreme deity who rules the universe, while the moon and stars are lesser deities, each controlling certain matters and destinies, an arrangement so similar to their own form of government that we may reasonably suspect that one was patterned after the other. In addition to these major spirits, every mountain, river and natural formation, as well as trees, rocks, vegetables and all living creatures are thought to have their own special "gods" or spirits, all of whom are subject to the special spirit controlling human beings and their destinies. Un-

like the majority of tribes, the Guaymís have few
evil spirits or "devils" to bother them, and these they
consider stupid and easily deceived. Hence there are
few ceremonies or observances for the purpose of
exorcising devils, and nearly all the Guaymí religious and ceremonial activities are devoted to pleasing
the beneficent gods and expressing gratitude for
benefits received. Strictly speaking, they have no
idols, but they are rich in fetishes, charms and proxies. The use of the latter has probably been carried
further by the Guaymís than by any other known
tribe. No Guaymí ever dreams of barring or otherwise securing the entrance to his home when he and
his clan desert the dwelling to attend some distant
festivity or for another purpose. Before leaving, he
places a rather crude wooden image, representing
the household god, in his doorway, and goes his way,
quite secure in the belief that the painted wooden
figure will act as his proxy and maintain guard over
the house and its contents until he returns. Moreover, he implicitly believes that this proxy is actually
possessed with his own spirit and that, should any
one have the courage to enter the house or do any
harm, the wooden sentinel will at once notify him by
a sort of mental telepathy. And of course, as the
belief is universal, no Indian, seeing the proxy on
guard, would dare ignore its presence.

It is during their dances and religious ceremonials
that these Indians carry the use of proxies to the
utmost extreme. While among the Guaymís I was
privileged to witness one of these ceremonials, in fact,
even to take part in, and, owing to my having successfully treated the presiding dance-chief and cured

him of colic so that he could proceed with the ceremonies, I was honored by being made a member of
the tribe with the rank of medicine-chief.

The ceremonial took place upon a flat-topped
mountain at an elevation of over five thousand feet
above the sea in the very heart of the Guaymí country. Here an immense ceremonial house or temple
had been erected and from far and near the Indians
had been summoned by means of message strings
(see Chapter XIV) sent out by couriers from the
various chiefs. I had become friendly with one of
the ranking chiefs, Neonandi, and had been living
in his house for some time. In his company and with
him to vouch for me, I was to be permitted to witness
some portions of the ceremony. Over three thousand
Indians, men, women and children, gathered at the
meeting-place, and as it was rumored that Montezuma was to appear in person, excitement ran high, but
as hour after hour passed without a sign of his approach it began to look as if the Guaymí king had
changed his mind. Then, from far off came the faint
sound of a cow-horn trumpet, and with shouts of
"Montezuma; Montezuma!" the Indians commenced
beating drums and blowing horns and whistles. I
had expected to see a wizened, wrinkled old chief,
but to my amazement he was a young man, well built
and very light-skinned, with regular features, a
dignified expression, broad forehead and intelligent
face. His costume differed in no way from that of
his subjects, but his crown of *quetzál* tail plumes set
off by a band of golden and scarlet macaw feathers
was a truly regal affair. With the arrival of Montezuma preparations were made to commence the cere-

monies. As the sun set, the Indians lighted flaring torches and gathered in a great throng about the ceremonial house. Drums boomed, flutes and whistles shrilled and rattles shook, until the combined sounds rose to a deafening roar. Then, slowly at first, but with ever increasing speed, the Indians commenced dancing round and round the temple, chanting in unison, keeping time to the throbbing drums and piping flutes, and alternately stooping low or leaping up in regular order until the moving stream of figures appeared like an immense serpent gliding in sinuous curves about the building. This, in fact, was exactly what it was supposed to represent, for the ceremonial was a feast in honor of the Plumed Serpent god of the ancient Aztecs. Suddenly the music stopped, and silently the dancers slipped away and vanished within the sacred precincts of the temple. From within came a weird chant, a wailing cadence, and the slow measured beat of drums. I was of course anxious to enter and witness what was taking place, but Neonandi cautioned me against it. The evil spirits were being driven out, he explained, and if I went near they might take possession of me.

Presently the music and chanting ceased, Neonandi touched my arm and, beckoning for me to follow him, led the way into the building. Within, the beams and rafters were draped with flowers, birds' skins, jaguar and ocelot pelts and streamers of dyed cotton cloth. In the center stood an altar-like table piled high with every variety of food known to the Guaymís and decorated with corn-stalks, flower-covered coffee-tree branches, sugar-cane flowers and brilliant orchids. Guttering torches cast a fitful glare over the scene and filled the temple with aromatic, resinous smoke. Round one side the men were seated, row after row of closely packed, savage-looking figures staring fixedly ahead, smoking their ceremonial pipes of carved stone. Between them and the central altar was a fire of huge logs, and over this girls were cooking thick unsweetened chocolate, while others stirred an immense pot of rice chicha. Moving silently about, other girls were passing the chicha and bitter chocolate to the men; and on the farther side of the altar sat scores of women, their long hair falling over their faces and their eyes fixed upon the floor. All about the altar were placed small earthenware effigies of birds, beasts, reptiles and fish, with a few human figures, some monsters that resembled ogres or devils, and many miniature clay pots, dishes and plates.

Following the short ceremony of adopting me as a member of the tribe, which was an amazing surprise on my part, the assembled Indians rose and commenced a slow wailing chant. The barbaric music was then resumed, while the old dance-chief (whom I had recently cured) took his place beside the altar carrying a "devil-stick" in one hand. Then, in perfect rhythm, the Indians began dancing around and around the altar, following the sinuous, snake-like formation I have mentioned. Every now and again one would shout the name of some beast, bird, person or spirit. Then, leaping aside from the line of dancers, he would seize a handful of food from the altar, thrust some into his mouth, stoop quickly and drop some into one of the tiny clay dishes, and toss the remainder into the fire. At the same time the dance-chief would pick up the image of the creature or being whose name had been called, together with the dish of food, and breaking them into bits, would throw the fragments into the flames. This continued until the last of the images had been destroyed. It was a strange, interesting and incomprehensible rite, but Neonandi willingly explained it. The images represented persons who, through illness or other causes, could not attend the ceremony; birds and beasts who could not be present, and mythological beings. According to Guaymí belief the spirits of these would enter their respective images and thus take part in the ceremonial by proxy. The food upon the altar was for them, but being unable to eat it while in their clay forms, the Indians acted as proxies while the dance-chief destroyed the images in order to release the spirits so that they might return to their own bodies. Then, in order to prevent evil spirits from taking possession of the images and causing trouble for their former tenants, he burned both the fragments and the food in the fire. In other words, the images served as proxies for persons, beasts and supernatural beings, and the dancing Indians acted as proxies for the proxies.

The ceremonies came to an abrupt end when the last of the clay proxies had been destroyed, and, leaving the temple, the Indians prepared for a stick-dance. In this remarkable dance, which is of a symbolic character, the participants pair off, one of each pair being armed with a six-foot pole several inches in diameter and sharpened at one end. While his partner dances about, back to him, he hurls the stick, the object being to knock the dancer's legs from under him. If he succeeds, the dancer must continue until he dodges the stick, whereupon it becomes his turn to throw the missile while the former thrower dances. Naturally, bruised and even broken legs frequently result, but serious injuries are rare, for every participant wears the stuffed skin of some animal upon his back in order to protect his spine. With from fifty to several hundred Indians dancing about and throwing the heavy sticks the fun becomes fast and furious, and football seems gentle by comparison.

On the following day the Indians took part in various sports and competitions: in archery, running, spear-throwing, etc. Much to my amazement I found that the Guaymís were still using the ancient spear-throwing-stick or atlatl of the Aztecs and that their name for it was *natlatdi*. Although they use powerful bows and long arrows, yet wherever it is possible to do so, they prefer the throwing-stick and spear, and, at distances up to thirty or forty yards, the spear thus thrown is more accurate than their arrows.

In their arts the Guaymís are extremely skilful. They spin and weave their native cotton into excellent cloth; their pottery, although rather plain, is well made, durable and well modeled. They make baskets of many forms and weaves and of many materials; they plait palm-leaf hats many of which are the equals of the famed so-called panama hats; they are good wood-carvers; their *chakaras* or pouches of pita fiber are so finely woven that they will hold water, and their beadwork is magnificent, the weave or stitch used being quite distinct from that of any other known tribe. They also manufacture many articles of horsehair, and they are the only Indians who, as far as is known, have ever invented a mechanical device. This is an arrangement for spinning or rather twisting horsehair and fibers into string and rope. It consists of a wooden frame with a rotating spindle equipped with a balance and operated by a bow and string. It is, in effect, a giant cotton-spindle fitted in a frame and operated on the principle of a bow-drill. As I have already mentioned, practically all the Guaymí decorative designs are of geometrical forms, Aztecan in character; but they have a wonderful eye for form and not infrequently reproduce human and animal figures with great fidelity. This is particularly true of the miniature terra-cotta figures used as proxies. Many of these are truly remarkable examples of modeling, and are so accurate in all their details that the species of bird, quadruped, insect or reptile is easily recognizable. This is the more remarkable inasmuch as these images are designed for temporary use only and are destined to be destroyed, and it would seem that a crudely made effigy would serve every purpose. But the Guaymís argue that as the images are to provide abiding-places for spirits they must be so true to nature that each spirit will at once recognize the figurine intended for it. Hence, in the case of the effigies representing human beings, every peculiarity, injury or deformity of the original is reproduced so that there can be no possible mistake as to the identities of the individuals they represent.

For musical instruments the Guaymís use drums, whistles of various kinds, cane and bone flutes, Pan's-pipes, *orcharinas,* some of clay and others made from dried seeds or nuts of a forest tree, cow-horn trumpets, rattles of several kinds, and a stringed instrument with a single string. Although their music is used primarily as accompaniments to dances and ceremonials, practically every man carries a flute, pipe, whistle or *orcharina* upon his person, and plays upon the instrument almost continuously as he moves about.

Strangely enough, these Indians are very deficient in traditions, myths and folk-lore, and, as far as I could learn, they have no tales to account for the origin of the various creatures as do most tribes, but are quite satisfied with their explanation that the spirits or deities, being all powerful, created things as they are.

Another peculiar custom of the tribe is their habit of smearing objects with a mixture of grease and soot when they are to be used for ceremonial purposes. Pots, dishes, baskets, images, musical instruments, stools, weapons,—every article or utensil used in a ceremony,—must bear smudges of greasy black. Black is symbolic of night or secrecy, and, as the Guaymís believed that the evil spirits are stupid and easily deceived, they smear black upon their various articles, feeling certain that the evil spirits will then be unable to see them, or at least cannot find a way to enter them. Ordinary soot and grease will not serve for this purpose, however. The pigment must be made from the charred bones of a jaguar or ocelot mixed with the grease from a snake. Here again, the Aztec influence comes to the front in the combination of jaguar and serpent in connection with sacred ceremonies, for both held prominent places in Aztecan mythology. And in addition there is the symbolic significance of the two creatures. The jaguar, being a night-prowler, is a symbol of secrecy, while the serpent is the symbol of wisdom and cunning. Somewhat similarly, to prevent evil spirits from taking possession of various articles, the Guaymís invariably break or change the design, color or pattern on everything they make. Sometimes this "devil-trap" is very obvious; but more often it is so cleverly concealed that it is difficult to discover. It may be merely a slight interruption in a line, an abrupt change of color, an extra figure, an alteration in the weave, or any one of innumerable methods of preventing a pattern or weave from being perfectly symmetrical.

Devil-fetishes, in the forms of small images, oddly shaped or colored pebbles or other objects are always carried by the Indians, while devil-sticks are always present before the houses or somewhere about the settlements. These consist of slender sticks split at one end and with a short stick placed in the slit, thus forming a sort of rude cross. There is no connection, however, between these and the Christian cross, the idea of the crossed devil-stick being to confuse or frighten evil beings. Whether or not the Guaymís ever indulge in human sacrifices or in cannibalism, I cannot say; but the neighboring Indians insist that they do, and they certainly hold symbolic sacrifices, using figurines of human beings and animals as offerings to their gods.

As might be expected, most of the ancient Aztec customs and observances have been lost or forgotten during the centuries that the tribe has been isolated. During all that time there have been the influences of the neighboring tribes to offset the inherited characteristics. The wonder is that any of the old survives. Yet, in their dialect, the Guaymís are distinctly Aztecan, and over forty per cent. of the words in their language are almost pure Nahuatl.

CHAPTER XI

THE visitor to the west coast of South America, who stops at the port of Salavery, Peru, is within a few miles of one of the most remarkable and important prehistoric cities of the New World. This is Chan-Chan, the capital of the once powerful Chimu Kingdom whose ruler was the Chimu-Capac or Great King of the Chimus. Long before the beginning of the Incan dynasty the Chimus had established themselves upon the Peruvian coast, and had conquered and cultivated the land from the present Ecuadorean border to the vicinity of the present city of Lima. Throughout this district, comprising approximately ten thousand square miles, the Chimus had established towns, villages and cities, had erected enormous walls and fortresses, had built great temples and palaces, had laid out roads, and had designed and carried out vast irrigation projects which would be a credit to any modern engineer. Many of these are still in use to-day.

They had attained to a culture or civilization superior, in many respects, to that of the Incas, and had developed certain arts and industries to a point never attained by any other American race. Their textiles were magnificent; their feather costumes, robes and head-dresses were beyond compare; their pottery was of the highest class; their wood-carving the equal of any, and while they did little or nothing in the line of masonry or stonework, but used adobe almost exclusively, they had invented a process of adobe sculpture which was not known to any other race. But it was in metal work that they had attained the highest and most remarkable skill. Not only did they smelt copper, gold, silver and even platinum, and form the metals into innumerable utensils, orna-ments, weapons, musical instruments and decorations, but they discovered the art of metal-plating. From the tombs and graves at Chan-Chan, and elsewhere within the Chimu district, have come many articles of metal which are actually astounding. Among these are masks, beads, ornaments and utensils of cop-per plated with gold; similar objects plated with silver, and silver objects gold plated. So perfectly and evenly is the plating done that any one exami-ning them would declare that they were electroplated if their origin were not known.

However, as it is beyond belief that the Chimus possessed any knowledge of electricity, we must formulate some other theory to explain their process of plating one metal with another. Possibly it was accomplished by some chemical process, although this seems as incredible as the electrolytic process would be. Possibly it might have been done by some method of dipping the object to be coated in molten metal; but in that case it would appear impossible that a thin copper or silver article would not instantly be melted and combined with the molten gold. It has been suggested that the objects were coated with some kind of adhesive or lacquer, sprinkled with metal-dust and burnished; but there are no indications of such a process having been employed, and no traces of any underlying preparation. The only plausible explanation appears to be that the plating was accomplished by means of fumes; that, by some manipulation of molten gold or silver, fumes were given off which deposited a metallic coating on another metal. But however it was done, there can be no question that it is a lost art.

Even in their ordinary metal working the Chimus showed the most remarkable dexterity and the greatest artistic taste and skill. Various methods were used. Metals were cast, beaten, welded, pressed, built up or spun into innumerable forms, and objects of large size were frequently made entirely of massive gold. In the American Museum of Natural History in New York City there is a small collection of specimens of Chimu gold-work which has no equal anywhere. Among these specimens are large pots or jars of solid gold, beautifully wrought and chased gold plates and plaques, and tall, gracefully formed vases of the precious metal. Gold, among the Chimus, had no intrinsic value apparently, but was prized for its ductility, its beauty and its enduring qualities. Though they possessed vast quantities of gold, yet, as far as is known, gold does not occur in the district they occupied. It is presumed that they must have acquired their supply from other tribes or races living in the gold-producing districts of the interior, or, possibly, from some other country.

Regardless of where and how they may have obtained their gold, there is no question about the vast amount in the possession of the Chimus. No one knows how much they had. The early Spaniards looted temples, cities, palaces and tombs of incredible quantities and kept no records. There are countless ruins and hundreds of thousands of burials which have never been excavated or robbed of their gold. During the four centuries that have passed since the advent of the Europeans into the district, *huaca,* or grave-digging for the sake of gold, has been regular and lucrative industry in the kingdom of the Grand Chimu. In most cases no records have been kept of the treasure thus obtained, and probably there is more gold remaining in the graves and ruins than has ever been taken from them. But some vague idea of the incalculable wealth of the Chimus may be obtained from the few available records in existence. Thus we know from documents still preserved in Trujillo that during the twenty-six years from 1566 to 1592 over two million dollars' worth of gold and silver was obtained from the Huaca de Toledo alone. Moreover, this represents only the amount upon which the Royal *quinta,* or one-fifth, was paid to the government, and no doubt a far greater quantity was removed surreptitiously and no tax paid upon it. Yet only a comparatively small portion of the tombs in the burial-mound known as the Huaca de Toledo have been rifled, and there are several other burial-mounds in the vicinity as large as this which have scarcely been scratched.

In addition to the gold and silver articles, these Chimu burials yield marvelous treasures in the form of textiles, pottery, copperware, feather costumes, carved woodwork, pearls, mother-of-pearl work and mosaics. Some of the examples of the latter are wonderful specimens of a highly developed art. There are vases, cups, ceremonial utensils, ear-plugs, breast-plates, wooden utensils and other objects of wood, clay and other materials highly and beautifully embellished by mosaic inlay work of bone, colored stone and mother-of-pearl, as well as of precious metals. There are ponchos and robes of the most magnificently woven textiles completely covered with pendent ornaments of gold, silver and mother-of-pearl, and there are weapons, utensils, vessels, crowns and musical instruments of solid silver.

Being a coastwise race and greatly dependent upon fishing, the Chimus, as might be expected, to large extent employed fish and marine creatures as motifs in their arts and decorations. But they were equally skilful in reproducing bird, mammal, vegetable and human forms. Much of their pottery, in fact the greater portion of it, was of this imitative type, and their so-called portrait jars have no equals anywhere. These were vessels of various shapes bearing heads, faces or entire figures of men and women as perfectly modeled and as accurate in every detail as any sculptures known to man. Every known type and every possible emotion were depicted upon these. Many were unquestionably modeled from life and were intended as portraits or busts of actual individuals, while others were probably caricatures or cartoons. Even these are carried out with a fidelity that is actually amazing. Not only do they serve to give us an accurate idea of the physical appearances of the Chimu people, but they illustrate exactly what the Chimus wore as garments and decorations, how they worked and played, the musical instruments they used, how they lived, cooked, cultivated the earth, fished, hunted and fought. They form, in fact, a pictorial record of the entire organization, occupations, life and customs of the race. And the vessels modeled to represent other forms, such as fruits and vegetables, marine animals, birds, mammals, insects and so forth, are just as true to life and as beautifully and accurately made. As there are many duplicates among these vessels it is evident that they were made in molds. In fact, such molds are often found and may still be used for forming vessels the precise counterparts of those produced by the Chimus centuries before Europeans landed in the New World. Just why the Chimus should have made so many of these portrait and effigy jars, and why they should have manufactured such an infinite variety of forms, has always been a puzzle. It has been surmised that they were ceremonial, and we know that some were. For example, one common form, showing a man with an exaggerated nose and accompanied by an ear of maize, was the corn-god, and it was customary to bury such jars in the fields when planting, so as to insure a large and successful crop.

Recently, however, Doctor Tello, of the Larco-Herera Museum of Lima, has suggested that these vessels may have served as records: that they were, in effect, words or rather hieroglyphic symbols in pottery form, and that, by some arrangement the secret of which is unknown, they were utilized much in the same manner as a child uses wooden alphabetical blocks. Each form, according to this theory, is a symbol signifying a certain idea or thought, and it is easy to understand how such a means of recording historical or other events might have been carried

out with these vessels. For example, suppose it was
desired to record a year in which locusts destroyed
crops and famine followed. A jar representing an
ear of maize could be placed beside a pot in the form
of a locust, and next to this could be placed a human
figure greatly emaciated and showing every sign
of being on the point of death from starvation.
Other symbols could be used to record the year, the
month or even the day of the disaster. Thus, with
the endless array of forms and variations, and the incalculable number of combinations possible with
these, any message, idea or event could be recorded
and conveyed. Such a theory would explain why so
many duplicates are found. On the whole it seems
a reasonable theory. But the objection to it is that
no one has yet discovered these imitative vessels arranged in any such orderly manner, nor has any one
yet been able to suggest any intelligible interpretation of such groups of vessels as have been found together.

In addition to these portrait and imitative natural
forms, there are many vessels representing, in quite
gruesome details, cadavers, skeletons, death's heads,
amputated limbs, malformations, wounds, tortures,
sacrifices and death throes. Others show surgeons
performing both minor and major operations, for,
despite the crude instruments available and the probable lack of all anesthetics and antiseptics, these prehistoric races performed many operations which
would be a credit to the medical profession of to-
day. Not only the Chimus, but many other
prehistoric races amputated limbs, trepanned skulls,
removed eyes, performed abdominal operations, re-

moved organs and filled, crowned and bridged teeth. Moreover, although there are no records to tell us what percentage of the patients died, yet we know from skeletons and skulls that many of the most serious operations were entirely successful. Large numbers of skulls have been found which have been trepanned, the area of bone removed varying from a very small amount less than a half-inch in diameter to huge pieces several inches square. Apparently the prehistoric surgeon considered trepanning a sort of universal cure-all, if we are to judge from the number of such skulls known. But it must be remembered that head wounds were, no doubt, the commonest type of injuries received by races whose weapons were largely axes, maces and slings. At any rate, despite the crude instruments used and the fact that in many cases the section of skull was removed by hacking, chipping or sawing the bone with sharp stones, the patients often survived. Many of the skulls show the bone healed about the edges of the incisions. It is difficult to say whether we should be more astonished at the skill or rather temerity of these prehistoric surgeons or at the fortitude of their patients who underwent the unspeakable agonies and tortures of such surgery and still survived.

A great many of the vessels are also of the so-called erotic type. In these every known form of social and solitary vice is portrayed with a realism and frankness that would put our most questionable sex plays and novels to shame, and which outdo any medical work. The purpose of these is as puzzling as the other forms described. Some claim that they were merely obscene and prove the makers morally a most degenerate race. Others declare they were merely representations of actualities and were added to make the molded records of the people complete. Others claim with equal reason that they were used in a more or less educational manner and were, in effect, pathological exhibits for the suppression of vice. Still others believe they were ceremonial and were used in sex-worship, while others find in them a symbolic significance and a use in expressing ideas in connection with other vessels when arranged in proper chronological order.

In addition to all these imitative and portrait forms, the Chimus made most beautifully painted and decorated pottery, often bearing carefully executed and accurately drawn scenes from their daily life. And, like several other races, they at times formed conventional and symmetrical designs by dissecting human beings and animals and employing the various parts to produce patterns and motifs which, at first sight, seem wholly made up of arbitrary forms. Many of these conventionalized fragments of anatomy might readily be mistaken for symbols or characters, and quite a number of persons have erroneously considered them pictographs or hieroglyphs, a few even going so far as to declare them Chinese characters.

A great deal of the Chimu pottery is of a fine red and white type while a very large proportion is of a peculiar, highly finished black clay.

As a rule, when we find a race excelling in one art or industry, we find the people deficient in some other art. But the Chimus—as well as most Peruvian prehistoric races—appear to have been masters of all trades. Their cities, although built of adobe, were well planned and laid out, and contained plazas, open courts, straight wide streets, fine buildings and imposing palaces and temples. Their forts, always placed at most strategic spots, were designed with a consummate knowledge of military science and were built with ramparts, salients, arrow-slits, parapets and ramparts strikingly like those of the medieval European fortresses.

Since the Chimus still existed (though wholly under Incan domination) at the time of the Spanish conquest, we know more of their habits, history, customs, dialect and other matters than of many prehistoric races in America. Thus we know that their language was the Mochica or Yunga which is still in use by some of the present-day Indians of the neighborhood. And we know that, according to Chimu tradition, the race came from somewhere in the north.

According to this tradition, the Chimus' ancestors arrived by way of the sea in a great fleet of rafts or canoes. They were no primitive savage people but were highly organized, possessed many arts and industries, and maintained an aristocracy and a court. Following the death of their first ruler there were eleven successors, until the time when the kingdom was abolished and the people established a true republic. This continued successfully for a very long period, or until a powerful feudal lord or chief in the Chicama Valley incited a revolt, and with his followers, overthrew the government and proclaimed himself the emperor or Chimu-Capac. Under his leadership the dominion was greatly extended, many tribes were conquered and made vassals of the realm under Chimu governors, and the Chimus even advanced into the nearer Andean valleys. Far to the north and south the Chimus exacted tribute, and the priests, kings and chiefs built up a ceremonial and religious state of such wealth and magnificence as has rarely been equaled in the world's history.

No doubt there is much truth in the tradition of the northern origin of the race. The Chimu skulls are of a marked northern type, and are similar to those of the Maya races. As no earlier primitive remains are known in the Chimu district we can place credence on the tale that they arrived on the coast as highly cultured, civilized people. Whence they came is a mystery, but it is not at all impossible, or even improbable, that they may have been the survivors of the race that was driven from Panama by the eruption of Guacamayo. (See Chapter VI.) Much of their traditional history, after their arrival in South America, is borne out by their arts, especially their pottery. The earlier specimens of ceramic ware show scenes depicting kings and court life, often most elaborate and magnificent. Later pottery is more conventional, and as scenes of court life and of rulers gradually disappear, scenes indicative of a different social organization appear, and there are decorations evidently recording the recurrent droughts, the disastrous floods and the other events which were of far greater interest and importance to the republican people than kings and courts. The earlier ware was largely red and white, then other and more generalized forms became abundant, until the typical local style again took prominence and once more depicted the royal personages and the pomp of a rich and powerful court.

We also know much of the home and public life of the Chimus, not only from a study of their remains and ruins, but from the writings of the early Spaniards who, occasionally, as in this case, were sufficiently interested in other matters than loot and saving souls, to record their observations. Thus we know that the Chimus were expert argiculturalists, and, although dwelling in a naturally arid and desert land, they cultivated and raised large crops of potatoes, maize, cotton and many other vegetables and fruits. In order to do this they were compelled to construct vast irrigation systems. In the vicinity of Chan-Chan the supply of water was obtained from the Noche River, and large reservoirs were constructed in order to conserve a supply of the priceless water during long dry periods when the river was low. One of the largest of these, known as La Manpuesteria is still in existence, and the aqueducts through which the water was led to the city and to the fields, as well as traces of the irrigation ditches, may still be seen. As Chan-Chan was a large and populous city covering an area of eleven square miles and housing nearly, if not fully, a quarter of a million inhabitants, a very large area of land was necessary in order to supply vegetable food for the people. Although much of the area once used by the Chimus for their fields and gardens has been occupied in building the city of Trujillo and its suburbs, and for the estates and haciendas of the Peruvians, a great deal has become dry and sterile, and at the lowest estimates we can feel certain that the inhabitants of Chan-Chan had

under cultivation fully ten times as much land as is
under cultivation in the district at the present time.

We know also that the houses of the common people were built of reeds, rough cobblestones or sun-
dried adobe bricks. The roofs were sharply pitched,
the walls leaned inward toward the tops and were
windowless, and reed or woven mats served as doors.
In cultivating the soil they used copper axes and hoes,
wooden implements and utensils made from bone and
shell. Their weapons were wooden clubs, copper
knives, daggers, spears and swords, as well as battle-
axes and maces, slings, and bows and arrows. They
wove their wonderful textiles of cotton, llama hair
and fibers upon crude wooden looms. They had
needles of bone and of cactus spines. The fishermen
used nets and sinkers, and went to sea in rafts or canoes of reeds known as *balsas*. For ornaments they
used feathers, beads of various materials, pearls,
seeds, bone, yarn and metal objects, and occasionally
agate, turquoise, crystal, lapis lazuli and other semiprecious stones.

The dwellers in the city lived on a much more lux-
urious plane. Here there were wide straight streets
flanked by high walls, stately houses, immense palaces,
magnificent temples and public buildings. Within
the confines of the walls surrounding the homes of the
rich and the aristocracy, were courtyards, patios,
gardens and baths. In many places there were large
reservoirs or tanks which still exist. One of these
measures six hundred yards in length by fifty yards
in width, while another is five hundred feet long,
one hundred and ninety-five feet wide and sixty feet
deep. Here in the city, the buildings were of *cascajo*

or coarse gravel mixed with a clay or cement-like mud to form a strong enduring form of adobe which has withstood the elements for centuries. The buildings were of massive construction, often forty feet from base to eaves, and with walls nine or ten feet thick at the bases tapering to four or five feet in thickness near the tops. The roofs were sharply pitched and were formed of hewn, hardwood timbers and reeds with a ridge of sun-dried adobe tiles. Like the walls, the doors were narrowest at the tops and were closed by reed mats and skins. In the gables, and in the centers of the walls, were circular window-like openings apparently for the purpose of providing limited ventilation and permitting smoke to find its way out. Here and there an important building or temple was raised on a mound above its fellows, and the walls of all the better class of buildings, as well as the great city wall, were elaborately decorated by pressed or molded bas-relief frescoes and friezes. These were in geometrical designs, in the forms of animals, conventionalized human figures, leaves, flowers, stars, circles and intricately interwoven lines. The backgrounds of these were painted in brilliant colors, bringing the designs out in bold contrasting relief and producing a most ornate and magnificent appearance. The finest of the buildings were of course the palaces, rectangular in form and some of them covering an area of over six hundred thousand square feet. One, which is unique, contained forty-five small rooms arranged in groups of five, each room being fourteen feet long, eight feet wide and nine feet high. Another encloses numerous galleries and small rooms lined with honeycomb-like niches in which the early Spaniards found richly dressed and gold-laden mummies which they promptly looted of their valuables. The "great room" of this palace was forty-five feet square; and adjoining it was an almost equally large living-room whose walls were completely covered with designs in relief and having many overlaid with gold-leaf.

A few years ago the visitor to Chan-Chan could trace the outlines of these various buildings, could wander about the palaces and courtyards, could reconstruct, in his mind's eye, the vast rich city as it was in the days of the Grand Chimu, and could marvel at the wonderfully complicated and beautiful sculptures covering the numberless walls and façades. But the rains of 1925 wrought sad havoc with Chan-Chan. Although the district is normally rainless, yet, at various periods within historic times, heavy rains have fallen along the ordinarily arid coast of Peru. Such rains also fell during the days of the Chimus, for the floods are recorded on the pottery.

These torrential downpours have done much to destroy the ruins. In 1701, 1720 and 1891 ancient Chan-Chan lost each time a portion of its painted walls, its adobe sculptures and its entirety. And between times earthquakes and vandals have done their part. On February 14, 1619, an earthquake destroyed every house in Trujillo within one minute. In 1687 another did almost as much damage. On January 6, 1725, the district was again largely destroyed, and in 1739 there was another disastrous quake. Through all of these the massive walls of Chan-Chan remained, although portions of the buildings were shaken down. But the heavy downpour of 1925 was the last straw. The walls which had endured for so many centuries crumbled and were transformed to mud, the sculptures were washed away, and to-day scarcely a trace of the ornate decorations remain, while the city is scarcely more than a labyrinth of broken-down walls and the débris of buildings.

The doom of Chan-Chan was sealed long before Pizarro set forth on his conquest of Peru, and, long before then, the Chimus had ceased to exist as a distinct civilization. With the coming of the Incas, filled with the ambition to extend their vast empire, the kingdom of the Grand Chimu was included in the list of prospective conquests. During a long period of peaceful easy life the Chimus had grown careless, lazy and lax in their defenses. Down upon them advanced the well-trained armies of the Inca. Many desperate battles ensued. Here and there portions of the Chimu Kingdom surrendered to the Inca, but the key to the heart of the kingdom was Paramonga where the Chimus held an almost impregnable fortress. It was built with three parallel lines of thick adobe walls, the outermost seven hundred feet long, the innermost six hundred feet in length, and above these extended salients jutting outward for ninety feet. Over and over again the Inca hurled his armies at the stronghold, only to be driven back. But strategy succeeded where force failed. Retiring to a spot in the foot-hills, the Inca constructed a dam across the river that supplied the Chimus with their water. Their fields withered and dried, their tanks and reservoirs were exhausted, but still they refused to surrender. Then from the Inca came a dire threat.

If the Grand Chimu did not surrender, he warned them, he would deprive them of the light of the sun as he had deprived them of their water. To the Chimus there was nothing impossible in this. A man powerful enough to do the one might do the other, and they bowed to the inevitable. Many were transported to distant Incan provinces. Others were placed under Incan governors, and nearly two hundred years before the coming of the Spaniards the kingdom of the Grand Chimu had ceased to exist and Chan-Chan was a deserted, half-destroyed city.

CHAPTER XII

NORTH of the kingdom of the Grand Chimu, in Ecuador and Colombia, are remains of two or more mysterious forgotten races whose works and attainments show a culture of the highest order. So little is known of these ancient races that it is difficult, if not impossible, to decide whether they possessed extremely advanced cultures or should be considered as having developed civilizations.

The Chibchas, at least, were as civilized in many respects as the Aztecs, the Chimus and many other races. Just who the Chibchas were, their racial affinities, their origin or their history are all hidden in the dim and distant past, and we have very little information regarding their customs, their lives, their attainments or their government, although they were still in existence at the time of the Spanish conquest of what is now Colombia. Their territory was the high Andean region of Colombia, and they were ruled, at the time of the conquest, by two kings or rather regents. One of these was the Zippa whose capital was in the vicinity of the present city of Bogota; the other was the Zoque whose capital was at Tunja. As was the rule with the Aztecs, the eldest brother of the regent, or if there was no brother the eldest nephew, succeeded to the throne, instead of the son of the ruler himself. This rule would indicate

239

that descent was by the matrilineal line, as is the case with many Indian tribes of the past and present. As among the Incas, monogamy was enforced.

The social organization was very complete, and there was a strictly observed code of laws with unusual and often severe penalties provided for nearly every offense or crime. An unfaithful wife was compelled to eat red peppers or be killed. If she chose the former punishment, and survived the ordeal, she was forgiven and her husband was forced to apologize to her. Men who showed fear or were adjudged cowards were forced to dress and act like women, and to do women's work. Blasphemy and many other offenses were punishable by death, and crimes or misdeeds which injured another resulted in the offender being compelled to serve as the slave of the injured party.

The Chibchas' houses were built of adobe with conical roofs of reed mats, and were placed in groups within high-walled enclosures guarded by watchtowers occupied by armed men. Honey formed a large part of their food, and they carried on an extensive trade in cereals which they exchanged for salt with the coastal tribes.

Their religion was a modified sun-worship. According to their mythology the moon was the wife of Bochica, the sun-god. As she was a most disagreeable sort of being, and was forever trying to destroy men, she was permitted to appear only during the night. Bochica, the sun-god, was a semihuman divinity, and the myths regarding him bear a most striking and remarkable similarity to the Aztec legends of Quetzálcoatl and the Mayan myths of Kukulcan. Human sacrifices were practised, the victims being trained and prepared for their fate for several years in advance. The Chibchas also held certain mountains and bodies of water sacred, and greatly venerated Lake Quatavita into whose depths they annually cast innumerable objects of gold, silver, platinum, etc. Several attempts have been made to drain the lake and recover the treasures it is supposed to contain, and while considerable numbers of images of gold and other metals have been obtained the efforts have mainly been unsuccessful. According to old Spanish accounts, the Chibcha dead were embalmed with resin and other preservatives, and, together with all the possessions of the deceased, were buried in wooden coffins covered with sheets of gold. They were so carefully hidden in secret tombs or caves that none has ever been discovered.

In their arts the Chibchas had reached a very high development. They wove excellent cloth and textiles of cotton and fibers; they made magnificent pottery; they constructed excellent roads and large temples. They were past masters at working gold, silver and even platinum, and they possessed a knowledge of some unknown and lost process of plating objects with precious metals which was only equaled by the Chimus. (See Chapter XI.) Although they never erected great stone buildings nor built large stone cities, as did the Aztecs, Mayas and Peruvians, and never approached those races in the extent and beauty of their stone sculptures, they were expert stone-workers and erected many well-carved stone columns or monuments.

Possibly they were of the same race as, or related

to, the Manabis who occupied the Pacific coast district of northern Ecuador, but from what evidences we have it would appear that the Manabis were a distinct race with a culture differing materially from that of any other ancient people of South or Central America. So little is really known of this race and its accomplishments that it is impossible to say whether they actually attained to a civilized state. The only remains they left were their remarkable stone sculptures, their pottery and their gold objects. No traces of their houses, buildings, temples or other structures have been discovered. It is assumed that they dwelt in flimsy cane and thatched houses, and that these have long since vanished. Their pottery is unusual and distinctive, the typical form being a baseless, elliptical-bodied jar with narrow mouth. Scattered over the area occupied by the race are numerous slabs and monoliths of stone elaborately carved and sculptured in low bas-relief, as well as many very remarkable stone seats or thrones. These vary in size from small affairs to immense chairs weighing half a ton or more. But all are alike in shape, being similar in form to the ancient Roman chairs, and with the bases elaborately sculptured. Even though these are made from a fairly soft volcanic rock, yet to hew and carve the material into the form desired must have entailed incredible labor and skill and a vast amount of time. If only a few specimens of these stone thrones had been found it would not be so amazing, but their number is astounding. Why any race should have made so many chairs, what purpose they served, why they were left scattered about hit-and-miss, are among the greatest mysteries of ancient American races.

However, it was in their metal work that the Manabis accomplished the most astounding results. Not only did they manufacture beautiful objects of gold of ordinary size, but they produced ornaments of gold of microscopic dimensions. In the Museum of the American Indian, Heye Foundation, in New York are many tiny particles of gold which appear to be natural grains or small nuggets. But when viewed through a magnifying-glass they are revealed as most perfectly and beautifully wrought beads. Many are elaborately engraved or chased, others are built up of several almost invisible pieces welded or soldered together, and all are pierced. It seems impossible that such minute objects, many smaller than the head of a common pin, could have been produced by human beings without the aid of a lens. The only solution seems to be that the Manabis actually made use of crude lenses fashioned from crystal, or else they possessed microscopic eyes and more adept and delicate fingers than any other race of men.

Despite the high attainments in art, engineering, astronomy and government which were reached by the Aztecs, the Incas, the Mayas and others, in a way these unknown, forgotten races of South America were more remarkable, and were unquestionably far more ancient. From the Chibcha district in Colombia to northern Chile, numerous races rose to a civilized state, vanished and were forgotten centuries before the first Montezuma or the first Inca saw the light of day. Indeed this area, much of which is to-day arid desert or even more sterile mountains, and which is so austere, so uninviting and so bare of the very essentials of existence, appears to have been the center of ancient civilizations for an immense period of time; the spot wherein the ancient Americans developed the most numerous and most diverse civilizations, and wherein the mysterious races of the dim past reached the highest attainments in social organization, in engineering and in many other lines.

Some of these races existed at the time of the establishment of the Incan Empire, and were conquered and made an integral part of the Incan confederation. But more had completely vanished before the coming of the first Inca, and, if we are to believe history and traditions, the Incan races had no definite knowledge of these pre-Incan peoples. No one dares even guess how long ago the first of these races rose from savagery and became highly cultured people. No one can say, with any degree of certainty, which of the civilizations is the most ancient. No one is absolutely sure whether all were offshoots of one race, whether the many civilizations were links in one chain of development, or if all were distinct. And no one can answer the riddle as to who they were, whence they came or why they vanished. All are shrouded in the deepest mystery. Even the Incas, the most recent of all, whose civilization was flourishing at the time of the Spanish conquest, are surrounded with mystery. We really know nothing of their history or their ancestry. We have only vague legends, traditions and allegories regarding these matters, and even these are lacking when it comes to the more ancient races and civilizations which preceded the Incas.

Everywhere, throughout Ecuador, Peru, Bolivia and even over the borders in Brazil and Chile, are scattered the ruins and remains of civilized people of whom nothing is definitely known. Over an area of more than one million square miles there is scarcely a square mile that does not contain evidences of once having been inhabited by races who reached a high state of culture, and many of whom performed almost incredible feats of engineering. Everywhere, among the Andean ranges and upon the deserts, are the ruins of temples, palaces, great cities, immense walls, massive fortresses, as well as hundreds of thousands of graves and tombs containing millions of mummies.

Although many archeologists have studied and excavated among these remains; although hundreds of thousands of specimens have been obtained, and although innumerable pamphlets, reports, and even ponderous volumes have been written regarding them, yet the surface has scarcely been scratched. There are ruins and remains beyond calculation which have never been examined; there are as many more which have never been seen by white men and by few of the native Indians. No doubt, somewhere in these ruins of long-vanished civilizations, in some crumbling palace or temple, or hidden in some tomb, is material that, when found, will solve the mysteries surrounding these forgotten people.

It is impossible even to calculate the number of the inhabitants who once occupied the area. For a stretch of more than one thousand miles north and south there is an almost endless chain of cemeteries and burial-mounds extending inland to beyond the Andes. In many of these the number of dead interred is almost beyond conception. The earth is literally filled with the dead, and there must be hundreds of millions of mummies within the area. These of course represent the accumulation of dead bodies through many centuries,—thousands of years in fact. In this dry land where it seldom rains, and in the nitrate-impregnated soil, bodies last indefinitely, and it is often impossible to determine whether a mummified body was interred five hundred or five thousand years ago. I say mummies; but in reality these bodies are not true mummies preserved artificially, but are merely the desiccated remains, the dried, shriveled cadavers preserved intact by the dryness and the chemicals in the soil.

Often they are in remarkably good condition, even the facial expressions being retained, but as a rule they are merely skeletons covered with shrunken, parchment-like skins, and with the hair remaining upon the heads. But if we cannot state definitely how long ago they were interred or who they were, we can be certain that they are the dead of many races or distinct cultures, that there were long lapses between the various eras of civilization, and we can determine with reasonable accuracy which culture certain mummies represent, and from them can learn much of the lives, customs, habits, religions, arts and crafts of their lifetimes.

These facts are established by what is termed stratification. In other words, by careful excavation of ruins, remains, burial-mounds and graves we find that the remains, human and otherwise, are distributed in more or less regular layers or strata. At times there will be several—as many as four or five— of these strata, while at other times there will be only one recognizable deposit. Often there is no distinct line of demarcation between two or more layers, while again there may be considerable depths of barren sand or earth between the strata of remains. In the former case we can safely assume that one culture superseded another or was a development of its predecessor, and hence the cultures represented were probably of the same race or people; whereas in the latter case we can assume with equal certainty that one culture or civilization disappeared and another took its place in the same locality after a gap of many years or even centuries, and that there is probably no racial connection between the two. Such a condition only adds to the mystery of the whole matter, however. Why, we may well ask, did one highly cultured or civilized race die out or disappear, and why, centuries later, should another race develop a culture or civilization of a different character in practically the same spot? No one can offer an answer. If each succeeding culture was more advanced than those preceding it we might think that the people profited by their forerunners' examples and improved upon them. But not infrequently the later cultures were inferior to those of earlier date and showed no proofs of having been influenced by them.

Prominent among these prehistoric mysterious cultures is that known as the Nasca from the fact that it centered about the Nasca district in and around the present cities of Pisco and Ica in central Peru. Here, over a vast area of desert country between the Pacific and the Andes, dwelt a race of people who developed a ceramic art in many ways unexcelled by any other prehistoric American race.

Their pottery, of which hundreds of thousands of specimens fill the great museums of the world, is easily recognized, and unlike that from any other portion of the world. Largely it is polychrome, usually colored in soft reds, browns, buff, white and black; beautifully modeled and finished, and remarkable for the variety of its intricate and complicated designs. It is in the thin delicate nature of the ceramic ware, the perfect firing and the truly artistic and beautiful polychrome designs that the Nascan pottery excels all other types. Although most of the Nasca ware is in the more conventional forms, such as plates, saucers, bowls, jars, cups and pots, there are a great many imitative pieces, resembling, in their fidelity to natural forms, the Chimu and Tiahuánaco pottery. But the Nasca ware is always recognizable by its coloration and is quite distinct from all others.

The Nascans also employed pottery for making many implements, utensils, etc., rarely if ever, formed of earthenware elsewhere. Among these are flutes, trumpets, horns, Pan's-pipes, bells, whistles and other musical instruments. Also, like many other races, they possessed the knowledge of "whistling jars," utensils so formed with double spouts that when liquid was poured from them they emitted a low, musical, whistling sound. In fact, there is scarcely any form of utensil which cannot be found among the Nasca pottery. In some respects, however, all the Nasca ceramic ware is much alike. With few exceptions it is made of a fine quality of clay rubbed to a satiny surface, but unglazed, and with few exceptions it is, when decorated at all, embellished with most cleverly executed paintings, each of which tells a story or is symbolic of some event. Often these designs are so involved and intricate that at first glance they appear meaningless, but once one becomes familiar with the style, the technique and the handling of the art, the motifs may readily be interpreted. As these, like the forms of the vessels themselves, are frequently duplicated, it may be that they conveyed thoughts, messages, or recorded events.

Aside from their unique and astonishing pottery, the Nascans were expert weavers, feather-workers, metal workers and wood-carvers. Their textiles, often finer than anything made by machinery, are found well preserved in the graves with the mummies. Much of the textile work is plain weaving, but the best, and a very large proportion of it, is tapestry in which the most elaborate and intricate designs in many colors are brought out by a sort of embroidery upon a woven base. So fine is much of this that it seems impossible to believe that it could have been done by human figures. Not infrequently the stitches are so small that they are almost invisible to the naked eye, and the designs seem at first sight to be painted upon the cloth. In their feather-work the Nascans sewed thousands of small, bright-colored feathers on to a woven background, and in this way made belts, headbands and even large ponchos and entire garments of the most artistically blended tints, and of surpassing beauty. Silver and gold were used extensively, and were beautifully wrought into innumerable forms for utensils, weapons and ornaments. Copper was seldom if ever used. Their woodwork, especially ceremonial staffs and spades, was most elaborately and intricately carved.

Nowhere in Peru or elsewhere are there such mummies as are found in the Nascan tombs. Not only are the bodies most perfectly preserved, but their wrappings and coverings are rich, elaborate and gorgeous. Ordinarily the Peruvian mummy is doubled up with the knees under the chin, is covered with a poncho or blanket, and, together with a few personal belongings and ornaments, is wrapped in layers of coarse sacking, quilted cotton and, outside of all, a coarsely netted container of rope. At times a mask of painted wood, of silver, copper, earthenware or even gold, may cover the face, and the body of a chief or priest may be buried with the insignia or feather head-dress used in life. But the Nascan mummies are of quite a different sort. Not only are they interred with the finest pottery, the richest garments and most prized weapons and ornaments, but in addition they are wrapped, bundled, decorated and disguised until they bear no outward resemblance to human bodies. The entire body is wrapped and roped into a bulky bundle, the wrappings covering head and all. On top of this is placed an artificial head covered with hair sewed in place, and with a mask of silver, gold or wood, painted, carved or chased, to represent the face of the deceased. Upon the head is placed a gorgeous feather crown, often with a fillet of silver or gold. The bundle is robed in the finest textiles and feather-work, and is draped with necklaces and ornaments of precious metal and semiprecious stones, until the whole looks like a badly proportioned, stumpy tailor's dummy fairly covered with feathers, gold and silver, tapestry and gewgaws.

With all their other attainments the Nascans seem to have fought shy of stonework. They were an agricultural and fishing race, as we know from the designs on their pottery and other remains; they dwelt in a warm equable climate, and they apparently had no need of stone dwellings. Like the inhabitants of the northern Peruvian coast districts, their temples, forts, buildings and walls were of adobe, and they erected no large stone monoliths or idols. Though in a desert district they placed large areas of land under cultivation, bringing the water for many miles by canals and ditches to irrigate their fields. They raised nearly every variety of vegetable, grain and fruit known to South America. Although, as far as we know, they were by no means as highly cultured or civilized as the Aztecs, the Mayas, the pre-Incas or the Incas, the Nascans were far above the level of savages or barbarians. They possessed all or nearly all the arts, and had a good fundamental knowledge of engineering. They had many industries of civilization, a complex religion, and possibly a symbolic recorded language. They were well organized socially and politically, and, did we know more of their home life and customs, we might find that they were a truly civilized race.

Until recently it was thought that they were the only highly cultured race that had existed in the disstrict, and innumerable theories had been suggested to account for their presence and culture. They had been linked theoretically with the still more ancient Tiahuánacans, with the pre-Incas and with many other cultures, but none of these theories seemed to fit in entirely with facts.* Recently, Doctor Tello made a most remarkable discovery in the Nasca district. A few miles from Pisco, on an outjutting cape, in a barren desert waste among equally forbidding hills, he discovered the remains of two great cities. Here, exposed by the drifting sand, he found massive buildings, houses, temples, walls and tombs of beautifully cut pink porphyry. Though very little of the remains has been uncovered or excavated, enough has been done to prove that these prehistoric cities were immense centers, the residences of thousands of people, and though so close to the Nascan district—actually within it, in fact—they are obviously the work of a distinct race and represent a different civilization. Their pottery, sculptures, textiles, woodwork, etc., are totally unlike those of the Nascans or any other prehistoric Peruvian race.

Excavations have proved that there were three distinct civilizations at these "pink" cities, the latest Incan, the next older pre-Incan and the oldest the unknown, immeasurably ancient civilization of the district. Among the numerous objects obtained from these oldest remains are vessels depicting llamas with five toes on the front feet, instead of two as in the llamas of the present time. Moreover, skeletons of five-toed llamas were found. This would seem to prove that these prehistoric people lived in the dim

*It has been claimed by some authorities that during the interval between the ancient pre-Incan (Tiahuánacan) and the Incan period, there was a time of anarchy and internal warfare, and that, during this time, the Mochicas arrived from southern Mexico or Central America and established the civilizations of Nasca, Chimu, Pachacamac, etc., superimposing their culture upon that of the pre-Incans. Although there is so far no real proof in support of this theory, yet the striking similarity of the Nascan sun-god and the Mexican sun-god, together with the Chimu legends of a northern origin, indicate that there may be a basis for the assumption.

past when llamas still possessed five toes—a time so remote that we cannot even hazard a guess at it. But many scientists are of the opinion that the five-toed llamas of the pink city people were merely freaks or were a special variety bred by these people and perhaps regarded as sacred because of their five toes.

Why these people should have erected stone cities, whereas all the other coastal races used adobe, is also a mystery. Certainly they had no more real need of stone buildings and dwellings than had the Chimus, the Nascans and the others, and surely it was not because stone was the most convenient material at hand. On the contrary, the stone was quarried and cut many miles from the site of the cities, and was transported with tremendous difficulty, and by herculean labor, across wide desert wastes. Thousands of people must have toiled for years to have accomplished this, and the quality of the buildings and the workmanship prove that they possessed an advanced knowledge of engineering, of architecture and of mathematics. That they were a numerous race is proved by the size of the cities, one of which is estimated to have housed over forty thousand inhabitants, by the number of burials and mummies, and by the amount of labor represented.

Here we face other mysteries. Why should such a numerous and highly cultured race have been confined to a restricted area on a comparatively small and isolated cape? Why should they have built two cities here, and never have spread to other districts? And whence did they come and where did they go? Did they come from oversea, bringing their arts and cultures with them, and settle down and

build their cities upon the spot where they landed?
Were they wanderers from the interior driven into
the deserts by savage tribes? Were they the decen-
dants of other cultured people who left no known
traces forming a connecting link between them and
the inhabitants of the pink cities? Were they driven
out by pestilence, enemies or by some great cataclysm
of nature? There are innumerable solutions that may
be offered in reply to these questions. For all we
know, the present desert may, in their time, have been
fertile, well-watered land, and with the climatic
changes people may have been compelled to abandon
the cities they had worked so hard to build. They
may have been conquered by some more powerful
and more warlike race, perhaps even by the earliest
Incas, and forced to move to some other portion of
the land. They may have been decimated by plagues
or epidemics, until not enough remained to keep up
the cities, and the survivors, finding life impossible
here, may have migrated elsewhere and lost their
identity among other races. There are just as many
theoretical solutions for the puzzle of their origin.
They may have come from some long-submerged,
mid-Pacific archipelago. They may have come from
the Oceanic islands or even from Asia, or they may
have been migrants from the north, south, or east.

It has been claimed by some that all the pre-Incan
races were of Oriental origin, that they were
Chinese or even Japanese, and several volumes
have been written to prove this theory. Vocabularies
have been compiled showing the striking similarity of
numerous words in the Quichua and Aimará dialects
and in the Chinese and Japanese languages. And

numerous examples have been cited of alleged Chinese and Japanese characters and inscriptions upon pre-Incan pottery, sculptures and metal work.

At first glance the proof appears to be conclusive. But a close study of the arguments and alleged proofs rather shatters one's faith in the theory. There are many times more words in the Quichua and Aimará dialects which bear not the slightest similarity to the Chinese and Japanese than the similar words compiled so carefully. Moreover, there are as many or even more that closely resemble—in fact are often identical with—words of the same meaning in the Oceanian dialects. And the superficial similarity of a few words among thousands is far from conclusive evidence of racial relationship. The various inscriptions and characters which are claimed to be Chinese or Japanese are most questionable. Some of these are obviously purely decorative motifs, and being composed of lines and dots, bear a superficial resemblance to Chinese characters. Others are apparently pictographs, and it is only natural that crudely and greatly conventionalized symbols for certain objects as used by one race should more or less resemble the symbols used as characters in writing by another race, even though there is no connection between them. In many cases, also, the sponsors of this theory have used vivid imaginations and have "restored" the so-called inscriptions to fulfil their own ideas as to what they should be. Finally, the originators of this theory admit that no two authorities agree as to the interpretation of the alleged Oriental characters, and not one of the translations offered has any real sense or meaning of importance.

Of course, on the other hand, it is not impossible nor even improbable that voyagers from China or Japan may not have visited the west coast of South America in ages past. They may have come in sufficient numbers to have established settlements, and they may have left some influence upon the people. Their words for certain objects, especially articles hitherto unknown to the natives, might have been adopted by the indigenous races, and some of their rather decorative characters might have been used by the natives, especially if they regarded them with superstitious reverence or looked upon them as magical, which would no doubt have been the case. But if the population of the district was entirely of Mongolian origin, if the country was settled by the Chinese or Japanese, and the cultures and civilizations were theirs, then it would seem that there should be distinctively Japanese or Chinese influence recognizable in the arts, the industries, the architecture and the other attainments of the pre-Incan races, and that Chinese and Japanese characters and inscriptions should predominate and should occur everywhere. This, however, is not the case. Among all the countless thousands of examples of pottery, metal objects, sculptures and textiles obtained from pre-Incan and Incan remains there are scarcely a dozen specimens that bear figures which, by any stretch of the imagination, might be considered of Japanese or Chinese origin.

Others have attempted to connect the pre-Incan races with the Egyptians, and with the famous "Lost Tribes" of Israel, and at least one authority has maintained that Peru was the Ophir of the Bible, that

King Solomon's mines were in the Andean region, and that the Indians are descendants of the people sent oversea by the famous Biblical king. Many have tried to settle the mystery of these races by claiming they were all of common origin and ancestry; that during thousands of years of wandering about, of living in various environments and under varying conditions of climate, they developed widely varying habits, cultures, arts and civilizations. But even if we accept this, which after all is the most plausible theory of the lot, it does not provide any answer to the greatest mystery of all: namely, where the original race came from and who they were.

Moreover, as I have mentioned before, the most ancient races that inhabited the district appear to have been the most highly civilized. There are no traces of a gradual evolution of their culture, no stepping-stones, as it were, from savagery or barbarism which can be credited to these races. Their only known remains prove them most highly advanced and civilized people, each distinct from all others, and presenting the greatest archeological puzzle of the entire world.

CHAPTER XIII

THE MYSTERY OF TIAHUÁNACO

FAR up on the Andean heights, nearly fifteen thousand feet above the sea, and a few miles from the shores of Lake Titicaca, are the remains of the oldest and most mysterious city in the New World. Here, on the very roof of the world, in a barren, bleak and dreary land, are the ruins of Tiahuánaco, once the mighty capital of a highly civilized people whose origin, history and fall are unsolved mysteries, whose feats of engineering seem almost superhuman, whose sculptures have no counterpart in the entire world, and who had vanished from the face of the earth centuries before the fall of Rome. The influence of their art and their religion extended throughout Peru, Bolivia and the Andean regions, and yet, as far as is known, they were a race apart, and in no other spot in the world are there sculptures, carvings and structures even remotely resembling those at Tiahuánaco. It is as if the entire civilization, the entire prehistoric race, had been confined to the one restricted area about Lake Titicaca, in fact, as though the people and their civilization had descended upon this spot from another world, and, as mysteriously, had gone back whence they came.

Although for hundreds, thousands of years, Tiahuánaco has been at the mercy of the elements and earthquakes; although the Incan people, the wild

Collas, the Spaniards, the Bolivians, the tourists, the treasure-seekers, the archeologists and the railway-builders have done everything within their power to destroy, desecrate and obliterate the work of the Tiahuánacans, and although the most remarkable and most priceless remains have been carried off, broken up or removed, still much exists of the prehistoric city, its immense temples, its stupendous buildings and its amazing monoliths. Fortunately, those portions of Tiahuánaco which have defied time and man through the long centuries are the portions which speak most eloquently of the high civilization and the incredible feats of the vanished race who dwelt and worshiped there.

The ruins are scattered over an area of several square miles close to the modern Bolivian Indian village of Tiahuánaco. The Guáyqui-La Paz Railway passes directly through their midst. In fact, the greatest destruction of these irreplaceable and priceless remains of a prehistoric civilization was wrought by the builders of the railway. Innumerable idols, monuments, sculptured monoliths and countless tons of stone from the ruins were broken up and used for ballasting the road-bed. Ruthlessly, cuttings were made through burial-grounds, and human remains, magnificent pottery and hundreds of archeological treasures were broken, destroyed and thrown away. But long before the railway was thought of, Tiahuánaco had suffered at the hands of innumerable vandals. The ancient Catholic Church, built by the old Spaniards, is largely composed of portions of the magnificent buildings and monuments. In front of the church stand two huge stone images or idols, broken in half in order to reduce them to movable proportions. Fully one-half of the squalid adobe huts of the village have door frames, steps or other portions formed from sculptured stones filched from the ruins. Wherever streets are paved the pavements are made from the cut stones of Tiahuánaco, and, outside the village, the farmers have utilized every bit of stonework they could transport to build the walls about their fields. Even those portions of the ruins which have been left have suffered. The finest idols and monuments have served as targets for the rifles of Bolivian soldiery; magnificent sculptures have been wantonly defaced, and the condition of these most ancient ruins in the New World is a disgrace to the Bolivian Government.

Although the ruins are now over thirteen miles from Lake Titicaca there are reasons to think that in the days when the city was occupied it stood on the shores of the lake itself or on an arm, or bay, for traces of what was apparently a dock or mole are to be seen just north of the principal ruins. If so the lake has receded and we must discard the theory that the city was destroyed and deserted owing to the lake rising and flooding the district.

It has also been claimed that the city was the product of two distinct races or civilizations, the more recent people having added to and reconstructed the original ruins left by a much more ancient race. But personally I can see no reason for this supposition, although there are evidences of the Incan people having used the site to some extent, perhaps merely as a shrine or for holding certain religious ceremonies. That they should have done so is quite probable, for

Tiahuánaco was a most holy city and was so regarded in Incan folk-lore and legends. Moreover, according to Garcilasso de la Vega, who doubtless had it from his Incan mother, Tiahuánaco was occupied for considerable periods by the Incas. Garcilasso even goes further and claims that the name, Tiahuánaco, was not the original name of the city, but was bestowed upon it by the Incas. According to him, a fleet-footed courier brought a message from Cuzco to the Inca at Tiahuánaco, and the latter, addressing the weary messenger as "Guanaco" in complimentary comparison with the famed speed of the guanaco, requested him to be seated, using the words *"Tiay, Guanaco."* (Be seated, Guanaco.)

This explanation of the origin of the name is far-fetched and unreasonable. In the first place, the guanaco is not found in Bolivia, but is a native of southern Chile, and the Inca would have been far more likely to have compared his messenger to the vicuña, with which he was familiar, than to the guanaco. Moreover, the word guanaco is of Mapuche and not Quichua derivation, while finally, guanaco has the accent on the penultimate syllable, whereas huánaco has the first syllable accented. As a matter of fact, the origin of the name, TIAHUÁNACO or TIAHUÁNACU is quite obvious and very simple.

In the Hualla (ancient Quichua) language, *huánacu* means dead, and *tihuánacu* would signify a place of the dead or a dead city. The name was undoubtedly bestowed by the Incans, just as the ruins of Chawin were so called owing to the fact that they were the work of past or dead persons, *chawi* meaning literally "a body that has lost its life (density)" and which, in its broader sense, is used for remains of any kind. The use of the word *huánacu* or its roots or derivatives, as applied to anything devoid of life or pertaining to dead persons, was common among the Incans. Thus the statues of the Incas at the Temple of the Sun in Cuzco were known as Chuqui-Huáncas, the burial-ground was called Huánacu-Pampa, etc.

Those who claim that two distinct civilizations built the city, point to the fact that two kinds of stone were used, one a gray arsenite or andesite, the other a reddish sandstone; that there are two types of art and sculpture in evidence, and that there are many half-finished stones and sculptures indicating that the workmen were forced to leave their tasks uncompleted, as if by a sudden attack or some other unexpected calamity.

But I fail to see how any of these facts prove the point. The fact that two varieties of stone were used means little if anything. It may have been the result of personal preference on the part of the architects or workmen. It may have been due to expediency, as for example when a monument or other piece of stonework was required in a hurry, and the sandstone could be cut and sculptured in a fraction of the time required to complete a monument in andesite. Moreover, there is no rule or order of sequence in the case of the two kinds of stone. Very often one may find two monoliths, or even two masses of building stone, one of sandstone and one of andesite, side by side and obviously cut and erected at the same time. Neither have I been able to find any distinct difference or any sharply marked line of demarcation in the sculptures, stone-carvings, decorations, etc. To be sure, there is considerable variation in the technical quality of the work, and, to some extent, in the prevailing designs and motifs used. But this is no more than might be expected as the result of individual variation in skill and artistic talent on the part of the workmen, and certainly not nearly so great a variation as we find in the arts of other races when we examine the results of their work through many centuries and innumerable generations. In fact, it is surprising that there is so little difference between the earliest, or apparently oldest, work of the Tiahuánacans and that of the latest period of their existence.

That many of the monoliths were abandoned half finished may point to some sudden catastrophe; probably to some overwhelming calamity that completely wiped out the inhabitants of the city, such a catastrophe as an earthquake, a volcanic eruption, a flood, a pestilence, or even a sudden attack by overwhelming numbers of some savage enemy. Even so it does *not* prove that the exterminated race was superseded by its conquerors or by any other race until the days of the Incas who, we know, had no hand in the building of the city or in its destruction.

Although the city originally covered a vast area, and was undoubtedly continuous over that area, the ruins are now more or less separated and divided into distinct sections which are commonly designated as Akapana (the Fortress or Hill of Sacrifices), Kala-sasaya (Temple of the Sun), and Tunca-Puncu (the Place of Ten Doors), besides several smaller groups, individual monuments, idols, etc.

The first and most prominent objects seen by the visitor to Tiahuánaco are several badly defaced, immense stone images close to the railway track, in their design and arrangement most strikingly like the similar monuments found at the ruined temple site at Coclé in Panama. (See Chapter VI.) A short distance east of these rises the truncated pyramidal hill of Akapana. It has been claimed that this hill, which is approximately one hundred and seventy feet in height, is entirely artificial, but my examinations and studies of the spot convince me that it is largely natural, and that, instead of being built up from the surface of the plain, together with several smaller hills about it, Akapana was originally much larger, and that much of the natural material was removed in order to give it and its neighbors the pyramidal forms desired. In form its base is rectangular, four hundred and ninety by six hundred and fifty feet, with each side almost mathematically in line with the respective cardinal point of the compass. Originally the sides, for a portion of their height at least, were faced with huge rectangular stone blocks and smaller rocks, but the greater part of these has been carried away by the natives for their own uses, while hundreds of tons of the walls were crushed and used as ballast for the near-by railway.

Originally, too, a huge water-basin occupied the top of the hill with stone conduits leading from it to the base, while an immense stone stairway gave access to the summit. All of these have been broken, thrown about or removed entirely, and from the portions remaining it is impossible to say whether Akapana was intended as a place of worship, a temple to the rain-god, a sacrificial pyramid, a fortress, or merely as a residence or lookout.

Far more interesting, because it is in a better state of preservation, is the so-called Temple of the Sun or Kalasasaya, about one thousand feet from the northern base of Akapana. Here the earth has been formed into a rectangular terrace rising about ten feet above the plain, and about five hundred feet by four hundred feet in size. Around the four sides, and spaced from sixteen to twenty feet apart, are stone monuments or phallic columns fifteen to twenty feet in height. In arrangement, form and every other detail these columns are almost identical with those of the temple site at Coclé in Panama. (See Chapter VI.) But here the similarity ends. There are no traces of the parallel rows of columns and idols as at Coclé, and no evidence that such ever existed at Tiahuánaco. Moreover, the temple terrace at Kalasasaya was originally completely paved, although all but a few of the stones have been carried off. The same is true of the huge stone idols or images that once stood within the enclosure, and only one immense, badly defaced idol still remains in position, its calm but battered face turned toward the rising sun. At the eastern side of the temple a broad stone stairway leads from the surrounding plain to the terrace. The steps, formed of single masses of stone about ten feet in width by twenty feet in length, are in a good state of preservation, as are the two huge monoliths standing like sentinels on either side.

It is evident that originally many of the columns surrounding the terrace supported lintels, timbers or slabs of stone, thus forming portals, or perhaps a

rude sort of colonnade, about the temple. Many of
the columns bear notches, depressions and carefully
cut mortises at or near their summits, which could
only have served to support timbers or capstones.
But all the capstones have long since disappeared.
In this connection it is interesting to note that many
of the stone monuments at the temple site at Coclé,
Panama (see Chapter VI), had similar notches, indicating that they, too, once bore lintels, probably of
timber, which have long ago vanished. But it is also
evident that many of the columns in Tiahuánaco, as
well as at Coclé, were complete in themselves, for
their summits are smoothly tooled and rounded and
are of the phallic type. Possibly, when originally
erected, the true monuments and the stone portals
alternated, but so many are missing and so many
more have been broken or defaced that this is impossible to determine. No doubt, when Tiahuánaco was
inhabited, there were many objects within the temple
which have now completely disappeared. Scattered
everywhere are fragments of idols and images,
broken stone conduits, bits of sculptured rock,
shattered remnants of highly decorated pottery, and
remains of what may have been stone altars or sacrificial stones.

But despite the ruin and wanton destruction that
have taken place, the most remarkable feature of the
temple still remains almost intact—the so-called
Gateway of the Sun, which stands at the western end
of the terrace. This monolithic portal is the largest
known example of stone-cutting in the entire world.
It is cut from a single massive block of andesite thirteen feet and five inches in length; seven feet and two

inches in height; eighteen inches in thickness, and
with a square doorway four feet and six inches by
two feet and nine inches in size cut through its center.
The western surface of the upper portal forming the
lintel is cut in a series of low bas-reliefs of severely
plain geometrical form, and with four deep niches
which were probably designed to hold small idols or
images, very likely of gold or silver. The lintel on the
eastern face is completely covered with beautifully
sculptured symbolic figures in bas-relief, and has two
deep niches, one on each side of the doorway. The
sculptured symbols or figures are arranged in a series
of equal-sized squares surrounding a representation of
a deity, supposedly the sun-god. In either hand the
semihuman figure bears a ceremonial staff or scepter, and the rays about his head terminate in miniature jaguar heads. Flanking this central figure are
the forty-eight squares, twenty-four on each side, arranged in three rows of eight figures each. All these
face the god as if running toward him, and each carries a small scepter or staff. The upper and lower
rows are semihuman figures with wings and crowns
and are identical in all respects. The figures of the
central row are repetitions of the others, aside from
the fact that they have condor heads. Below all these
is a line of sixteen carvings consisting of twelve human heads in flat relief flanked by two condor heads.

No one has been able satisfactorily to explain or
interpret this remarkable sculpture which is unquestionably of great ceremonial or symbolical significance. According to the ancient Peruvian mythology,
a giant condor-god carried the sun across the heavens
each day; and he is often represented battling with

a jaguar, the god of darkness or night, thus symbolically representing the eternal conflict between night and day. In all probability the sculptures upon this Gateway of the Sun represent the supreme deity or sun-god with the various lesser deities paying him homage. Although this elaborate symbolic carving is most interesting it is by no means so remarkable as the ornamental design and niches on the opposite side of the huge block of cut stone. So accurately and perfectly cut are these, so geometrically and mathematically true, that it is impossible to detect an error even by the use of calipers, a millimeter rule and a draughtsman's triangle. The same is true of the doorway itself and of all the innumerable geometrical sculptures at Tiahuánaco. How any human beings could have cut this hard andesite rock to such perfect angles, with such true sharp edges, and often to a depth of six or eight inches from the surface, unless they possessed steel tools and most accurate mathematical instruments is perhaps the greatest mystery of the ruins.

Scattered about the plain near the temple are the remains of several other buildings, monoliths, etc., but, with the exception of the so-called sacrificial altar, all have been mutilated and destroyed until their original forms and purposes are unrecognizable. The altar, as it is commonly known, is a single block of stone squared on the four sides, deeply hollowed to form a basin-like depression on the top, and with a narrow groove or opening on one side. If it actually was used as a sacrificial stone it is a most unusual type. I am inclined to believe that it was never intended for such a purpose, but was probably a basin or font for holding holy water or oil or for some similar religious or ceremonial purpose.

Separated by nearly a mile from the other ruins is the Tunca-Puncu or Place of Ten Doors, the largest, most impressive and most remarkable remains of all. At first sight these ruins appear to occupy the summit of an artificial mound about fifty feet in height and two hundred feet square. But in reality the "mound" consists of the ruined masonry and foundation-stones of the enormous building which have fallen in and have been partly covered with débris and drifted sand. Possibly the base of the structure was formed of stone slabs and blocks filled in with earth, but excavations show the tooled and cut stones extending far below the summit of the present low hill. Formerly Tunca-Puncu was known as the Palace of the Incas, but it antedates the first Inca by many centuries, and its true purpose can only be surmised. Perhaps it was a regal court; it may have been a sort of forum, a tribunal of justice or even a temple. To-day it is such a complete ruin that it is practically impossible even to determine its original form. Its most salient and striking features are its stupendous slabs of stone, its innumerable, magnificently sculptured cornices, columns and blocks, and its gigantic stone steps. Only those portions too massive for transportation remain. Many of these are of incredible size, the largest single block measuring thirty-six by seven feet and weighing from one hundred and seventy-five to two hundred tons, while slabs weighing forty or fifty tons each are everywhere.

Bordering the edges of some of these largest slabs

are immense stone platforms cut into square seat-like forms. It is possible that these served as thrones or that thrones were placed in them, but it is more probable that they were designed to hold statues or idols. Also, on the edges of every large stone slab and block, are seen deeply cut grooves in T-shape with holes drilled into the stone at the ends of the cross grooves. In many places, where the stones lie side by side, these mortised recesses are in line, and it is at once evident that they were designed to hold metal keys or staples for binding the blocks together. Heretofore it has been assumed that the staples were of copper, but several have been found among the ruins within the past two years and these are of solid silver. From their shape and the hammer marks upon them it is obvious that they were cast or forged in squarish or oval section, and, after being inserted in the grooves, were hammered in until the metal spread and was thus locked immovably in the slots.

Unquestionably the removal of these metal keys caused the collapse of this stupendous structure, and the fact that the metal used was silver and not copper accounts for the Spaniards taking the trouble to remove them. The inconsiderable amount of copper that would have been secured, provided the staples had been of copper, would not have been worth the time and labor involved in extracting them, and I think it safe to assume that all the metal keys used in this huge structure were of silver. Copper is by no means abundant in the vicinity, while silver is, and the latter metal, being much harder and stronger than copper, would have been better suited for the

purpose. Undoubtedly the Tunca-Puncu was partly
in ruins when the Dons arrived at Tiahuánaco, and
if so the Spaniards could have obtained only those
staples which were exposed and accessible. But
there must have been hundreds of the silver keys
buried under the massive stones and used in the
foundations of the building. No doubt they still remain there, as secure from molestation beneath those
one-hundred-ton blocks of sandstone as though in a
safe deposit vault.

Originally the Place of Ten Doors must have been
a beautiful and ornate structure, for fragments of
sculptured stone are scattered everywhere. In every
case, however, the designs are formed of straight
lines, squares and severe but graceful geometrical
forms. On many the carving is in bas-relief, in as
many more it is incised, but in every case there is
no slightest flaw in the true, sharp, mathematical
accuracy of the stone-cutting. Occasionally a stone
is seen with the swastika design, and crosses are very
numerous. Much controversy has been aroused over
these, but it must be remembered that the swastika
is one of the most ancient designs known to human
beings, and that simple crosses are even older. In
some cases, too, it is evident that these deeply cut,
cross-shaped niches were designed to hold timbers or
even stone lintels or slabs, and several fragments of
stone have been found with the ends accurately cut
to fit the niches.

Perhaps the most puzzling objects among these
ruins are two immense stone disks or wheels which I
discovered on my last visit to Tiahuánaco. One of
these is completely buried under the fallen masses of

stone and only its edge is visible, while the other was concealed under small fragments and is now completely exposed. It is about seven feet in diameter, about sixteen inches in thickness, and has a square hole in its center. It is made of the same stone as the ruins themselves and its surfaces show the same type of tool marks and the same character of workmanship. Had I seen such an object in any other locality I should have passed it by as a Spanish millwheel or *arastra*. But, as far as is known, there never was an *arastra* at Tiahuánaco, and there never was any reason for one. Moreover, the summit of the Tunca-Puncu hill with its ruins is the last place in the world where such a mill would be erected, while the fact that the stone wheels were buried under the ruins would indicate that they were there before the stones fell apart, and hence long before the arrival of the Spaniards.

Hitherto it has always been claimed that no American race ever discovered the wheel, and one of the greatest archeological puzzles has been how the prehistoric Americans accomplished many of their feats without it. Such a feat, for example, as the transportation of the innumerable gigantic blocks of stone at Tiahuánaco for distances of many miles. But if the stone disks at the Place of Ten Doors are actually prehistoric wheels, the problem would be greatly simplified. With a wooden rotating axle fitted to such wheels, slabs or blocks of stone could be slung from the axle by means of ropes and could readily be trundled across the plains and deserts, for the sixteen-inch tread of the wheels would prevent them from sinking into the earth or sand. With the extreme scarcity of timber in the vicinity, and with no wood of sufficient size for constructing a large wheel, stone would be the only available material, and a stationary wooden axle with the wheels rotating upon it would have been out of the question. The wood would have been ground and worn away in a very short time, as there would have been a tremendous amount of friction. But by using greased ropes or even twisted withes as slings, and a rotating axle with squared ends secured immovably in the wheels, these problems would have been overcome.

Oddly enough, while excavating the ruins at Coclé in Panama (see Chapter VI) I uncovered two immense stone disks very similar to those at Tiahuánaco; but assuming them to have been of Spanish origin I gave them no attention. Possibly they too were of prehistoric origin, and we may yet discover that the wheel was by no means unknown to the ancient civilized races of the New World, but was used when necessity demanded it.

Aside from their marvelous stonework, the Tiahuánacans had developed many arts and crafts to a high degree. Their pottery was beautifully designed and finished and was far superior in form, color and firing to that of the later pre-Incas and the Incan races. A great many of the vessels are of the effigy or portrait type, and from these we can obtain an accurate impression of the physical characters of the Tiahuánacans and their customs. In every case the beautifully modeled faces show the race to have differed but slightly in features from the highest types of the living Indians of the district. Occasionally one is shown with features of a Mongolian type, but as a whole they have straight eyes, broad intelligent foreheads, prominent, well-formed and slightly aquiline noses, thin lips and a calm, dignified, intelligent expression. Often they are shown with one cheek distended from chewing coca, the leaf so universally used by the Andean tribes of to-day—proof that the use of this stimulant dates back to the most ancient times. Frequently, also, the heads are shown with a close-fitting cap with ear-tabs, identical in form to those of the living Indians, while full-length figures and paintings show that the Tiahuánacans used ponchos, sandals, ear-plugs and other articles of dress and adornment such as are still in daily and universal use in the region. In fact, many of the effigy jars might have been models from life of some present-day inhabitant of Bolivia, and it is highly probable that the latter are, at least partly, descendants of the race which inhabited this most ancient of American cities.

But during the long centuries that have passed since Tiahuánaco was a thriving, holy city the aborigines have degenerated sadly and have become much mixed. In Bolivia they are mainly of the so-called Aimará race, while in Peru the so-called Quichuas predominate. But these divisions are more linguistic than racial, and both the Aimarás and Quichuas are so named from their languages instead of vice versa. The Quichua tongue was the official language of the Incan Empire and was forced upon the people by the Incas, while the Aimará dialect was adopted by countless distinct tribes in the dim past. The Aimará language is considered the most ancient in the New World, and was probably the dialect used by the Tiahuánacans. The fact that it is so widely diffused and still persists proves how far-reaching and wide-spread must have been the power and influence of the prehistoric Tiahuánacans. Otherwise it would have become mixed with the various tribal tongues or lost altogether, ages ago.

We have other evidences of the vast dominion and influences of the mysterious civilization of Tiahuánaco. Everywhere, throughout the Andean region, along the coasts, and for thousands of miles north and south, we find remains of prehistoric cultures showing unmistakable proofs of Tiahuánacan influence. And always, these are in the most ancient or lowest strata, thus proving that the Tiahuánaco civilization was beyond question the most ancient civilization in South America, and hence in the western hemisphere. But when, at what period in the history of the New World, this civilization thrived, no one can say. It is folly even to guess at the date when Tiahuánaco was in its glory. It must have antedated the Christian era by many centuries; it must have required hundreds of years to lay out and construct the city and its stupendous edifices, and the civilization must have been flourishing for ages before it attained its culmination at Tiahuánaco. To develop such an advanced and far-reaching civilization must have required an almost immeasurable time, and unless the Tiahuánaco civilization was brought, fully developed, from some unknown distant locality, the highlands about Lake Titicaca must have been inhabited by civilized human beings long before the Children of Israel fled from Egypt, perhaps before the infant Moses was hidden among the bulrushes.

Unlike the Israelites, who left us a history, however inaccurate it may be, of their times, the Tiahuánacans left nothing but their ruins, their utensils and their language. It is even doubtful if they left any human remains to aid us in solving the mystery of their identity. Many skeletons and skulls have been found in and about Tiahuánaco, it is true, but it is questionable if any of these are those of the builders of the city. Many are unquestionably those of the much later Incan inhabitants of the district; others are of men and women who, as proved by the inferior character of the pottery and artifacts associated with them, were not of the highly civilized Tiahuánaco people, and until some epochal discovery is made, Tiahuánaco will remain the most fascinating mystery of all the prehistoric American cities.

CHAPTER XIV

THE INCANS AND PRE-INCANS

*(See end of chapter for pronunciation
of Incan names.)*

EVERY one knows of the Incans, but comparatively
few possess any correct or definite knowledge of the
civilization destroyed by Pizarro. The popular misconceptions are due to the fact that much if not most
of the public's knowledge of the Incans has been obtained, either directly or indirectly, from the books
of Prescott and other authors whose accounts are, as
a rule, greatly exaggerated and far from accurate.
Prescott's *The Conquest of Peru* has become a classic,
and yet, in the light of our present-day knowledge, we
know that it is far from the truth in many respects.

Unquestionably Prescott intended his book to be
accurate, but he was woefully handicapped. He had
never visited Peru nor the west coast of South
America, he knew nothing of the Incans at first hand,
and his information was all obtained from outside
sources. A large portion was culled from the works
of Garcilasso de la Vega, the historian, who was the
son of an Incan princess and a Spanish soldier and
who might have been expected to possess a first-hand
and intimate knowledge of his maternal ancestors.
But, as a matter of fact, it was quite the contrary.
From the lips of his Incan mother this historian

heard the story of the race, it is true, but he also heard countless myths, legends, folk stories and allegories. Fact and fiction became inextricably mixed, and Prescott and others assumed that all was true history. The errors, the exaggerations and the purely fanciful features have been so long accepted as facts that to-day it is next to impossible to separate one from the other or to correct the long-established errors.

Even the word Inca is misconstrued, improperly used and misapplied. It is almost universally used as a racial name, and people speak of the "Incas" as they do of the Sioux, the British or the Germans. But there is not and never was such a race as the "Incas." The word Inca merely signified a ruler or king, or rather a particular dynasty, and it is just as erroneous to refer to the ancient or modern aborigines of Peru and its vicinity as Incas as it would be to call the British "Kings" or the Germans "Kaisers." But it *is* perfectly correct to speak of the Incan Empire, the Incan civilization or the Incan confederation, just as it is correct to speak of the Kingdom of Great Britain, or the German Empire. And just as the British or the former German Empires consisted of a number of states, races and cultures confederated and dominated by a line of hereditary kings, so the Incan Empire consisted of a vast number of distinct races, tribes and cultures consolidated and ruled by the regal Incas. In fact, I might carry the simile even further, for, like the royal family of England and of many European countries, the Incas were of a different race from their subjects. Finally, although we are accustomed to refer to all

the ruins, remains, mummies and works of ancient
civilized races in western South America as Incan,
the true Incan Empire was comparatively young at
the time of the Spanish conquest, and the greater
portion of the remarkable remains of prehistoric
civilizations which are scattered over Ecuador, Peru
and Bolivia are not attributable to the Incan culture.
Ages before the first Inca saw the light of day, the
countries which the Incas afterward ruled had been
inhabited by highly cultured and civilized races whose
works far excelled those of the Incan civilization.
Who these people were, whence they came, why or
when they disappeared are all unsolved mysteries.
We know that their numbers were vast, that they
were highly organized and industrious; that they had
attained to astounding heights in their knowledge of
engineering, mathematics, architecture, astronomy
and arts, that they performed feats which are so inexplicable that they appear almost supernatural;
that in many respects no race, ancient or modern, has
ever excelled or even equaled them, and that they had
completely vanished unknown centuries before the
commencement of the Incan dynasty.

Fortunately for us, they inhabited a land where
climatic and other natural conditions are the most
favorable for the preservation of organic matter, and,
as a result, their works, their manufactures, their
utensils and implements, their garments and even
their bodies have remained almost intact through
hundreds, thousands of years. From these remains
we have obtained a good idea of their lives, customs,
social organizations, religions, arts, habits and home
life. We cannot, with any great certainty, declare

how many of these distinct civilizations existed, which was the oldest, or whether they followed a more or less evolutionary order, or whether long periods elapsed between them. Even the Incan races at the time of Pizarro knew nothing of these predecessors of their own civilization, and, aside from vague and obviously mythical traditions or legends, they could throw no light upon their history. Hence, aside from one or two exceptional cultures, all of these prehistoric people are classed merely as pre-Incas, and as the majority of true Incan and pre-Incan remains are found side by side, or are hopelessly mixed, it will serve our present purposes to treat them together.

When the Spaniards arrived on the west coast of South America, they found the country from Ecuador to Chile inhabited by vast numbers of highly cultured and civilized people under a king or emperor known as the Inca. At that time the ruling Inca, Atahualpa, had recently been victorious in a civil war and had taken his brother, Huascar, prisoner. According to the Incan tradition, there had up to that time been thirteen Incas reigning over the empire, the first Inca and the founder of the empire having been Manco-Kapac who, with his sister-wife, Mama-Ocllo, appeared on the scene from Lake Titicaca and declared themselves the Children of the Sun. At the spot now known as Cuzco they established their capital and laid the foundations for a vast confederation that eventually extended for more than three thousand miles north and south and from the Pacific coast to beyond the Andes; an area of more than twelve hundred thousand square miles, containing upward of twenty million people,—the largest area and the largest population under one government existing in the New World prior to the Spanish conquest.

Following Manco-Kapac, the hereditary Incas were: Sinchi-Roca; Lloque-Yupanqui; Mayta-Kapac; Kapac-Yupanqui; Inca-Roca; Yahuar-Huakac; Wira-Kocha; Inca-Yupanqui and his twin brother Pacha-Cutic who ruled jointly; Tupac-Yupanqui; Huayna-Kapac, Cusi-Huascar and his half-brother, Atahualpa.

But it is obvious that the tradition regarding Manco-Kapac is largely if not wholly allegorical. Assuming that each Inca reigned for fifty years, which is highly improbable if not impossible, then the Incan Empire could not have existed for more than six hundred years before the arrival of the Spaniards. And it is utterly preposterous to believe that a civilization and a communism such as Pizarro found could have been built up and developed in six centuries, even if the Incans had borrowed from their predecessors, of which there is no real evidence. Whatever may be the truth regarding Incan history, whether the empire had been in existence for six hundred or six thousand years prior to the European invasion, there can be no question regarding the heights it had reached. Fortunately for us, the Incan Empire was still flourishing at the time, and innumerable accounts of the people, their customs, life, government, religion and other matters were written by Spanish priests and others who recorded their personal observations, and whose invaluable works are still in existence.

Although, as I have said, the most stupendous and

amazing works of the ancient Peruvians and their
neighbors antedate the Incan dynasty, and while a
vast amount of undeserved credit has been given the
Incan people for their engineering, mathematical
and other attainments, the races under the Incas had
attained almost unbelievable heights in many ways.

To students of sociology they are of the utmost
interest, for nowhere else in all the known history of
the entire world, has there been such a complete and
successful communistic society. Individuality and
freedom of thought, life and action were all sub-
servient to the community. From birth to death, the
lives, actions, tasks, social status, homes, marriages
of the people, and even the destinies of the offspring,
were planned, regulated, ordered and carried out according to inexorable laws. Every individual, other
than those of royal blood or the priesthood, was a
mere cog in the mighty wheel of the empire, and
every individual was a numbered, tagged unit of the
whole. At birth a man's or a woman's place in the
scheme of things was ordained. At five years of age
every child, male or female, was taken over by the
government and reared and trained for the occupation, the position or the task to which his entire future life was to be devoted. A man was forced to
marry when he reached the age of twenty-four, and
eighteen years was the age limit for spinsters. Once
married, neither husband nor wife had any say as to
the future of their children.

If spinners were needed the girls were trained as
spinners; if soldiers were required the boys were
trained as soldiers. If an agricultural community required additional members, the requisite number of

men and women were taken from some community where there was an excess of people and were transported to their new homes where they were forced to remain. Aside from the privileged classes, every one was equal, both socially and in worldly goods. All shared equally, all contributed equally to the support of the government, the army, the state, the religion and the community.

Each town, village and hamlet carried on its own particular allotted art, trade, industry or occupation. One village might be devoted entirely to carding wool, another to dyeing the yarns, another to weaving. By this method trade and intercourse were established, and to this day the custom still prevails to a large extent among the Indians. It is not unusual to find the inhabitants of two villages a few miles apart journeying fifty miles or more to a market town and there bartering their goods with one another, to return, often side by side, to their homes; but never dreaming of strolling from one village to the other to exchange their wares.

Law and order were rigidly enforced; there were penalties provided for every misdemeanor and crime, and many of these, judged by our standards, were far out of proportion to the offenses. So strictly enforced were the Incan laws that Mancio Sierra, writing from Cuzco on September 15, 1589, declared that at the time of the conquest the Spaniards never found a thief, a liar nor a sluggard in the entire empire. The most serious crime was blasphemy, directed at the sun, the priests or the Inca. For this the penalty was death, following the most fearful tortures. A Virgin of the Sun or any nun

who violated her vows was buried alive, and the village where she belonged was utterly destroyed, together with many of its inhabitants. Murder and
adultery were punishable by death or torture. Theft
or dishonesty resulted in the culprit's being branded
for life. Liars and scandal-mongers were flogged for
the first offense, beaten with a club at the second, and
had their tongues nailed to a board for the third offense. Incorrigibles were put to death, and petty
offenses were punished by floggings, or, in some cases,
the offender was forced to carry a heavy stone where-
ever he went, the duration of the period varying with
the seriousness of his offense.

Human sacrifices were absolutely prohibited under
heavy penalties; the killing, maiming or imprison-
ment of captives taken in war was prohibited, such
prisoners being deported to some remote district
where they were given their liberty and a plot of land
and were transformed into useful citizens. Divorces
were granted for various causes, such as adultery,
habitual misbehavior, brutality, immorality, etc.
They were also given for reasons of state and were
then compulsory, whether or not desired by either
or both of the interested parties. Either the prefect,
the priest or the tribal chief could enforce divorces.
Polygamy and polyandry were prohibited, but the
Incas were wise enough not to interfere too much
with the local customs of their colonies and provinces.
Just as the British Government permits its Indian
subjects to follow their own religious observances and
domestic customs unhindered, so the Incas permitted
the inhabitants of their conquered provinces to follow many of their tribal and time-honored customs,

provided they did not clash with the national laws. Hence, in many localities, especially in the eastern districts about the Amazon tributaries and in the tropical Montaña, polygamy was in vogue. As far as is known, polyandry existed in only one locality—at Torontoy—and this was from necessity rather than choice. The eastern frontier was frequently attacked by the savage Amuenshas and Campas, who made more than a hundred raids upon the outlying Incan towns, and, in 1499, successfully attacked the fortress of Ollantay. On these invasions the savages killed all males and carried the women away as captives. As a result, the few survivors were largely men who fled to Torontoy and there established a new settlement. To meet requirements and conditions, polyandry was adopted, each woman having two, three or four husbands. Moreover, as these fugitives were closely related, the polyandrous unions were frequently contracted between brothers and a sister. When word of these conditions reached the Inca he used the strongest measures to suppress the custom, transporting members of the colony to other districts, breaking up unions of near relatives, forcing the people to marry individuals from other localities, and inflicting the most severe penalties for any violation of the new order of things.

Although under Incan laws men and women were compelled to marry, still they were at liberty to choose their own mates. The courtship and marriage customs varied somewhat according to tribes and districts. Often the girl was bought, at least symbolically, by the youth. At other times she was—quite voluntarily—abducted and hidden by her lover who then visited her home, paid for her with presents and chicha, and asked her parents to consent to his keeping her. Following this there was a period of eight days of "proof," or a short trial marriage, during which time the groom could reject his bride if she did not come up to expectations physically or in her ability to sew, weave or perform the domestic duties of a wife. Girls who were not adepts at the essential arts and industries were soon found out and rejected, until they were forced by the requirements of the law to become proficient in wifely duties.

Widows were much preferred to virgins owing to their greater experience and skill in household duties, and were known as *chuqui-sonkos* or hearts of gold. Widows, however, never married widowers, though whether they preferred the single men or whether the widowers preferred maidens, is uncertain. In those localities where there was a superabundance of single men, the *camachicue* or prefect had them lined up in the plaza facing the file of marriageable girls, and each was forced to select a girl. In case a man desired a particular girl who already had been chosen by some other youth, he was obliged to content himself with the next best.

Naturally, in a confederation built up of innumerable distinct races, a common language was required, and hence the Incas forced the people to acquire the Quichua dialect, and Quichua became the recognized tongue of the Incan Empire, even though the people retained their own local dialects in some places. Naturally, too, one of the results of the communistic government was to create an enormously wealthy and elaborate Court and a large, powerful and wealthy priesthood, for a large proportion of all products, manufactures and returns from labor went to the Inca and to the priests. Under the law, the head of each family received a portion of land, comparative to the size of his family, a certain number of llamas, or alpacas if in a pastoral community, or the equivalent in other possessions. But the fruits of his own and his family's labors and industry were not theirs to do with as they pleased. Everything was divided into three portions: the first for the Inca; the second for the "Sun" or Church; and the third part for the community or people. But it must be admitted, to the credit of the Incas and the priests, that once the two-thirds allotted to them were acquired there were no further demands upon the people. From the government's share all public works were carried out, all expenses of the enormous army, of wars and of conquests defrayed, all the pomp and luxuries of the royal family paid, all the costs of maintaining a complex, expensive and ceremonial religion taken care of. Moreover, in the case of outlying tribes and races which had been brought under Incan dominion, but formed no truly integral part of the Empire, the annual tribute or taxes they were forced to pay were equally divided among State, Church and commonwealth. Largely this tribute was in the form of gold, precious and semiprecious stones, copper, silver and other riches. It was mainly from these outside sources that the Incan people secured the incredible quantities of precious metals and gems which so aroused the cupidity of the Spaniards, and led directly to the destruction of the Incan Empire.

The empire, however, was already on the decline.

Despite the fact that the communistic government had proved the most successful of its kind in the history of the world, and had prospered and increased to stupendous proportions, there was constant and increasing unrest among the people. Already there had been numerous revolts and bloody civil wars, and had Pizarro not arrived when he did, in all probability the empire would have ceased to exist as an entity in a short time. And had it not been that the Incans were engaged in civil wars and rebellions, the Spaniards would have had far from an easy task to conquer them.

If we are to believe Incan traditions, and no doubt there is much of truth in them, Manco-Kapac and Mama-Ocllo (or whoever were the founders of the Incan Empire) found raw material with which to build up a civilization when they first arrived upon the scene. Long before the Incan dynasty began, the pre-Incan civilizations had vanished, and the natives had largely reverted to barbarism. To be sure, the Chimus in the north had their own civilization, with the great city of Chan-Chan as their capital, and there were scattered cultural centers in the Rimac Valley, about Pisco, along the coast, and perhaps elsewhere.

Starting at Cuzco as their headquarters, the first Incas developed the nucleus of a new civilization, promulgated laws, instructed the people in arts and industries, and amalgamated many diverse tribes. The facts that these supposedly divine persons appeared suddenly and from nowhere, claiming to be the son and daughter of the sun; that they possessed a knowledge of matters unknown to the natives, and that they were of such superior intellect, all indicate that they were of a distinct race from the inhabitants of the country, perhaps survivors of the pre-Incas or the Tiahuánacans. We must accept this theory or else believe that they were inspired and possessed some of the divine attributes accredited them in the legendary lore of the Incans, for there appears to have been no slow and gradual development or evolution of culture following their appearance. Rather, it was an abrupt and entirely revolutionary order of things, exactly as though the laws, customs, arts, sciences, industries and social organization of the new régime had been brought, ready-made and fully developed, from another sphere or unknown land.

Very rapidly the empire was extended. Cuzco became a great and populous city. Magnificent temples were built, stupendous engineering feats were carried out; millions of acres of arid desert lands were brought under cultivation by means of immense irrigation systems, and rich cities were established in many places. Although the industries, arts and other features of the new civilization were influenced by or copied from those of the pre-Incas, there was practically nothing in common with the civilization of these earlier people, any more than our own civilization has any direct connection with that of the Egyptians or the Chinese, even though we borrow and use Egyptian and Chinese motifs for many purposes. From the small beginning near the shores of Lake Titicaca, the Incan power spread north, south, east, and west; but it was not until the accession of Huayna-Kapac, the eleventh Inca, that the empire reached the zenith of its power, extent and wealth.

Huayna-Kapac was an ambitious, indomitable empire-builder, a soldier, a statesman and a conqueror who may well be likened to Julius Cæsar or Napoleon. It was his dream to extend the Incan Empire to include all of the then known world. Under his reign the boundaries of the empire were pushed in every direction for thousands of miles. The Chimus were conquered and reduced to mere vassals, and Chan-Chan was destroyed. Southward the triumphant irresistible armies of the Inca swept on to central Chile, and northward the Incan legions penetrated to northern Ecuador and subjugated every race and tribe they met. The powerful kingdom of Quito was conquered, and the daughter of the dethroned and captive king was espoused by the victorious Inca. Huayna-Kapac even penetrated the tropical Montaña district beyond the Andean plateaus, and although he never completely conquered the savage jungle tribes of the district, many of them were forced to pay annual tribute to the Inca. Aside from offensive and warlike campaigns, immense public works and improvements were conceived and carried out by this Inca. But as with Rome, the power, the wealth, and the oppressions of Huayna-Kapac's reign proved the last straw, and the long-smoldering fires of discontent and revolt burst into flame in scores of places throughout the empire.

Of the union of the Inca with the Quito princess, a son, Atahualpa, had been born. Although his half-brother, Cusi-Huascar, was the elder and the legitimate heir to the Incan throne, yet Atahualpa was the favorite son of the Inca and, upon the death of Huayna-Kapac, he was given Quito, while Huascar was made Inca of Cuzco. Once the empire was thus divided its doom was spelled. Hitherto each sporadic revolution had been confined to a certain district and to a small portion of the community, and the uprisings had been easily crushed. But now the entire empire was split into two factions. Each of the two brothers was jealous of the other's power; open war between them broke out, and although Huascar was killed and Atahualpa was victorious, his triumph brought about his own downfall and death. By deceit and trickery he was made a prisoner by Pizarro who promised him his liberty in return for a vast ransom in precious metals. But when the greater part of the treasure had been handed over to the Spaniards,* they violated their pledges and executed the betrayed Inca on the flimsy pretext that it was just punishment for having caused the death of Huascar.

In most cases the Dons grossly exaggerated the amount of treasure or loot they obtained from their conquests. But no man could exaggerate the amount of riches in the possession of the Incas. The quantity of gold they had accumulated was almost incredible, and even the Spaniards, already accustomed to finding wealth beyond their wildest dreams, could not believe their eyes when they looked upon the stupendous quantities of gold, silver and gems in the Incan temples and palaces. The woodwork of the Temple of the Sun at Pachacamac was fastened together with gold nails and when, at Pizarro's orders, these were

---

*The ransom paid over consisted of sufficient gold to fill a room measuring nine by seventeen by twenty-two feet with twice the amount in silver in addition.

removed, they were found to weigh more than thirty-two thousand ounces, roughly a value of over half a million dollars in our money. Many of the most valuable objects in this temple had, however, been hidden from the Spaniards and had been secreted in and about Lurin. These, as far as is known, have never been recovered. The riches contained in the Temple of the Sun at Cuzco were far greater and were almost beyond belief. Were it not that the records of the Dons and all contemporaneous accounts, as well as Pizarro's official reports, agree, we would be forced to regard the stories of the temple's riches as the most fanciful fiction. The amount of loot taken from this temple by the Spaniards in 1535 totaled more than twelve million dollars in our money, and this was but a tithe of the treasures which had been in the temple a short time previous. Incalculable amounts of gold, silver and gems had been taken away in the vain attempt to ransom Atahualpa, and even more had been hurriedly removed and hidden to prevent the sacred objects from falling into the hands of the invaders. Some of this hidden treasure was found by the Spaniards, but much more has never been recovered.

Among the articles which were eventually found and shipped to Spain was the immense image of the sun, a golden disk with silver rays tipped with immense jewels. This was hidden in the Willca Pampa and, forty years later, was found by accident and was sent to King Philip II of Spain by the Viceroy Don Francisco de Toledo, together with a letter dated the ninth of October, 1572. Another golden sun of much smaller size was found in the temple and, for a long time, was mistaken for the original image. So numerous and so large were the pearls and precious stones possessed by the Incans that the Dons could not believe them genuine and put many of the gems to the "test by hammer" breaking them into pieces, most of which were later converted into rosaries and other religious objects by the priests.

Most of the gold, silver and precious stones in possession of the Incas was obtained in the form of tribute from innumerable subject tribes. But vast quantities were secured from extremely rich placer workings, especially those of the Marañon district near Laurikocha, Chuac, Raín, Chuquis, Pampamarca, Quihuilla, Chuquipampa, Patas, etc. A great deal also came from the Quimsa Wiri mine between the Cascay and Cayumba Rivers, which is one of the almost fabulously rich "lost" mines. Incan records state that from the mines of the Camanta Mountains, two hundred and fifty carriers transported over ten tons of gold to be used in making the immense gold chain that Huayna-Kapac ordered to commemorate the birth of his eldest son, Huascar. This was the famed chain, seven hundred feet in length, which was to be a portion of the ransom for Atahualpa. When word of his death was received the treasure was hidden by the Incans. Some legends say it was sunk in the Lake of Urcos, others that it was hidden in a cave near Sorata. In addition to this chain there were seven thousand loads of gold of seventy-five pounds each, being brought from Chuquis for Atahualpa's ransom. This was concealed in a pit or cavern near Piscobamba. This almost inconceivable treasure, having a value of nearly one hundred and sixty million dollars, has never been found. Taken altogether, the gold of the Incas was probably the greatest accumulation of the precious metal the world had ever known prior to the time of the conquest.

Gold, however, was valued only for its beauty, its ductility, its imperishable nature, the ease with which it could be worked and the fact that its color was symbolic of the sun. It had no intrinsic nor monetary value, and it was used solely for ornaments, decorations, religious vessels and other objects, for ceremonial articles, and even for implements and utensils for utilitarian purposes. As goldsmiths, the Incans never approached the perfection of the Chimus, the Mayas, the Aztecs or many of the more primitive and less cultured races of Central and South America. As a rule, the true Incan metal work was rather crude. The bulk of the real Incan gold and silver objects are very thin, and are hammered or beaten into shape, the designs or patterns upon them being sometimes incised or engraved, and at other times pressed or hammered out like repoussé work.

In addition to gold and silver, the Incans used copper, or a natural bronze alloy, extensively. Many of their tools and weapons, as well as ornaments and images, were of these metals, and various methods were employed in forming them. Many were cast, others were forged or hammered into shape, and occasionally welding or soldering was employed. Most of the really fine metal work ordinarily attributed to the Incans is in reality of pre-Incan origin. But as it is often impossible to determine whether a mummy, a grave or a specimen is Incan or pre-Incan, usually they are all called Incan.

Thus, at Pachacamac, the holy city near Lima, we know from stratification examinations that there were five distinct and separate cultures. Nearest the surface we find the typical Incan remains in the form of pottery, textiles, etc. Below these is a strata recognized by a peculiar black ware. Under this are remains of an earlier culture whose ceramics were mainly white and red painted in black. Still deeper is the purely local culture, while beneath all we come upon remains exhibiting the classical Tiahuánaco features.

Yet, ordinarily, Pachacamac is referred to as an "Incan" city, and all objects from its graves and ruins are called Incan. As a matter of fact, Pachacamac is one of the oldest cities in the western hemisphere, and it antedates the Incas by thousands of years. Possibly it was built and originally occupied by the Tiahuánacans; but for all we know to the contrary, it may have been in existence even before their advent. For centuries before the dawn of Incan civilization, Pachacamac had been a sacred or holy city, and from far and near pilgrims had journeyed to it from every direction in order to worship and make offerings in its Temple of the Sun, or to find a last resting-place within its sacred precincts. Even after it had come under Incan dominion, the pre-Incan religion survived in this great holy city.

Although built of comparatively perishable adobe or sun-dried bricks, yet the city has survived, and, despite its ruined state and the desecrating hands of vandals and treasure-seekers, one may still obtain a good idea of its size, its plan and its architectural details. And to a person with an imaginative mind it is not at all difficult to reconstruct and revisualize it as it was in its heyday. Although it now occupies a barren desert area, there are reasons to think that, in its day, Pachacamac was surrounded by fertile, productive lands and green fields. The ruins cover an area of several square miles of low rounded hills and narrow valleys, and spread upward on a steep, high, partially artificial pyramidal eminence surmounted by the Temple of the Sun. One can still trace the many well-graded, straight streets, the large plazas, the courts and market-places, the palaces and temples, the innumerable residences, the shops and storehouses. Within the roofless buildings, beside the walls in the open desert, are thousands of graves. For hundreds, perhaps thousands, of years the vast population of the city, as well as hundreds of thousands of pilgrims, died and were buried at Pachacamac, so it is little wonder that the entire spot is an immense necropolis. And as for centuries, scientists, treasure-seekers, curio hunters, vandals and tourists have been excavating and disinterring the mummies, it is not surprising that Pachacamac to-day presents the appearance of a vast charnel-house. Everywhere are scattered mummy-wrappings, human bones, skulls and masses of human hair, as well as broken pottery, odds and ends of textiles, cotton-spindles and other objects cast aside by the seekers after treasure and curios. In many places the skulls and bones are piled in windrows, and one can scarcely walk a dozen yards without treading upon human remains.

From Pachacamac vast quantities of specimens of Incan and pre-Incan handiwork have been obtained, and no one can even guess at the aggregate worth of

gold, silver and other valuables that have been secured from the burials in and about the ruins.   But
as was the case throughout the Incan Empire, the
majority of the inhabitants were poor and possessed
little or nothing in the way of precious metal.   Such
things were reserved for royalty, the priests and the
aristocracy, and only occasionally is a mummy found
which bears golden ornaments.   But before the coming of the Spaniards, Pachacamac itself was fabulously rich in gold.   Pizarro heard tales of the city's
treasures when at Cajamarca in 1522, and it was directly due to these stories that he came to the Rimac
Valley.   At that time the Temple of the Sun, rising
above the city, was fairly filled with gold and silver
in the form of holy vessels, ornaments, idols, images,
decorations, offerings, a golden altar and an immense
golden sun.   Everything of this sort that they could
find, was stolen by the Dons and cast into the melt-
ing-pot, thus robbing the world and science of what
were probably the most priceless archeological
treasures in the history of the world, for the massive golden objects at Pachacamac were largely of
pre-Incan origin and may have dated back to the
first inhabitants of South America.

Pachacamac was not, however, the only city of importance in the vicinity, or near the coast of what is
now Peru.   Everywhere in the Rimac Valley, along
the coastal plain, back in the hills and in every valley
from Chan-Chan to Mollendo and beyond, are the
remains of large, well-built cities; everywhere are
adobe walls, immense mounds, the ruins of villages
and of temples.   Countless more have completely
vanished, the adobe of which they were composed

having disintegrated through the action of the elements; in countless other cases the material has been removed and used for other purposes by the Peruvians.   Also, throughout this entire district there are innumerable cemeteries of vast extent containing millions of graves.   The necropolis at Ancon near Lima is world-famed; between Lima and Callao, near Miraflores, are numbers of immense burial-mounds containing hundreds of thousands of bodies buried in small, cell-like tombs of adobe bricks. At Pueblo Viejo, Punta Piedras, Chancay, Lambayeque, Pimentel, Paramonga and, in fact at or near every settlement on the entire coastal plain, there are extensive cemeteries.

No one can positively say who the people were who dwelt in these ancient cities, cultivated the valleys, and buried their dead in the mounds and graves. That they must have occupied the territory for ages and must have been very numerous is obvious from the number of burials and their stratification.   That they must have been a highly cultured and industrious race is proved by their arts, industries and engineering feats.   Water was carried by canals and aqueducts for hundreds of miles to irrigate the fields; bridges and roads were constructed, stupendous mounds and edifices were erected.   They were experts in the ceramic arts, wove marvelous textiles, worked metal to some extent, and evidently had a complex and highly developed social organization. Possibly they far antedated the Incas and even the Chimus; perhaps they were civilized by the earlier Incas.   But it is obvious that they were of several races or tribes, and to some extent adhered to

their racial customs, even if they were united in
a confederation. The remains show cultural
and racial differences; the types of architecture vary
in different places; and the burial customs were often
distinct even within an area of a few miles. In some
places the dead were interred in tombs in immense
mounds, in others the bodies were buried in the sand
of the desert, in still others the graves were walled or
lined with stones, while in some localities the dead
were placed in stone tombs or even in caves. But
in one respect all were alike. All employed adobe
for building. Not a single stone edifice is known
in the entire district, and not a single stone idol,
image or monument of any size has yet been found.
In the more northerly sections the remains and
artifacts show a distinct Chimu influence; in the
south there are signs of Tiahuánacan influence;
but whether these outside influences were introduced
directly or indirectly it is impossible to say. But we
do know that at the time of the Spanish conquest the
entire area was under Incan domination; that the inhabitants whom the Spaniards found in the Rimac
and other coastal valleys were subjects of the Inca,
and that, in arts, customs and other respects they
were to all intents and purposes Incan.

Inland, in the Andes and on the trans-Andean plateaus and valleys, there are innumerable ruins and
vast cemeteries, proving that these regions also were
inhabited by an immense population for incalculable
ages. But the ruined cities, the walls and the buildings of these areas differ strikingly from those near
the coast, inasmuch as they are all of stone. This
does not necessarily indicate that the people were of

a different race. On the dry, warm, practically rainless coastal area, adobe served every purpose, and was the simplest, most available and cheapest material for building; but in the bleak, cold, Andean regions, where rains are heavy and protection from the sleet and snow is required, adobe would have been worse than useless, and stone was the only available material that would answer. But from other evidences than their buildings there is every reason to think that the coastwise and mountain people were distinct races, although all were consolidated and became one commonwealth under the Incas. Like their predecessors, the Incan people followed out the use of stone in the highlands and adobe in the lowlands; but their stonework was poor, crude and miserable in comparison with that of the pre-Incas. Nowhere else in all the world are there such amazing and inexplicable examples of masonry as are to be found in the pre-Incan ruins about Cuzco, near Lake Titicaca, and elsewhere in the Andean regions of Peru and Bolivia.

Moreover, it is an absolutely unique form of masonry and does not even remotely resemble the stonework of any other known race. This in itself would go far toward proving that the people who erected these cyclopean walls and buildings were of an unknown race. Such an entirely distinct type of building is not evolved nor invented all at once. Stranger yet, as far as is known, there are no remains showing traces of an archaic or evolutionary form of this masonry, as would most certainly have been the case had the art been developed in the district. No cement or mortar was used in this type of construction, and none was needed. The enormous blocks of stone, sometimes weighing more than twenty tons, were cut, faced and fitted so perfectly that even to-day, after the lapse of countless centuries, it is impossible to insert a six-thousandth of an inch gauge between the stones. No two blocks are alike in shape or size, but each is most accurately fitted to those about it. No expert modern mechanic, working with steel tools, the most highly perfected machines, and micrometer gauges, could produce results in metal more minutely accurate. The structures, and each individual block of stone to be used in them, must have been planned and laid out beforehand. It would have been impossible to have fitted the blocks as the artizans proceeded with their labors. No sane man can believe that a twenty-ton stone was pecked here and there, dropped into position, hoisted out and trued and cut over and over again, until a perfect fit was obtained. Even if we can imagine such endless herculean labor being performed, it would have been impossible in many cases owing to the fact that the stones are locked or dovetailed together. Although some of the stones are fairly square or rectangular and with six faces, many are irregular in form, and some have as many as thirty-two angles. The only way in which such complex forms could have been fitted with such incredible accuracy was by cutting each block to extremely fine measurements, or by means of a template, a process which would indicate that these prehistoric people possessed a most thorough and advanced knowledge of engineering and the higher mathematics. Evidently, too, the construction of these stupendous walls was neither very difficult nor

very expensive, for they are everywhere in and about
Cuzco and its vicinity, and often where a roughly
built wall would have served every purpose. In
nearly every case they slope slightly inward toward
the top, and rarely do they show any signs of ornamental or decorative work. So strong and enduring
are these structures that the Dons, despite their utmost efforts, found it impossible to tear them down,
so they made the best of the matter by erecting their
own buildings within or upon the ancient walls. For
this reason the finest examples are still preserved, although often concealed by cheap stucco or masonry.

Ordinarily all of these walls and buildings are referred to as Incan, but in reality the true Incan masonry was of an inferior type. The stones used were
much smaller than those used by the pre-Incans, they
were more carelessly and loosely fitted together, and
not infrequently mortar or cement was used between
them. In many places the later Incans' work covers
the ancient masonry of their predecessors, and in such
cases, where a portion of the more recent masonry
has been removed, the contrast between the two
types is very striking

Beyond doubt, the Incans found many of the pre-
Incan structures in fairly good condition when they
occupied Cuzco and its vicinity, and merely embodied
these in their own buildings. Thus the famed Temple of the Sun at Cuzco, now included in Santo Domingo Church, is always referred to as Incan. But
the most beautiful and remarkable features of this
ancient temple are of typically pre-Incan origin. It
is obvious that the Incans, finding the temple ready
made, repaired it, added to it and made use of it as

their own place of worship. Although the Spaniards transformed the temple to a Christian church,
and added a deal of European embellishment and
adornment to it, yet the greater portion of the structure still remains that of the prehistoric unknown inhabitants of Peru.

Architecturally this Temple of the Sun is one of
the most remarkable buildings in the entire world. It
is built of immense blocks of amazingly fitted stone,
no two of which are exactly alike in size or shape, but
which are so accurately designed and cut that the circular interior with its radii is mathematically and
geometrically perfect. No engineer of our times,
equipped with the most delicate of instruments and
the most modern appliances and mathematical tables,
could excel the work of the long-vanished designers
and artizans who constructed this remarkable temple.

In the days when the Incas held sway this temple
presented a sight which would have made Aladdin's
cave look tawdry by comparison. The walls, outside
and inside, were completely covered with plates of
burnished gold. The gardens were filled with trees,
shrubs and plants of silver and gold. Among the
leaves and branches of precious metals were birds,
animals and insects of gold and silver, and even the
fountains, the tools and the implements of the gar-
dener's trade were of the same metals. But dazzling
and marvelous as was this amazing garden, the interior of the temple was a thousand times more wonderful. Upon one wall, above where the Christian
altar now stands, was an immense sun of massive
gold studded with jewels which flashed and scintillated in the sunlight until the eyes of the marveling

Dons were blinded with their brilliance. Opposite this glorious sun was a huge representation of the moon wrought of polished silver, while about these two chief luminaries were the stars of silver and gold, with an arching rainbow of gold tinted in some remarkable manner to imitate the natural prismatic colors.

Beneath the wondrous image of the sun were seated the mummies of the Incan emperors wrapped in their robes and mantles of tapestry and feathers, their false heads adorned with golden crowns, golden masks representing their features, gold and jeweled ornaments upon their breasts, and with ornate staffs and symbols of office before them. And opposite them beneath the silver moon were the mummies of their queens and princesses, attired in all their most prized robes and richest jewels together with twelve life-sized solid gold statues of the dead Incas. Golden and silver images of deities and mythological beings were on every side. Priceless ceremonial and religious symbols, utensils, vessels and ornaments filled the immense room. Marvelous draperies and textiles covered floor and walls, and gorgeously attired priests offered up prayers and sacrifices to the sun-god.

The twelve golden statues of the deceased Incas, together with many other gold, silver and jeweled ornaments and vessels, including most of the objects from the marvelous garden of the Temple were ordered brought to Cajamarca to ransom Atahualpa. But they never reached their destination. Some were concealed when the Incans heard of Pizarro's treachery and Atahualpa's death, but the greater

portion were hidden by the orders of the Incan
priests who were partizans of Huascar and who
could not see the holy vessels and ornaments of the
temple turned over to the Dons to save the life of
Atahualpa whom they regarded as a usurper. Quite
a number of the hidden objects were found by the
Spaniards, but the twelve golden statues and the
greater part of the objects from the garden have
never been discovered.

Even the hardened Spanish campaigners, satiated
with wonders, glutted with treasure, stood gazing
with incredulous awe when they first entered this
Temple of the Sun. For a space they could not believe their eyes. Before them were greater riches,
more gold than they had ever imagined in their wildest dreams. But they were there to rob and despoil,
not to admire. Ruthlessly the precious symbols were
torn from their places; the regal mummies were
thrown down, hacked to pieces and their regalia and
ornaments torn off. Holy vessels were battered and
smashed. Priceless tapestries were wantonly ripped
to bits and destroyed. Magnificent rugs, and textiles
such as the world had never seen, were cut and hacked
to pieces with swords and daggers, and were used as
wrappings in which to bundle up the golden loot.
Struggling, fighting among themselves, each striving to gain the lion's share of treasure, the mail-clad
soldiers trampled jewels and images, battered and
hammered golden utensils into shapeless forms more
easily carried, and stripped the temple and its
marvelous garden of every vestige of precious
metal and precious stones. Heedless of the beauty,
the art, the incalculable value of their loot, the con-

tents of the temple, the golden plates which had covered its walls, the amazingly wrought trees, birds and other objects in the gardens, were cast into the melting pot and transformed to bullion. Of that vast treasure of the Temple of the Sun, all that remains intact to-day are a few bent and battered plates of thin gold that once formed part of the covering of the outer wall, and which were dropped, trodden into the earth and overlooked by Pizarro's men.

Throughout the immeasurably ancient capital of the Incas, and everywhere throughout the empire as well, it was the same story. Every object of intrinsic value was seized by the Dons. Everything that hinted of paganism and that could be destroyed was destroyed by the priests. Countless palaces, temples and other buildings were torn to pieces to provide material for erecting Spanish churches, the cathedral and other structures.

But the massive walls that had withstood the elements, the earthquakes and the wear and tear of thousands of years were beyond the power of the Spaniards to destroy. By dint of immense labor and hundreds of toiling enslaved Indians they managed to knock holes in them here and there, to pry a few stones loose, and to remove the uppermost tiers of blocks. But the results were not worth the labor and time expended, so the Dons erected their own flimsy, ugly edifices upon the summits of the pre-Incan works or fitted their dwellings, like parasitic growths, within them. But the magnificent walls still remain, hemming in the narrow, dirty, cobbled streets; forming the foundations of rows of squalid huts; rising majestically above offal-strewn corrals and markets; frowning down upon honking motor-cars and padding llamas; enduring, indestructible reminders of the strange civilization that flourished in Peru when Spain was a wilderness and the Spaniards were naked, cave-dwelling savages.

Outside of the city there are even better preserved remains of the Incas and pre-Incas. Overlooking the city from the summit of a high hill, is the famous fortress of Sacsahuamán, built of stone blocks as accurately and carefully fitted as the finest of the temples, but of stupendous size. Even more astonishing is the fortress of Ollantaytambo with its walls built of blocks of stone twelve to eighteen feet in height and six to eight feet square, and yet trued, cut and fitted as precisely as though formed by machinery. Then there is Macchu-picchu, the wonderful fortified city long hidden from the memory of man within the jungles; Viracocha with its gigantic walls; the magnificent palace of Manco-Kapac, and countless other pre-Incan and Incan ruins, all testifying to the almost incredible engineering ability of these ancient races.

Scattered about the country, sometimes upon the hilltops, sometimes in the valleys, are strange round towers of perfectly fitted stones, commonly known as *chulpas*. These structures, which are about thirty feet in height by ten feet in diameter, are mysteries. Although popularly regarded as tombs or burial-towers, and although mummies and many objects have been found in some of them, there is little evidence to prove that they were erected solely to serve as burial-places for the dead. Possibly they were used as watch-towers, or for signaling, or they may have been observatories like the towers of the Mayas.

The pre-Incans and the Incans were well up in astronomy, and the Incans had a perfect calendar similar in many respects to those of the Mayas and Aztecs. The Incan year consisted of twelve *quillas* of thirty days each, with five days added at the end of each year. As the *quillas* were computed from the moon's rotation, instead of from the sun's, and as the monthly moon rotation is completed in three hundred and fifty-four days, eight hours and forty-eight minutes, the Incan months or *quillas* of thirty days, plus the additional five days, brought their year very close to the solar year, and to make it exactly coincide an extra day was added every fourth year, precisely like our system of leap-years. Unlike the Aztecs and the Mayas, who regarded the odd five days as unlucky or evil, the Incans made their five days an occasion for holidays and rejoicing. They were looked upon as days entirely apart from ordinary time, and as so much gained each year,—a sort of extra dispensation granted by the sun-god to enable the hard-working, oppressed people to enjoy themselves for a space until the new year commenced, and they were entirely devoted to merrymaking, to dances and to pleasures.

It was during this period that the drama-opera of *Ollantay* was given, perhaps the most remarkable dramatic and musical composition ever produced by an ancient race. The scenes were laid in and about the prehistoric city of Ollantaytambo. To this day the play is still given by the Peruvian Indians, although not in its complete or original form, and much of its haunting music has been adopted throughout the civilized world. (See Chapter XV.)

As far as is known, the astronomical instruments and devices of the Incans and pre-Incans were of the simplest character. By means of a sun-dial-like arrangement, or *Intihuatana,* consisting of a cone surmounting a large rock on which were cut marks dated as the sun festivals, the sun's course, the hours and all important dates were determined by the position of the shadow cast by the cone-shaped gnomon. For determining the solstices, the equinoxes and many other dates, stone columns were used. These were arranged in four groups of two each and were known as *Pachacta unanchac.* They were set perpendicularly upon high hills, two being placed toward the east and two to the west. By marking the extreme variations of sunrise and sunset, the declination of the sun could be measured, and the solstices determined whenever the sun passed beyond the central pair of columns. Probably the pre-Incans and Incans possessed various other means of obtaining astronomical data; instruments and devices of which we know nothing, and which may have been utterly destroyed by the Spanish priests, who regarded them as devices of the devil, or which may have been lost during the centuries that have passed.

To the Incans the time of the solstices was of the utmost importance, for the Peruvian summer solstice, the first of September, was not only their New Year or "Birth of the Sun" but was also the birthday of the Inca regardless of the actual day of his birth, for, being considered a "son of the sun" his birthday anniversary was coincident with that of the sun itself. The observance of the Incan New Year or Birth of the Sun was the most important and holy ceremonial of the Incan religion, and is graphically described by an Inca prince named Checo who was baptized by the Spanish priests and christened Domingo. At seventy years of age he imparted a great deal of information as to Incan customs to the Viceroy Toledo who was greatly interested in gathering knowledge of Incan history. His description of the ceremony, translated from the old Spanish, is as follows:

"From his palace the Inca was carried in his golden litter or *Juantu,* that was covered with diamonds, turquoise, amethysts, rubies and emeralds, and was lined with the finest robes and pillows of feathers and down, by his bearers and was surrounded by thirty-two guards of the race of the *Lucanas* who claimed the privilege of this honor. He was clothed in rich robes of fine cloth with a wide border of fine embroidery in silver and gold. In his hand he carried the *Champi* of gold, which was an elegant mace in the form of an axe, and was his scepter. His hair was cut short around his neck but for two fingers (plaits) falling by his ears, and was confined by a band called *llauto,* a diadem of bright colors that bore above it two red plumes of the bird *pillco-pichiu* rising above two other plumes of white from the eagle, in two bunches above the forehead. On the left side of the diadem came another royal symbol called *huasca-payalla* that was in the form of a plate of gold set with gems. Covering his ears were oval shells of gold. About his neck was a collar formed of fifty-two emeralds each the size of a pigeon's egg, and from this collar were hung topazes of greatest size that were carved to represent the sun and the moon and the fifty-two phases of the moon. Beside the Inca was his woman and sisters and cousins. With them went the Virgins of the Sun, the chief of the holy men [high priest] the chief of the court of princes, the wise men [council] and governors and lords and officers of the warriors, together with all the nobles, the governors of provinces, the centurions and the chiefs of cities and provinces. The sentries, to the number of two thousand *Cañarias* and two thousand *Chachapoyas,* with their painted wooden shields and garbed in bright-colored ponchos and with great lances, occupied niches, like windows without openings, round about the city, the walls, the Inca's house and the plazas. The great orchestra consisted of three hundred and seventy-five *taquicamayocs* with *pincullus* and *queñas, antaras, pututus, charancos, quepas, huancaras* and *tinyas.* [These instruments were in the nature of flutes, pipes, little organs, guitars, cornets, trumpets and drums.] The music they gave was plaintive and sad. As the sun rose above the mountains of Sallac and Piquicho, where is the castle of Sacsayhuman, it was watched by fifty thousand and more as it moved toward the temple. At sight of its rays, cries and hurrahs of joy arose. At this solemn moment the Inca rose from his litter, and facing the sun, raised his first finger to the height of his mouth. At once a great silence came, and the Inca pronounced the words: *"Capak-inti-illariymin,"* and the multitude in chorus replied: *"Punchao-pacariyrcum,"* which was the chant of the great arrival of the sun of the morning on the day of *Capak-Raymi* when the sun-lord reached nearest to the land and thus told the people of the coming of a new year. Ending the chant, the escort and holy men sang victoriously with the people in chorus, passing the chant from place to place until it resounded from the mountains in its echoes. At the close of the chant, from various parts of the city where they had been already allotted, maidens famed as singers, accompanied by other virgins, sang together five chants to the sun, the moon, the stars, the rainbow and the Inca, the last verses of each song being given by one thousand five hundred acolytes arranged for this solemn day about the temple of Kori-Cancha. The chants ended, the Inca drank with the chief holy man a great drink of chicha from a sacred golden cup called a *pacha* formed to represent the sun and other figures, and from which the chicha ran through a path or gutter to a spout whereof the Inca and the chief holy man of the temple sipped. Then all went within the temple and the Inca made obeisance [or *mucha*] to the gods and to his ancestors, until the rays of the lord of the day struck upon his gold image, whereupon the sacred fire was lighted by the Inca who held in his hand a mirror and reflected the rays upon charred cotton.

"Then from this fire the Virgins of the Sun struck other fires and kindled the sacred fires throughout the temple, and with great shouts the people hurried to light their fires, for since the coming of the night before no light or fire had been left burning in the land. Great rejoicings were made through the day, and in place of water chicha ran from the fountains, and at the plazas and on the streets were great jars of chicha from which all who desired might drink their fill, for this day was the birthday of the Inca and the birth of the sun, the great *Inti,* and the New Year of the people of the land."

One of the greatest obstacles in the way of learning many important matters concerning the Incans and pre-Incans is the fact that, as far as is known, they had no written or recorded language. Many carvings, sculptures and specimens of pottery have been found which, at first sight, appear to bear hieroglyphic or symbolic inscriptions. But most of these, upon scientific examination, prove to be highly con-

ventionalized representations of objects of a purely
decorative character. There are a few, however,
which are difficult to explain on this hypothesis, and
which may prove to be true inscriptions. Notable
among these are the sculptured stones at Sahhuayacu, about one hundred and eighty miles northeast of
Cuzco, in a district probably never under Incan dominion. In one of these there are twenty-four
characters, all but seven of which are repeated two or

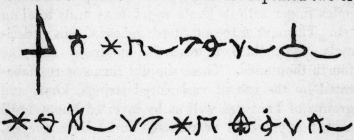

Pre-Incan "Inscription" at Sahhuayacu, Peru.

more times, much as if they were true letters and
formed words. The great trouble is that the same
characters seldom appear in the same sequence or
relation on any two glyphs. Moreover, were the
inscriptions carved by some race possessing a
written language, it is remarkable that so few inscriptions were made. And as identical or similar
characters are not known upon the ruins, monuments
or ceramics of the civilized races of the country, it
would seem more probable that they are of a symbolic or pictographic character and the work of the
savages of the district.

For sending messages and for recording certain
events, the Incas used a complex system of knotted
colored strings or cords called *quipos*. Records of
Imperial property were kept by means of decimal

knots on the *quipos*. Large and small knots of various colors recorded the births, deaths and marriages in each district. Various combinations of knots and colors recorded important events, and a trained corps of men—bookkeepers, we might say—were kept busy making and translating the *quipo* records. The *quipo* owed its origin to an evolution of the human hand, the strings representing the fingers and the knots the joints. The thinnest cord represented the index finger with its knots or joints as units totaling ten. The next or second finger indicated tens or decimals. The third represented hundreds, and the fourth thousands. These simpler forms were elaborated by the use of varicolored strings, knots and groups of knots, as well as by inverted knots, until almost any record or message could be conveyed. For keeping accounts or recording business transactions special strings were used. These were known as *hankos* and *chaaras*. Credit accounts were kept on the *hankos,* which were often of pearls or gems, while debit accounts were kept on the *chaaras,* usually of seeds, shells or beads. The *hankos* consisted of one hundred pearls or other objects strung decimally on a cord with a pendent string carrying nine pearls or units. The *chaara* was similarly arranged. In effect these were much like the abacus. Another method consisted of a wooden tray divided into ten compartments. Ten pebbles in a compartment signified one hundred, and by the simple method of taking pebbles from a compartment on the credit side of the tray and depositing them in the corresponding compartment on the debit side, accounts of almost any size could be accurately kept.

'Although nominally an absolute monarchy, yet the Incan Government was, in many respects, republican. In addition to the Inca, there were the tribunal of princes or *Apu-Auquis,* composed of men of royal blood, and the cabinet of four wise men presided over by a president or *Apu-Tucuy-Ricac,* who acted as chairman and respresentative. In Cuzco these were appointed by the Inca; but in the outlying districts they were elected annually by the inhabitants, the nominees being men who already had been in the service of the Inca. Any unanimous decision of the four was absolute and could be revoked or revised only by the *Apu-Auquis,* or tribunal of princes. In addition to the central federal government, each district or colony had its own mayor or governor, *Curaca,* and each village or town had its own prefect or *Suyuyoc,* as well as its local council or board of aldermen known as *Auquis,* who acted as a sort of grand jury, court and governing body all in one. The Incan princes were commonly known as *Huancos,* or "Golden ears," from the fact that they wore gold ear-coverings. This custom had an interesting origin. A son of the Inca Pacha-Cutic lost one of his ears during a desperate battle and, in order to hide the mutilation, wore gold plates or shells over the ears. To commemorate the prince's bravery, and in order that he might not be conspicuous, the other princes adopted the gold ear-coverings, and they became recognized as an insignia of nobility.

The Incas, and their descendants of to-day, were, like most Indians, extremely superstitious and believed implicitly in omens and signs. Stubbing one's toe against a bit of fallen masonry signified that one's wife was untrue. A vulture, alighting over a door and spreading its wings to the sun, was a sign of an accident to the owner of the house. A fox or a snake crossing a road in front of a traveler presaged an unlucky journey. Bringing an amulet from a distant spot was an omen presaging the appearance of a new variety of potato. The Incans also believed that trepanning a person's skull always resulted in a new variety of potato, and, oddly enough, there is no other part of the world where there are so many varieties of potatoes as in Peru, and nowhere else was trepanning so widely practised. In Incan days, if the current of the Desaguadero River flowed from south to north, it was thought to indicate an uprising of the Karanca or Kallaca tribe. The tribute demanded of the Uros and Kellay-Senka tribes consisted of a species of parasitic insect prized as a delicacy by the Incas. If this tribute was not punctually paid it was deemed a sure sign of an approaching uprising among the Karas in the south. If more cocks than hens were hatched from eggs the approaching end of the world was foretold.

Sorcerers, of course, flourished, and many if not most of the priests claimed to be able to forecast events for years to come. No doubt many of these men were hypnotists and charlatans, but it is an indisputable fact that many of their prophecies *did* come true. If we are to believe the statements and writings of the Spaniards, the Incans possessed certain powers which are inexplicable. According to innumerable observers and historians, as well as Incan traditions, the Incan races had an uncanny and seemingly supernatural ability for conveying and receiving accurate information over long distances. If we are to credit the apparently unvarnished accounts, it was as remarkable in its way as wireless telegraphy or mental telepathy. An Indian could and often did know exactly how many men or horses were approaching long before they could be seen or heard; he could tell where or in what direction a friend or an enemy was traveling, and he could perform many more equally mysterious feats.

Even to-day some of the living descendants of these people possess the same weird power. According to my friend, Dr. Juan Durand, who has devoted many years to a study of Incan history, traditions and life, he personally has witnessed such feats. One night, while at an Indian hut at Raco, the Indian owner placed his ear to the floor and told Doctor Durand the exact number of men in a platoon of soldiers who were passing at a distance of more than three kilometers from the spot. Another Indian at Panao, without rising from his couch, stated the number of men on foot and the number of mounted men traveling on a distant road, and even told the order in which they moved and the direction in which they were going.

In 1896, while between Cayumba and Monzon, Doctor Durand's Indian carriers deserted; but without faltering or hesitating, other Indians gave the exact route the fugitives had taken and followed them for eight days across deserts, mountains and rivers where there was no sign of a trail or spoor, often cutting across country, and found them exactly where they had foretold.

Personally I have never witnessed demonstrations

of this sort, but I have repeatedly visited Indians in the most remote spots only to find that they expected me, that they had full information regarding my party and equipment, and had known these facts long before I had arrived. And I have often been informed of events by the Indians when they could not, by any possibility, have received word by any ordinary means, and later I have always found their information absolutely correct. According to historians and to Doctor Durand, the Peruvian tribes claim that they are able to receive such information of distant events by their ability to "read" the barking and howling of their dogs, and that this knowledge of the dogs' language thus enables them to receive information and full details of matters of which, otherwise, they would know nothing. In all probability this is merely an explanation to satisfy the curiosity of the white man, and the real solution still remains a mystery.

But it is no more of a mystery than how the pre-Incans cut their cyclopean stone blocks, how they transported their monoliths over long distances, or how they accomplished many other of their feats. In several places in Peru, and even in Bolivia, there are immense monuments and images formed of a stone which, as far as is known, does not occur within hundreds of miles of their present sites, the nearest deposits of the rock being in Ecuador, fully fifteen hundred miles distant. One such monolith is Saycunin or La Piedra Cansada near Ollantay. This immense stone, known also as El Monolito Abandonado (the Abandoned Monolith) measures nearly seventeen feet in length, ten feet in width and three

feet in thickness.* It is of a peculiar rock identical
with the formation about Chimborazo in Ecuador,
and which, it is claimed, does not exist anywhere in
the vicinity of Ollantay. According to the Indians
and to Incan tradition, the Saycunin was quarried at
Quito, and the monolith, saddened at being carried
so far from home, wept blood which still adheres to
it, (it is marked with a red piroxene oxidization) and
at last exclaimed: "Saycunin! I am weary!" At
this manifestation of its supernatural character, the
cacique, Urcon, dropped dead, and the stone was left,
abandoned by the terrified Indians, at the spot where
it still rests about a mile north of Ollantay.

Of course this is a purely fanciful and allegorical
myth invented by the Indians or their ancestors of
Incan days to account for the immense stone with its
blood-like stains lying by the roadside. As a matter
of fact, there are several similar monoliths of the
same material which also were abandoned in the vicinity. But there is no denying that they are of a stone
unknown even to the Indians of the district, but
identical with formations in Ecuador. Possibly the
pre-Incans who cut these huge stones knew of a near-
by quarry which has not been rediscovered, or perhaps they exhausted the supply of that particular
mineral. But there may be a basis of truth in the
ancient legend, and it would not be beyond the
bounds of possibility that these immense monoliths
actually were cut in distant Ecuador and dragged
overland to Peru. It would have been a herculean

---

*The largest stone idol recorded was that of the Willca-Huaman which was
over fifty feet in length by twelve feet in diameter. This was destroyed
by the Jesuit priests, and it is recorded that it required thirty men working
steadily for three days to reduce it to fragments.

task, it is true, a task that would have required many years to accomplish, and yet it would have been no more difficult, no more astonishing than many of the feats which we know these ancient Peruvians actually accomplished.

Among these was the construction of the marvelous Incan road, a splendid highway stretching from Quito, Ecuador, to southern Chile, a distance of over three thousand miles in a direct line. No race, not even the Romans, ever equaled this feat of prehistoric road-building. The highest ranges of the mighty Andes; the deepest, most impassable canyons, the most fearful precipices, the widest deserts, the snow-capped peaks and the foaming torrents were treated as though non-existent. Vast abysses were spanned by suspension bridges, their immense cables of fiber and hair ropes fastened in holes cut through solid rock. Gorges were filled with masonry to form immense causeways. Mountains and cliffs were pierced by tunnels which are still in use. The loftiest ranges were surmounted by the most perfectly computed gradients and hairpin curves, and throughout much of its length the roadway was paved and surfaced with asphalt, and to this day some portions of it are still used as a motor highway. At intervals side roads branched off to east and west as far as the Amazonian jungle and the seacoast. Here a second "King's Highway" ran north and south along the shore.

At regular distances of about twenty miles were rest-houses or stations for messengers, while every forty miles there were "Imperial Inns." These served as storehouses for food, supplies and equip-

ment for the army or for relief of villages in case of
famine; as eating-places for the army when on the
march; and as stopping-places for the Inca when
traveling. There was also a series of sentry stations,
watch-towers and forts, as well as a system of signal
fires or lights by means of which the men on watch
could transmit messages from one terminus of the
road to the other in an incredibly short time. At the
time of the revolt of the Caras at Quito, word was
sent by means of these signals, and news of the uprising was received in Cuzco four hours after the rebel-
lion broke out. One of the duties of the watchers at
these beacons was to signal an eclipse of the moon.
The Incans believed that during eclipses the moon
was suffering the agonies of childbirth and, as soon
as the signal of an approaching eclipse was sent out,
everybody beat drums and shouted prayers and sup-
plications to aid the planet in her trouble.

Throughout the entire length of the road there
were mile-posts showing the distance to the next rest-
house, and transportation over the road was as rapid
as over the railways to-day. Fresh fish caught on
the coast reached Cuzco within thirty hours—six
hours sooner than by way of the Mollendo-Cuzco
Railway (Southern Railroad, of Peru). From Lake
Urubamba, fish caught in the morning reached the
Incan capital the same afternoon, and the fruits and
vegetables of the coastal districts reached Cuzco within fifteen hours.

In their ceramic arts these races reached a high development, but as a rule the true Incan pottery is
far more utilitarian than artistic, as might be expected of a communistic civilization wherein industry

and art were regulated and controlled by law, and individual talent and genius counted for nothing. But that the Incan people were not lacking in artistic temperament, inventive genius, dexterity and imagination is abundantly proved. In their later years, a short time before and after the Spanish conquest, the Incas developed a remarkable and unique art in woodwork. Cups, vessels, utensils, and many other objects were highly and beautifully embellished with colors applied like lacquer or enamel. Even to-day, after a lapse of centuries, the colors upon these are bright and fresh. Chemicals have little if any effect upon the pigments used, and they resist the action of all ordinary known solvents. No one has yet been able to learn the secret of their composition or to duplicate them, and we may consider the work as a true lost art.

Moreover, even if the later Incas were not noteworthy as pottery makers, their textiles were wonderful, although the true Incan textiles never equaled or approached those of the pre-Incans. Many of these are more finely woven than would be possible on any machine-loom to-day, and examples are known in which there are three hundred threads to the inch. The types and weaves of these textiles are practically numberless. They vary all the way from the heaviest, coarsest blankets, rugs and ponchos to the finest, most delicate fabrics as thin and soft as silk. Many were of the tapestry class, others were tied or knotted, and others were direct warp-and-woof weaving. The dyes used have never been equaled, and to-day, after having been buried for centuries in the desert sand and in stone tombs, the colors on these remarkable fabrics are as pure, clear and bright as on the day they were first woven.

In patterns and designs these ancient textiles vary endlessly. Usually they are of a more or less geometrical type with human and animal figures, flowers and other forms represented in a rather "cubist" manner; but magnificent, graceful, curved and involved patterns and scrolls are not unusual. A peculiar feature of a great majority of the pre-Incan textiles is the predominance of the "six-unit" type of design. In these every sixth figure in the pattern is a repetition, the key-design consisting of certain distinct forms which are thus repeated over and over again, number one becoming number six, number two number seven, and so on. But as the coloring may vary to almost any extent in every figure, and may never be repeated, the design appears to be endlessly varied until it is carefully analyzed.

Some of the finest specimens of these textiles have been obtained from the Island of the Sun in Lake Titicaca, where they were found enclosed in a remarkable stone chest cut from a single block of rock. Here, where Incan tradition says that Manco-Kapac and Mama-Ocllo first appeared, there are remains of two distinct cultures. One of these is a primitive inferior type known as the Chulipa while the other is a highly advanced Cuzco form. Hence there is reason to think that the pre-Incan civilization actually had its beginning in this district, and that there is a groundwork of truth in the Incan legend, even if the chronology is at fault.

Recent investigations indicate that this allegorical myth of Manco-Kapac being the first Inca owed its inception to a confusion of names and personages. Among the folk tales and legends of the Peruvians there is frequent mention of Wira-Kocha (the Creator of the Lake) as the semisupernatural being who was responsible for the cyclopean architecture of the pre-Incas. His divine power was supposedly derived from the Kuntur Ticsi (Conder God) and as Kuntur-Ticsi-Wira-Kocha he was venerated as a deity. But he had no connection whatever with the eighth Inca who assumed the name of Wira-Kocha.

Although the Incans and pre-Incans are commonly referred to as sun-worshipers, the religion of the earlier race was distinct from that of the Incan people of later years. The pre-Incan supreme God or Creator is almost invariably represented as a puma or jaguar, more or less humanized, and surrounded by symbols of divine power. Usually these consist of condors, jaguars, fishes and snakes, the first three being symbolic of the god's dominion over air, earth and sea, while the serpents are symbolic of the sun's rays and indicate the god's dominion over heaven. It was not until the reign of Huayna-Kapac, the eleventh Inca that the later sun-worship was fully established, and even then the pre-Incan religion persisted, especially at Pachacamac and at other ancient holy cities.

The Incan sun-god was a being who suffered and died at the time of solar eclipses, but was reborn each time, and he was thought to be subject to a supreme divinity known as Pacha-Kamac or the Creator of the Universe, whose abode was *hanak-pachac* or heaven. The Incas also believed in a hell or *haek-pachac* presided over by a devil called Supay. They believed in a resurrection and an after-life, with a heavenly existence as a reward for being good, and everlasting tortures in the nether world for sinners. Unlike the Aztecs and the Mayas, they had comparatively few minor deities or gods, those that they believed in being in the nature of sprites, dryads, fairies and supernatural beings rather than deities. The similarity of the Incan religion and the Christian faith is most remarkable. Just as we believe in a supreme God, and in Christ His son who suffered and died and reappeared, so the ancient Peruvians believed in a Creator and a divine humanized son. And just as we worship both God and Christ, so the Incans worshiped their Pacha-Kamac and their sun-god, or Inti. We may go even further and compare the Incas themselves, who claimed to be direct descendants of the sun-god, to the various modern kings and emperors who claim "divine right" to reign and are referred to as "heaven-born."

And when the eighth Inca, whose real name was Socsoc, assumed the name of Wira-Kocha, it was because he attributed his power and his triumphs to divine intervention, and wished publicly and officially to proclaim and perpetuate his faith in this manner. But it is very easy to understand how the Indians, confusing the Inca Wira-Kocha with the divinity Wira-Kocha, built up an imaginative and allegorical mythological tale in which they traced the genealogy of their rulers to the sun-god himself. As a matter of fact, the genealogy of the Incas, from Manco-Kapac to Huascar is well known and is as follows:

INCA NAME OR TITLE	ACTUAL NAME
1 Manco-Kapac Inca	Panaca Chima
2 Sinchi-Roca Inca	Panaca Raurac
3 Lloque-Yupanqui Inca	Panaca Hahuac
4 Mayta-Kapac Inca	Panaca Usca Mayta
5 Kapac-Yupanqui Inca	Panaca Apuc Mayta
6 Inca-Roca Inca	Panaca Willca Quirau
7 Yahuar-Huakac Inca	Panaca Aucac
8 Wira-Kocha Inca	Panaca Socsoc
9 Inca-Yupanqui Inca*	Panaca Iñaca
9 Pacha-Cutic Inca*	Panaca Hatun Iñaca
10 Tupac-Yupanqui Inca	Panaca Kapac Tupa
11 Huayna-Kapac Inca	Panaca Tumi Pampa
12 Cusi-Huascar Inca	Panaca Huaycac
13 Atahualpa Inca	half-brother of Cusi-Huascar Inca

NAME OF EMPRESS	NAME AS PRINCESS
Mama-Ocllo	Huaco
Mama-Kora	Chimpu
Mama-Chahua	Wuarqui
Mama-Cuca	Ichi Urma
Mama-Kori Illpay	Kahuac
Mama-Micay	Cusi Chimpu
Mama-Chicya	Ipa Huaco
Mama-Runtu Kayan	Kayan
Mama-Ipa Huarcu	Ipa Huarcu
Mama-Anac Huarcu	Anac Huarcu
Mama-Chimpu Ocllo	Chimpu Ocllo
Mama-Pahua Ocllo	Pahua Ocllo
Mama-Chuqui Llantu	Cantar Chuqui

But whether this royal line actually descended from the immeasurably more ancient rulers of the

---

*Twin brothers who ruled together.

pre-Incans and the semimythical Wira-Kocha, or whether they were a different stock who erected a new civilization upon the remains of a much greater one, we cannot say and we may never know.

PRONUNCIATION OF INCAN (QUICHUA) NAMES

Although the Quichua (Incan) words and names I have used are spelled phonetically, it is practically impossible to convey the exact sounds and pronunciations by means of our alphabet, and a few words of explanation are necessary in order to give an idea of the Quichua pronunciation of sounds as represented by our nearest equivalents in letters.

All vowels have the broad, soft Spanish sounds.

Double *l* (*ll*) should have almost the Spanish sound of *elyay* with a slightly more distinct *l* than in Spanish.

K is an explosive guttural approximating *k-y!* Thus the word *ako* is pronounced more as if spelled *aky-o* or even *aq-qo*. At times a slightly softer or less guttural *k* is used, and this I have indicated by substituting the letter *c* which should have about the same sound as our own *k*.

S has the normal English sound except when final, in which case it is pronounced as *ys*. In the Quichua, the terminal *s* does *not* denote the plural, but means "named" or "called," as *huara-s*. But for simplicity and to avoid confusion, I have as a rule employed *s* to denote a plural, thus slightly Anglicizing the words. For example: the plural in Quichua is denoted by adding the word *cuna* or many, and hence the plural of *chasqui* would be *chasqui-cuna*. But for our purposes it may just as well be written as *chasquis*.

Qui and *Que* have Spanish sounds of *key, kay,* etc.

O always has the English sound, as does *u*, and these

two letters, as well as *e* and *i,* may be interchanged or transposed without affecting the meaning or correct pronunciation of a word, owing to the fact that in Quichua these four vowels are scarcely pronounced and vary in different localities. Thus *Quichua* may be *Quechua; cuca* is the same as *coca; quipo* or *quepu* is equally correct. *Huanacu* or *Huanaco* does equally well; *Apachita* is the same as *apacheta* and *quincha* may be spelled *quencha.*

J and *h* are practically silent or slightly aspirated. As, during the Colonial period, the Spanish influence was very strong, certain words, which, in pure Quichua, begin with a pure vowel sound, have now become universally pronounced as if spelled with the Spanish *j.* Thus the word *amuy* can only be expressed in its present form as *hamuy* or *jamuy.*

W and *v* are so much alike that they are interchangeable and, as a matter of fact, their pronunciation is far better expressed by the Spanish *hui* or *hue* than by either of the consonants.

Finally, we must remember that the Quichua tongue of the Incan Empire was by no means a pure language, but was more or less a conglomerate combination of many dialects. Hence it varies greatly in different localities, each tribe having adopted many of its own words and names, and pronouncing the Quichua as they would their tribal dialect. In the south the Quichua is strongly influenced by the Aimará, in the north it contains many words of the Chimu or Yungas, and in the trans-Andean regions of Peru it is combined with the Huanca tongue. Often, too, many Spanish words have been adopted into the Quichua. Probably the purest Quichua is used in the vicinity of Cuzco.

CHAPTER XV

THE CHILDREN OF THE SUN

WITH the murder of Atahualpa by the Spaniards, the Incan Empire came to an end. Cuzco was occupied by the Dons, looted of everything of value, and made the headquarters for raiding-parties which carried death, destruction and inhuman brutalities far and near. Wherever the Spaniards found a city, a temple or a burial-place containing gold it was robbed, desecrated and wantonly destroyed. Thousands of the peaceful, industrious and docile Incan people were subjected to unspeakable tortures, forced into slavery, or ruthlessly killed. From central Chile to northern Ecuador, and from the Pacific to the head-waters of the Amazon, the country literally ran with blood. Only the valiant Mapuches of Araucania, and the wild and savage tribes of the Montaña forests were able to hold their own against the invaders. The wonder is that any of the Incan races survived.

How many thousands succumbed to hardships, hunger and abuse, as they toiled as slaves in mines and elsewhere, will never be known. How many thousands were transported to other lands or were butchered outright, no one can say. Yet they not only managed to survive, but they maintained their racial integrity, remained to a large extent of pure blood, and even retained their arts, customs, habits, language and social organization. Indeed, with the overthrow of Spain's power in America, and the slight betterment of their condition, they rapidly increased in numbers, until to-day over seventy-five per cent. of the total population of Bolivia, over sixty per cent. of the population of Peru, and probably seventy per cent. of the population of Ecuador are Indians of unmixed blood who are direct descendants of the Tahuantisuyo or "Children of the Sun," as the Incan people called themselves.

While all have traits in common, and while all retain many of the characteristics of the Incan organization, they keep their tribal distinctions and vary considerably in different sections of the land. Throughout Peru, and over a large part of Ecuador, they speak the Quichua of the Incans, and are commonly classed as Quichua, while the majority of those in Bolivia speak the ancient Aimará tongue and are ordinarily called Aimarás. But among both the so-called Quichuas and the Aimarás there are a great many tribes and sub-tribes, the precise number and names of these being known only to the Indians themselves.

Among the better-known tribes of the Aimarás are the Collas, inhabiting the country east of Lake Titicaca; the Chutas about Cochabamba, and the Yungas of eastern Bolivia. The more noteworthy of the Quichua tribes are the Huancas in the district about Huancayo and Ayacucho; the true Quichuas about Cuzco, and the Monteros of the country west of Lake Titicaca, as well as the Chimus about Trujillo and the "Incas" near Oruro, Bolivia.

Although a person familar with these Indians can

distinguish members of the various tribes at a glance, to the average man all appear alike. Owing to the forced mixture and amalgamation of tribes when under Incan rule, there are no sharp physical distinctions between the tribes, or even between those of Quichua and those of Aimará stock. Broadly speaking, the Quichuas are shorter, lighter-colored and with more prominent cheek-bones and foreheads, and longer heads than the Aimarás. The average Quichua is more of a yellow than a brown, and has fairly thick lips, often a straggling beard and mustache, and is frequently of a pronounced Mongolian type. But the Quichua characters vary greatly in different localities and among different tribes. Many of those near the coasts have dark-brown skins, round heads and broad noses. Near Arequipa there is a small tribe with black skin, sharply aquiline noses and thin lips. The Huancas are often pale olive with finely chiseled features, while enormous, hooked noses are not unusual. As a rule the Aimará is a bronze or brown in color and is taller, more slender and with a sharper nose and more receding forehead than the Quichua. But the Aimarás vary almost as much as do the Quichuas. Many have well-developed beards, many are strikingly Polynesian or Malaysian in appearance, and gray or light hazel eyes and brownish-black hair are not uncommon. Both races, when dwelling at considerable altitudes, have rosy-red cheeks, often actually purple, but owing to their lighter skins the Quichuas appear to have redder cheeks than the Aimarás.

In temperament the two races are totally different. The Quichua is invariably docile, quiet, peaceable, industrious and firmly wedded to the soil, whereas the Aimará is inclined to be surly, aloof, turbulent, quarrelsome, restless and is a husbandman only by force of circumstances. But the most interesting feature of both races is that they live and dress in practically the same way as did their ancestors in Incan days, and carry on the same arts, professions and industries. Though the costumes differ in details in various localities and according to tribes, they are, aside from these minor variations, the same everywhere, and as a whole are the same as in Incan days. The man's costume consists of trousers or drawers of heavy, hand-woven woolen cloth, a shirt, sometimes a jacket and even a vest, a poncho, a tightly fitting woolen cap, and sandals. He may or may not wear a hat, which may vary from an Indian-made felt affair, patterned after the hat of the white man, to a highly ornate and decorative head-piece precisely like those shown in the contemporaneous pictures of the Indians in Incan days.

The women wear innumerable bright-colored petticoats and blouses, quite obviously patterned after the corresponding garments of their white sisters, but they still retain the short poncho, the gay-colored woven belt, the embroidered gauntlets, the *manta* and the beautifully colored woven square of cloth which, knotted about the neck, forms a bag-like receptacle in which is carried anything and everything from foodstuffs to infants.

There is probably no hardier, more patient or more industrious race than these Andean Indians. Living, as they do, in a cold, forbidding, bleak and almost sterile land; accustomed for innumerable generations to hardships, unending toil and the barest necessities of life; descended from ancestors who were oppressed by the Incas and enslaved by the Span-iards, and treated more like beasts than human beings by the whites of to-day, these Children of the Sun live and seem contented and happy under conditions which would be impossible for any other race.

Wherever there is a tiny patch of soil, no matter how poor, it is intensively cultivated. Every tiny valley is tilled, every hillside and mountain where there is a scraping of soil is terraced with farms and gardens from base to summit. And where nothing can be grown the Indians graze their flocks of sheep and their herds of llamas and alpacas. Their homes are mere hovels of stones or adobe, their beds a few hides or a thin layer of straw upon the bare earth. Their food is frozen potatoes, barley and tough dried meat, and their fuel, llama dung or the dried *yaretta* plant. Here and there the Indians may be seen culti-vating their land with steel hoes, but ninety times out of a hundred they plow with a crooked stick and use a short-handled, awkward, heavy-bladed hoe exactly like those of Incan and pre-Incan days, to use which the Indian has to bend almost double. Never do these Indians waste a moment of their lives. From daylight until dark the men and boys labor in the fields or drive their llamas to market laden with the few products of their industry. From daylight to dark and later the women and girls tend the flocks, weave ponchos, blankets and cloth, or help the men in the fields, and wherever they may be, whatever they may be doing, the women, unless their hands are otherwise occupied, are ceaselessly, constantly spinning wool into thread by means of primitive spindles. The only breaks in their monotonous, hopeless lives are the weekly trips to market, and often this trip entails a long and weary journey across mountains and deserts for fifty to one hundred miles or more.

As mentioned in another chapter, the old Incan custom of each village or settlement being confined to one industry still prevails to large extent, and the inhabitants of two neighboring villages will take the products of their labor for many miles to a market and there exchange with one another. Upon these trips, and whenever the Indians are traveling or working, they constantly chew the coca leaves. When masticated with a bit of lime or wood ash a small amount of cocaine is produced, and this serves to allay hunger and weariness and enables the Indians to endure hardships and to cover distances that would be impossible under any other conditions. It is not unusual for an Indian to carry a load of two hundred pounds for twenty to fifty miles across the highest mountains without apparent fatigue, and in Cuzco and other cities the Indian porters may often be seen trotting along the streets and bending under the load of a piano or an immense packing-box of machinery or other goods.

In temperament the Andean Indian, especially the Quichua, is quiet and sentimental, and gives the casual observer the impression of being sad, depressed and hopeless. Considering the endless centuries during which these people were ground down, oppressed and brutalized, it would not be surprising if they had become pessimists. But, as a matter of fact, they are far from depressed or hopeless. At the times of fiestas and dances, on Saints' days and market days, they are gay, happy and enjoy life to the utmost. To be sure, their utmost consists largely of gossiping, dancing and getting drunk on the vile rum of the traders and unprincipled shopkeepers of the towns. But fortunately these Indians seldom become boisterous, disorderly or quarrelsome when under the influence of alcohol. They become unusually gay, dance and sing, talk a bit loudly and thickly, and in the end fall asleep. Fortunately for them the women usually remain sober and look after their helpless menfolk. Often several women may be seen dragging and helping some staggering, wabbly-legged fellow toward his distant home. If he is too far gone, their lord and master may be uncere-moniously packed on to a burro or llama and carried off like a sack of meal. But it cannot be denied that their history of ceaseless oppression has left them with a heritage of sadness. Their music is always of a plaintive, wailing character and they are fond of depressing rather than cheerful pictures, stories and songs. But their hard life and harder past have not made them either callous or hard-hearted. On the contrary they are very kind and are excessively fond of their families, their homes and even of their live stock. Very seldom will an Indian kill a fowl or any domestic animal for his own use, and if the stranger purchases such he must buy it alive and do the slaughtering himself out of the Indian's sight. In fact, if the Indian desires a fowl, a pig or any other creature for food, he will travel a long distance and trade or purchase it from some one else, even though he may own plenty of live stock himself.

As in prehistoric days, every creature is supposed to possess a spirit or soul, and each has its own special fiesta day. Originally, no doubt, these feast days of the various domestic fowls and quadrupeds were dedicated to Incan or pre-Incan divinities. But with their veneer of Christianity, the Indians nowadays have adopted the days of Catholic Saints as the feast days for their domestic creatures. On these days the animals, to whom the day is dedicated, are washed, brushed, decorated with ribbons and ornaments, and a dance and feast are held in their honor. As the llamas are the most important beasts of all, it is natural that they should be treated with the greatest respect and should have the greatest fiestas. To the Indians the llama is like a member of the family. Every attention is shown him, he is tenderly cared for, decorated with bells, beautifully woven trappings and ribbons, and if he dies or is killed the Indians are inconsolable and mourn his loss as they would the loss of a child.

The religion of these Indians is a strange mixture of Christianity and sun-worship. On nearly every hut one may see a cross, but invariably, adjoining the symbol of the Christian church or somewhere near it, is the Incan sun. Although the rites of the Catholic Church are meticulously followed, and children are baptized and christened with Spanish names, and although mass and confessions are always attended, still the Indians cling in their hearts to the religion of their ancestors. Just how much actual faith they have in Christianity, and how much of their devotion to the Church is to satisfy the priests and for the sake of personal benefits and protection, it is difficult to say. But it is certain that they feel a lingering doubt as to the efficacy of the white man's religion and believe in playing safe by holding to the religion of their forefathers as well. In many places they always carry images of their own gods with them when they go to church, and the age-old ceremonials and rites of their race are still kept up, although nowadays they are held upon the Holy Days of the Catholic Church.

Yet few of them have any clear idea of the religion and the beliefs of the Incans, or possess real traditions of their past, and few of their caciques or chiefs are of royal Inca blood. Here and there one finds an individual or a family, even an entire village or community, claiming direct descent from the Incas, and near Oruro in Bolivia the members of a small tribe of Quichua stock call themselves Incas. Also, throughout Peru and Bolivia, there are certain individuals and families with enormous hooked noses commonly known as the "Inca nose" and whose possessors claim to be of royal blood. Unquestionably there must be many hundreds, perhaps thousands of these Indians in whose veins flows blood of the Incas, and there are a few Indians who are well known to be lineal descendants of Atahualpa or Huascar. One of these is recognized as such by many of the Bolivian tribes, another is employed in the Lima Country Club, but as a rule the Indians recognize no authority save that of their own caciques and the national government officials.

Though the present-day Indians do not approach the high quality of the textile and ceramic arts of their ancestors, still their textiles excel those of all other American races, not even excepting the Navajos of our Southwest. Woven from wool, llama hair or alpaca upon the crudest of hand-looms, their cloth, rugs, blanklets and ponchos are more durable, more beautiful and better in every way than anything yet produced by machinery. Formerly only vegetable and mineral dyes were used, but, most regrettably, aniline dyes are now utilized to larger extent. In their patterns and designs the Indians follow the motifs of their Incan and pre-Incan ancestors, even using the "six-unit" system in many cases. As a rule the patterns are combinations of various geometrical designs with human, bird and animal figures, together with the representations of the ancient deities. The Andean goose, the condor, the llama and the jaguar, all prominent in Incan and pre-Incan mythology, are common motifs, and often one finds the sun-god, the condor-headed god and other semihuman mythological beings embodied in the designs.

As already mentioned, certain villages are devoted exclusively to the manufacture of certain things. The inhabitants of one may spin or card wool, those of another may weave nothing but rugs, those of another may produce only ponchos; still others may devote themselves to woodwork; those of another to rawhide articles, those of still another may turn out pottery and nothing else, and so on. In many cases the people do not even weave the rugs, blankets and ponchos for their own use, but depend upon purchasing or trading them from others, though as a rule a certain amount of textile work is done in every community. About Cuzco, the Indians are primarily agricultural, and few of the women know how to use a loom, whereas about Huancayo and Ayacucho weaving is the leading industry.

In their ceramics these Indians have sadly degenerated in most places, and the modern ware, with few exceptions, is coarse and far from attractive, although following to some extent the old Incan and pre-Incan forms. About Trujillo, the descendants of the Chimus still make pottery vessels in effigy forms; portrait jars are common in several localities; in the vicinity of Cochabamba and La Paz much of the modern pottery follows Tiahuánaco forms and decorative motifs, and in the neighborhood of Sicuani in Peru the Quichuas produce very beautiful pottery with a high glaze, but unfortunately imitate European forms and designs.

Like most Indians, both the Quichuas and Aimarás are wonderful imitators, and are able to reproduce almost any object they see and examine. Working entirely by hand and with the simplest and crudest of tools, these Indians manufacture shoes, boots, hats, harness, furniture, musical instruments, toys and innumerable other articles which find a ready sale in the cities.

The Indians, however, are by no means confined to their own arts and crafts. Practically all labor in Bolivia and Peru is performed by Indians. They are the miners, artizans, mechanics, household servants, locomotive engineers, conductors, sailors, laborers, drovers, herders, and in fact are represented in every trade and profession. Without the Indians, the countries could not exist, and should the Indians refuse to work or strike *en masse,* business would come to a standstill, not a wheel would turn, and the inhabitants would starve to death.

President Leguia of Peru said, in a recent conversation with me:

"The Peruvians [and the Bolivians also] must learn that the Indians are the most important people in the country from an economic view-point. Without them nothing can be accomplished and the future prosperity and progress of Peru [and Bolivia] will depend largely upon the welfare of the Indians."

At present they are little more than slaves in the countries they once owned and ruled. But they are by no means lacking in intelligence, and, given proper living conditions, fair treatment, an even chance and an education, they are capable of rising to any height, as is proved by the many famous and prominent men of pure Indian blood in South America. Among their numbers are lawyers, artists, scientists, generals, merchant princes, bankers, statesmen; men of every calling and profession, even presidents of republics, and it would not be at all surprising if ere long descendants of the Incans should again rule the lands where dwell the Children of the Sun.

In the foregoing chapter (Chapter XIV) I have mentioned the musical talents of the Incan races, and, have referred to the drama of *Ollantay,* a classic of the Indians, which has been copied and borrowed by many of the modern composers.

Much of the Incan and pre-Incan music has never been written or printed, but is played by the Indians by ear. The favorite instrument of the present-day Quichuas and Aimarás is the *queña* or Incan flute, made either from a bone, a hollowed piece of wood or a natural reed. Pan's-pipes, flageolets and trumpets of cows' horns are also used as solo instruments, while the "bands" consist of drums, horns, flutes, Pan's-pipes, rattles, mandolin-like instruments with the body formed from the carapace of the armadillo, guitars, and at times native harps. A remarkable instrument, used by some of the Aimará tribes of Bolivia, is a gigantic form of Pan's-pipes. In this the tubes are of wood constructed like the pipes of an organ, and are from three to ten feet in length. As no one man could possibly expel enough air to operate all of these huge pipes, and as he could not move rapidly enough from one mouthpiece to another, the instrument is played by four or more Indians, each playing one or two of the pipes. The music produced is loud and penetrating but exceedingly sweet and mellow in tone.

The present-day Indians of the Peruvian and Bolivian highlands are born musicians, and it is seldom that a man or a boy is without his beloved *queña*. As they walk along, bending under their burdens; as they drive their llama trains; as they hurry toward some fiesta or dance, they continually play the plaintive, peculiar music of their Incan ancestors upon their Incan *queñas* or their Pan's-pipes. And wherever a boy or a man is tending the flocks of sheep, cattle, llamas or alpacas, the centuries-old airs of the Incans will be heard, filling the rarified mountain air with their melodies. Often, so bird-like are the notes, the stranger searches the stone-riddled fields and the barren hillsides for some unkown feathered songster, until he catches a glimpse of a brown-skinned mite wrapped in a tattered red poncho, and perched upon some outjutting rock overlooking the flocks and herds grazing upon the sparse dry herbage.

Much of the best-known and most popular Incan music has been rearranged to suit the piano and other conventional instruments, and has been published in Peru. In the following pages some of these are given, together with the Spanish versions of the songs. Among these are examples of love-songs, and several of the themes from the famous *Ollantay*.

Ollantay

YARAVI 1

Ollantay

KASHUA

344

Ollantay

YARAVI 2.

Ollantay

HUAYNO

Funerales de Atahualpa.

Cuando el Indio llora

Jazz- Camel.

SUSPIROS DEL CHANCHAMAYO
YARAVI

con sentimiento.   arr. por A. MILES DE MUZGO

A_mor_ci_to nue_vo qui_sie_ra ten_er, pe_ro no lo ten_go por no

pa_de_cer Soy pa_lo_ma tris_te que aprendo a volar don_de cierra la noche me pon go á llo_rar.

Chanchamayo de ja_ me pa sar mi_ra que tus chun_choe me van á fle char; Soy pa_

lo_ma triste que aprendo á volar don_de cierra la noche me pon go á lle_ rar.

HUAYNO

Ligeramente.

Mu cha-cha bo - ni ta lu - nar en la ca - ra Si eres sol-

te - ra dame tu a - mor; mu - cha-cha bo - ni - ta del lin-do lu - nar!...

Mas si hasdado a alguno tu vida y tu a - mor........ ve - te bien le - jos, lejos de

mi mu-chacha bo-ni-ta del lin-do lu-nar.....

An - da co-ra-zón por - fia - do. ten ver-güenza de que - rer....

á quien no te -co - rres - pon - de y se bur-la de tu a - mor.........

Co - ra-zon que no has a - ma - do

tu no sa bes el do - lor........ de un corazón des - ga - rra - do

por amarguras de a - mor...

BIBLIOGRAPHY

BIBLIOGRAPHY

AA, P. VAN DER. *La galerie agreable du monde* . . . *America.*
Vols. 63-66, Leyden, 1729.

ACOSTA, JOSEPH DE. SOC. J. *Historia natural y moral de las
Indias.* Madrid, 1608.

Album histórico civilización Nazca-Peru, Edad de Bronce.
Lima, 1921.

ALONSO DE SANTA CRUZ. *Islario general de todos las islas del
mundocon un prologo de D. Antonio Blazquez.*
Madrid, 1918.

ALVAREZ DE ABREU, A. J. *Victima real legal* . . . Madrid, 1769.

*Amazonas River. Relación del primer descubrimiento del Rio
de las Amazonas, por otro hombre, del Marañon
hecho por la Religión de neustro Padre San Francisco, por medio de los Religiosos de la Provincia de
S, Francisco de Quito.* Madrid, about 1642.

Annaes do XX Congreso Internacional de Americanistas.
Vol. I. Rio de Janeiro, 1924.

ANSON, G. *Voyage autour du monde.* Paris, 1764.

*Antiguedades Mexicanas. Publ. por la Junta Colombina de
México.* Mexico, 1892.

ARENAS, PEDRO. *Vocabulario manual de las lenguas Castel-
lana y Mexicana.* Los Angeles, 1793.

*Art precolombien. Poteries du Mexique du Costa Rica de la
Colombie et du Perou. Etoffes du Perou. Pierres
sculptees. Amulettes et bijoux.* Paris, 1927.

AVILA, FR. DE, del orden de S. Francisco. *Arte de la lengua
Mexicana.* Mexico, 1717.

BAESSLER, ARTHUR. *Ancient Peruvian Art.*

BANDELIER, AD. F. *Notes on the Bibliography of Yucatan,* etc.
Worcester (Mass.), 1881.

Baranda, J. *Recordaciones históricas*. Mexico, 1907.

Bardin, J. C. *Yucatan Develops a Truly American Art*. Bull. Pan Amer. Union. Washington, July, 1926.

Basalenque, Fr. D. *Historia de la provincia de San Nicolás de Michoacan*. Mexico, 1673.

Beisswanger, Konrad. *Am Lande der heiligen Seen. Reisbilder aus der Heimat der Chibcha Indianer*. Nuremberg, (no date).

Benzoni, H. *Novæ novi orbis historæ, id est, rerum ab Hispanis in India occidentali*. Geneva, 1600.

Berattelse, Kort. *Om Wast Indien eller America*. 1875.

Bernardino de Sahagun. *Historia de las Cosas de Nueva España*. Published for Mexican Government by Francisco del Paso y Troncoso.

Bertonio, P. Ludovico. *Vocabulario de la lengua Aymará*. Leipzig, 1879.

Arte de la lengua Aymará. Leipzig, 1879.

Beyer, Hermann. *Apuntes sobre el jeroglífico Maya-Ek "Negro."* Anales del Museo Nacional de Arqueológia. Mexico, 1925.

Apuntes sobre el jeroglífico Maya Muluc. Memoria y Revista de la Sociedad Científica Antonio Alzate. Mexico, 1926.

Las dos estelas Mayas de Chila Chis. El Mexico Antiguo. Mexico, 1926.

La inscripción del lintel 30 de Yaxchilan. Mexico, 1927.

La cifra diez en el simbolismo Maya. Revista Mexicana de Estudios Históricos. Mexico, 1927.

Dos fechas del palacio de Palenque. Mexico, 1927.

La cifra tres en el simbolismo Maya. Mexican Folkways. Mexico, 1927.

Bingham, Hiram. *Types of Machu-Picchu Pottery*. Amer. Anthropologist, N. S. Vol. 17, April-June, 1915.

Blom, Frans. *Notes from the Maya area*. Amer. Anthropologist, 1924.

Archeological and ethnographic expedition to Middle America, Tulane Univer., New Orleans, 1925.

BORDONE, BEN. *Isolario nel qual si ragiona di tutte le isole del mundo . . . copia delle lettere del prefetto della India alla Ces. Maesta rescritte* (the first account of Pizarro's arrival in Peru). Venice, 1537.

BOURKE, CAPT. JOHN G. *Scatalogic Rites of All Nations.* Washington, 1891.

BOWMAN, ISIAH. *The Andes of Southern Peru.* Amer. Geograph. Soc. New York, 1916.

Brasseur de Bourbourg, popol vuh. Le livre sacre et les mythes de l'antiquitie américaine. Paris, 1861.

BRINTON. *The Maya Chronicles.* Philadelphia, 1882.

BROWNELL, C. DE W. *Indian Races of North and South America.* New York, 1853.

BRY, TH. DE. *Great Voyages.* Part VI. Frankfort, 1594.

BUNKER, FRANK F. *The Art of the Mayas Revealed by Excavations at the Temple of the Warriors, Chichen-Itza, Yucatan.* Art and Archeology. Washington, 1927.

BURKITT, ROBT. A. *A Journey in Northern Guatemala.* Museum Journal. Philadelphia, 1924.

CALLEGARI, GUIDO V. *Copan la metropoli dei Maya, Scienza per Tutti.* Rome, 1925.

CAROCHI, H. *Compendio del arte de la lengua Mexicana.* Mexico, 1759.

Cartas de Indias. Publicadas por primera vez el ministerio de fomento. Madrid, 1877.

CASO, ALFONSO. *Las ruinas de Tizatlan.* Mexico, 1927.
El teocalli de la guerra sagrada. Mexico, 1927.

CASTELNAU, COMTE FRANCIS DE. *Expédition dans les parties centrales de l'Amerique du sud . . . de Lima et de Lima au Para.* Paris, 1850.

CASTILLO, BERNAL DIAZ DEL. *The True History of the Conquest of New Spain.* Translated by Alfred P. Maudsley.

CATHERWOOD, F. *Views of Ancient Monuments in Central America*. London, 1844.

CERVANTES DE SALAZAR, FRANCISCO. *Crónica de Nueva España escrita por Cronista de la Ciudad de Mexico,* etc. Madrid, 1914.

CHARNAY, D. *Les anciennes villes du noveau monde*. Paris 1885.

CIECA, DE LEÓN, PEDRO. *Parte primera de la crónica del Peru*. Seville, 1553.

CIECA, F. LOPEZ DE GOMARA. *Historia de Peru . . . y conquista de Yucatan*. Venice, 1560-99.

Codex Borbonicua (facsimile). *Avec un commentaire explicatif par E. T. Hamy*. Paris, 1889.

Codex Borgia (facsimile). Rome, 1898.

Codex Fejervary, Mayer. *Seler, E. elucidations of*. Berlin, London and Paris, 1901-02.

Codex Magliabecchiano XIII (facsimile). Rome, 1904.

Codex Nuttall (facsimile). Cambridge, Mass., 1902.

Codex Osuna (facsimile). Madrid, 1878.

Codex Peresianus (facsimile). Paris, 1888.

Codice Kingsborough (facsimile). Madrid, 1912.

Codice Maya (Cortesiano). Museo arqueolog. nacional, Madrid.

Codice Mendoza (facsimile). Mexico, 1925.

Colección de documentos ineditos relat. al descubrimiento, conquista y colonización de las posesiones España en America, sac del Real Archivo de Indias. Madrid, 1864.

Colombia prima or South America. London, 1807.

COLUMBUS, CHRISTOPHER. *Letter of Columbus to Rafael Sanchez*. Published in Barcelona, May, 1493.

COOK, HAROLD J. *Glacial-Age Man in New Mexico*. Scientific American. New York, July, 1928.

CORLETT, DUDLEY S. *The Art of the Mayas*. Art and Archeology. Washington, 1924.

CORONELLI, V. *Ordinum religiosorum in ecclesia militanti . . . Eques dictus Auricularis in Peruano*. Venice, 1715.

CORTES, HERNANDO. *Historia de Nueva España.* Mexico, 1770.

Costumes of America. Paris, 1780.

DAMIANUS, J. S. J. *Synopsis primi sæculi Soc. Jesu.* 1641.

DE LA CARRERA, FERNANDO. *Arte de la lengua Yunga.* 1644. Reprint, Univ. San Marcos. Lima, Peru, 1920.

DELAFIELD, J. *An Inquiry into the Origin of the Antiquities of America.* New York, 1839.

DIAZ DEL CASTELLIO, B. *Historia verdadera de la conquista de la Nueva España.* Madrid, 1632.

DIEGO LOPEZ DE COGOLLUDO. *Historia de Yucatan.* Merida, 1867.

DIESELDORFF, E. P. *Kunst und Religion der Mayavolker im alten und heutigen Mitelamerika.* Berlin, 1926.

DOMENECH, MANUEL. *Mexico tal cual es . . . obra escrita en Frances por Manuel Domenech.* Queretaro, 1922.

DURAND, JUAN E. *Leyendas Incaicas.* Antofagasta, Chile, 1923.

EMERSON, E. R. *Indian Myths.* Boston, 1884.

ESTABROOK, E. F. *The Pueblo Indians.* Santa Fé, 1927.

FANCOURT, CHARLES ST. JOHN. *The History of Yucatan from Its Discovery to the Close of the Seventeenth Century.* London, 1854.

FARABEE, WILLIAM CURTIS. *Indian Tribes of Eastern Peru.* Peabody Museum of American Archeology and Ethnology. Cambridge, 1922.

FERNÁNDEZ DE NAVARRETE. *Colección de los viages y descubrimientes que hicieron por mar los Españoles.* Madrid, 1829.

FERNÁNDEZ, MIGUEL A. *El Templo de los Tigres, Chichen-Itza.* Ethnos. Mexico, 1925.
El juego de pelota de Chichen-Itza, Yucatan. Anales del Museo Nacional de Arqueología. Mexico, 1925.

FEWKES, J. WALTER. *The Katcina Altars in Hopi Worship.* Washington, 1927.

FIELD, HENRY. *The early history of man with special reference to the Cap-Blanc Skeleton.* Field Mus. Nat. Hist. Chicago, 1927.

FOSTER, J. W. *Prehistoric Races of the United States of America.* Chicago, 1874.

FREJES, FR. FRANCISCO. *Historia breve de la conquista de los estados independentes del imperio Mexicano.* Guadelajara, 1878.

FREZIER, A. F. *Reis-Beschryving door de Zuid-Zee langs de kusten van Chili, Peru en Brazil.* Amsterdam, 1718.

GAGE, TH. *Nouvelle relation contenant les voyages dans la Nouvelle Espagne.* Amsterdam, 1721.

GAMIO, MANUEL. *Las excavaciones del Pedregal de San Angel y la cultura arcaica del valle de México.* Lancaster, Pa., 1920.
Cultural Evolution in Guatemala. Art and Archeology. Washington, 1926-27.
La población del valle de Teotihuacan . . . su evolución etnica y social. Mexico, 1922.

GANN, THOMAS. *In an Unknown land.* New York, 1924.
Mystery Cities. Explorations and adventures in Lubaantum. New York, 1925.
Maya Jades. Proceedings Twenty-first Intern. Congress of Americanists. Göttenborg, 1925.
The problem of America's Oldest Civilization; Lubaantum. Illus. London News. October, 1925.
Ancient Cities and Modern Tribes. New York, 1926.
A New Maya Stela with Initial series date. Man. London, 1926.
Slowly the Past Emerges. Scientific American. New York, June, 1928.

GARCIA, CUBAS A. *Atlas pintorescó e histórico de los E. U. México.* Mexico, 1885.

GARCIA, GR. *Origen de los Indios del Nuevo Mundo.* Madrid, 1729.

GARCILASSO DE LA VEGA. *Histoire des Yncas, rois du Perou.* Amsterdam, 1737.

GASTELU, ANT. VASQ. *Arte de la lengua Mexicana.* Los Angeles, 1726.

GATES, WILLIAM E. *El sistema de cronología Azteca,* Point Loma, Cal., 1913.
　　Linguistic Concepts in Prehistoric America. Point Loma, Cal., 1913.

GAYTON, A. H. *The Uhle Collections from Nieveria.* Univ. Cal. Pub. Vol. 21, No. 8. Berkeley, 1927.

GAYTON AND KROEBER, A. L. *The Uhle Pottery Collections from Nazca.* Berkeley, 1927.

Gazzettiere Americano. Livorno, 1763.

GILBERTI, MAT. *Arte de la lengua Tarasca o de Michoacan.* Mexico, 1558.
　　Diccionario de la lengua Tarasca. Mexico, 1559.

GOMEZ, ROBELO RICARDO. *El significado esotérico de algunas símboles Nahuas.* Mexico, 1925.

GOODRICH, SAMUEL G. *History of the Indians of North and South America.* Boston, 1856.

GORDON, G. B. *Examples of Maya Pottery in the Museum of the University of Pennsylvania, etc.* Philadelphia, 1925.

GORDON, THOMAS F. *The History of Ancient Mexico.* Philadelphia, 1832.

Guia para visitar la ciudad arqueológica de Teotihuacan. México 1927.

GUZMAN, D. J. *Interpretación de la escritura hierática de Centro America. Estudio sobre el sistema gráfico de la lengua Maya.* Boletén de la Academia Salvadoreña. San Salvador, 1925.

HAKLUYT, RICHARD. *The Principal Navigations, Voyages, etc. of the English Nation.* London, 1927.

HAMY, E. T. *Galerie Américaine du Trocadero.* Paris, 1897.

HARCOURT, R. et M.d'. *La céramique ancienne du Perou.* Paris, 1924.

Harrisse. *Biblioteca Americana Vetustissima.*

Hartman, C. V. *Archeological investigations in Costa Rica.* Stockholm, 1901.

Helps, Arthur. *The Spanish Conquest in America.* London, 1855.

Herrera, A. de. *Descripción de las Indias occidentales.* Madrid, 1601.

Herrera, Moises. *Las representaciones zoomorfas en el arte antiguo Mexicano.* Mexico, 1925.

Esculturas zoomorfas y fitomorfas de Tlotihuacan. Mexico, 1919.

Historia de las Indias. Madrid, 1875-76.

Hodge, F. W. *The Six Cities of Cibola 1581-1680.* Santa Fé, 1926.

Hoffman, Frederick L. *Mexico's pre-Colombian Remains.* Bull. Pan American Union. Washington, 1927.

Holton, Isaac F. *New Granada: Twenty Months in the Andes.* New York, 1857.

Hoornbeck, J. *De Conversione Indorum et Gentilium libri duo.* Waesberge, 1669.

Horn, G. *De originibus Americanis,* Book IV. Hague, 1652.

Hrdlicka, *Anthropological Work in Peru in 1913.* Smithsonian Misc. Collections. Washington, 1914.

Humboldt, Alex. von. *Historische Hieroglyphen der Aztecken, im Jahr 1803, im Konigreich Neu Spanien.*

Humboldt, A. de, et A. Bonpland. *Voyage aux régions équinoxiales du nouveau continent.* Paris, 1807.
Vues des Cordilléres et monuments des peuples indigénes. Paris, 1810.

Imbelloni, Jose. *Deformaciones intencionales de cráneo en Sud América.* Buenos Aires, 1925.

Ingersoll, Ernest. *Colorado Antiquities. Discovery of Ancient Stone Houses and Remains of Indian Life.* New York Tribune, November 3, 1874.

Irving, Washington. *The Life and Voyages of Christopher Columbus.* New York, 1892.

IZCUE, ELENA. *El arte Peruano en la escuela.* Paris, 1926.

JESKE, JOHN A. *The Grand River Mound Group and Campsite.* Bull. Pub. Mus. Milwaukee. Milwaukee, 1927.

JOYCE, THOMAS A. *An Example of Cast Gold Work from Palenque.* Proceed. of the Twenty-first Intern. Congress of Americanists. The Hague, 1924-25.
The Paccha of Ancient Peru. Journ. Royal Anthr. Inst. London, 1922.
The Hieroglyphic Stairway at Naranjo, Guatemala. Ibid, 1925.
South American Archeology. New York, 1912.
Report on the Investigations at Lubaantum. British Museum Quarterly. London, 1927.
Maya and Mexican Art. London, 1927.

JUDD, NEIL M. *Middle American Expedition of the Archeological Society.* Art and Archeology. Washington, 1927.

KARSTEN, RAFAEL. *The Civilization of the South American Indians with Special Reference to Magic and Religion.* New York, 1926.

KINGSBOROUGH, LORD. *Antiquities of Mexico.* London, 1830.

KREICHGAUER, DAM. *Anschluss der Maya Chronologie an die Julianische.* Anthropos. St. Gabriel Modeling bei Vienna, 1927.

KROEBER, A. L. *Archeological Explorations in Peru.* Part I. *Ancient Pottery from Trujillo.* Field Mus. of Nat. Hist. Vol. II, No. I. Chicago, 1926.
The Uhle Pottery Collections from Chancay. Univ. of Cal. Publ. in Amer. Arch. and Ethn. Berkeley, 1926.

LA CONDAMINE, C. M. *Relation abrégée d'un voyage fait dans l'interieur de l' Amerique méridionale.* Paris, 1745.
Augm de la relation de l'émeute populaire de Cuenca au Perou, etc. Frankfort, 1779.

LARDE, JORGE. *Arqueología Cuzcatleca.* Contrib. al III Congreso Cientifico Panamericana. San Salvador, 1924.

Cronología arqueológica de el Salvador. Revista de Etnología Arqueológía y Linguística. San Salvador, 1926.

Las Casas, B. de. *Relation des voyages et des découvertes que les Espagnoles ont fait dans les Indes occidentales.* Amsterdam, 1698.

Las Casas, Fr. Bartólome. *Bartólome Las Casas. Collección de tratados 1552-1553.* Buenos Aires, 1924.

Ledon, Luis Castillo. *La fundación de la Ciudad de México; 1325-1925.* Mexico, 1925.

Lehmann-Nitsche, Roberto. *Mitologia sudamericana XII, La astronomía de los Mocovi.* Buenos Aires, 1927.

Lehmann, W. U. H. Doering. *Kunstgeschichte d. alten Peru.* Berlin, 1924.

Leighton, Morris M. *The Cahokia (Ill.) Mounds.* Univ. Ill. Urbana, 1923.

León, Nicolás. *Los Tarascos.* Mexico, 1904.

Lindblom, K. C. *The Use of Stilts, Especially in Africa and America.* Stockholm, 1927.

Linne, Sigvald. *The Technique of South American Ceramics.* Göttenborg, 1925.

Locke, L. Leland. *A Peruvian Quipu;* Contr. Mus. Amer. Indian, Heye Found., Vol. VII, No. 5. New York, 1927.

Long, Richard C. E. *Some Maya Time Periods.* Proceed. Twenty-first Intern. Congress of Americanists. Göttenborg, 1925.

A link between the Earlier and Later Maya Chronologies. Man. London, 1924.

Lothrop, Samuel K. *Tulum, an Archeological Study of the East Coast of Yucatan.* Carnegie Institution. Washington, 1924.

The Museum's Central American Expedition. Indian Notes. Mus. Am. Indian, Heye Found., New York, Jan. 1925.

Pottery of Costa Rica and Nicaragua. Contr. Museum of Am. Indian, Heye Found. New York, 1926.

Stone Sculptures from Finca Arevalo, Guatemala. Indian Notes. July, 1926.

LUCAS, FRED. W. *Apendiculæ Historicæ.* London, 1891.

LUNA, CARLOS. *Apuntes sobre arqueología nacional.* Sociedad de Geografía y Historia de Guatemala, 1925.

MADISON, HAROLD L. *Mound Builders.* Cleveland Mus. Nat. Hist. Cleveland, 1925.

MARTYR, P. 1533.

MASON, GREGORY. *The Shrines of a Vanished Race.* World's Work. New York, November, 1926.

Silver Cities of Yucatan. New York, 1927.

Rebuilding America's Sacred City. Popular Mechanics Magazine. New York, April, 1927.

MASON, J. ALDEN. *Native American Jades.* Mus. Journ. Philadelphia, March, 1927.

Mirrors of Ancient America. Ibid. June, 1927.

Use of Tobacco in Mexico and South America. Field Mus. of Natl. Hist. Chicago, 1924.

MAUDSLEY. *The True History of New Spain.* Hakluyt Society. London, 1908.

MAYA. *Maya architecture.* Bull. Pan Amer. Union. Washington, August, 1926.

MAYA. *Handschrift, Die, der & Kgl. offebtl, Bibliothek zu Dresden.* Dresden, 1892.

McBRIDE, GEORGE McCUTCHEN. *The Agrarian Indian Communities of Highland Bolivia.* Amer. Geogr. Soc. Research. New York, 1921.

MEAD, CHARLES W. *Peruvian Art, as Shown on Textiles and Pottery.* Am. Mus. Nat. Hist. New York, 1925.

MEBA, RAMON. *Arqueología; Monolitos.* Mexico, 1924.

MENDIZABAL, MIGUEL O. DE. *El Lienzo de Jucutacato. Su verdadera significación.* Mexico (Museo Nacional) 1926.

MEXICO. *Museo Nacional de Arqueologia, Historia y Etnografía.* Album de colecciones arqueológicas arregladas por Franz Boas. Mexico, 1921.
Opiniones y juicios críticis sobre la obra La población del valle de Teotihuacan, etc. Tacubaya, 1924.
Informe general de los trabajos, realizados de septiembre de 1925 a augusto de 1926. Mexico, 1926.

MICHENER, CARROLL K. *Heirs of the Incas.* New York, 1924.

MOOREHEAD, WARREN K. *Exploration of the Etowah Mound.* Philips Acad. Andover, 1925.
Fort Ancient; the Great Prehistoric Earthwork of Warren County, Ohio. Andover, 1908.
The Origin and Development of the Pueblo Cliff Dweller Culture. 1920.

MOREDA, JOSE DE. *Relación histórica y cronológica de las Compañias Coloniales para Indias occidentales.* Cartagena (Colombia), 1764.

MORICONI, UMBALDO A. *Da Genova ai deserti dei Mayas.* Bergamo, 1902.

MORLEY, SYLVANUS G. *The Earliest Mayan Dates.* Proceed. Twenty-first Intern. Congress of Americanists. Göttenborg, 1924.
Chichen-Itza, an Ancient American Mecca. Nat. Geographic Magazine. Washington, January, 1925.
New Light on the Discovery of Yucatan and the Foundation of the New Maya Empire. Am. Journal of Archeology. Concord, N. H., 1927.

MORSS, NOEL. *Archeological explorations on the middle Chinlee (Arizona)* Mem. Amer. Anthr. Asso. Menasha, Wis., 1927.

MOSSI, H. *Diccionario Quichua-Castellano y Castellano-Quichua.* Sucre, 1860.
Gramática de la lengua general del Peru (Quichua). Sucre, 1856.
Gramática del idioma Quichua. Sucre, 1860.

Mound Builders. The Greatest Monument of Prehistoric Man; Cahokia or Monks Mound. East St. Louis, Ill. (no date).

MUSEUM OF AMERICAN INDIAN, HEYE FOUNDATION. *Indian Notes.* 1925-28.

NELSON, NELS C. *The Dune Dwellers of the Gobi Desert.* New York, 1926.
Prehistoric Man of Central China. New York, 1926.
Archeological Research in North China. Menasha, Wis., 1927.

NOGUERA, EDUARDO. *Los altares de sacrificio de Tizatlan.* Tlazcala, Mexico, 1927.

NOVELLA, GUSTAVO. *Clasificación del estilo Maya entre los demás estilos de arquitectura que se conocen.* Anales de la Sociedad de Geografía y Historia de Guatemala. Guatemala, June, 1925.

NUTTALL, ZELIA. *The Aztecs and Their Predecessors in the Valley of Mexico.* Philadelphia, 1926.

ORBIGNY, A. DE. *Voyage dans l'Amerique méridionale; Bresil, Uruguay, Argentine, Paragonie, Chile, Bolivia, Perou.* Paris, 1826.

ORDONEZ DE ZEVALLOS, P. *Historia y viage del mundo . . . a América.* Madrid, 1691.

OVIEDO Y VALDES, GONZALO FERNÁNDEZ DE. *La historia general de las Indias.* Seville, 1535.

PACHECO CRUZ, SANTIAGO. *La tumba del tesoro. Leyenda Yucateca escrita en el ingenio Dziuche por el Sr. J. Baltazar Perez. Vertida a la lengua Maya.* Merida, 1913.

PALACIOS, ENRIQUE JUAN. *Interpretaciones de la piedra del calendario.* Mexico, 1924.

PALACIOS, ENRIQUE JUAN. *La piedra del Escudo Nacional de México.* Mexico, 1927.
Informe mensual al C. Director de Arqueología. Boletín de la Secretaria de Educación Pública. Mexico.

PALEVECENO, ENRICO Y IMBELLONI, J. *Dos notas preliminares sobre la lengua Quechua.* Buenos Aires, 1926.

Pan American Union. *Summary of archeological work in the Americas in 1926.* Washington, 1927.

Pedrahita, Fern. L. *Historia general de la conquista del Nuevo Reyno de Grenada.* Hamburg, 1688.

Penafiel, A. *Teotihuacan. Estudio historía y arqueología.* Mexico, 1900.

Peralta, M. M. de. *Costa Rica, Nicaragua y Pánama en el siglo XVI.* Madrid, 1883.

Perez, Franc, ord. S. Aug. *Lengua Otomi.* Mexico, 1834.
M. *Arte de el idioma Mexicano.* Mexico, 1713.

Pinda, Juan de. *Anales de la Soc. de Geogr. y Hist. de Guatemala.* 1925.

Poeppig, A. *Atlas zur Reise in Chile, Peru und dem Amazonenstrom. 1828.* Leipzig, 1835.

Popenhoe, Wilson and Dorothy. *Quirigua, an Ancient City of the Mayas.* Unifruitco Magazine. May, 1927.

Pottery of Costa Rica and Nicaragua, Contributions from the Museum of the Amer. Indian, Heye Found. Vol. VIII.

Prescott, William H. *The Conquest of Peru.*
The Conquest of Mexico.

Quintana, A. de. *Arte de la lengua Mixe.* Mexico, 1733.

Ragguaglio D'alcune missioni dell' Indie Occidentali. Rome, 1592.

Raveneau de Lussan. *Journal du voyage fait à la mer du Sud avec les flibustiers . . . en 1684.* Paris, 1690.

Relacao. *Individual e verdadeira da extrema ruina, que padeceo a cidade dos reys Lima.* Lisbon, 1747.

Revista de Costa Rica. San Jose, 1919-25.

Reygadas Vertiz, Jose. *Ruinas de Zayi.* Anales del Museo Nacional de Arqueología. Mexico, 1925 (April-June).

Ricketson, Edith B. *Sixteen Carved Panels from Chichen-Itza.* Art and Archeology. Washington, 1927.

RICKETSON, OLIVER G. *Burials in the Maya Area.* Amer. Anthropologist. July, 1925.

A "Greenwich Observatory" of Prehistoric America. Illus. London News. London, November 20, 1926.

RIVET, PAUL. *Le peuplement de l'Amérique precolombienne.* Milan, 1926.

Les Malayo-Polynesiens en Amérique. Paris, 1926.

Les origines de l'homme Américain. Paris, 1925.

Les éléments constitutifs des civilisations du Nord Ouest et de l'Ouest Sud-Américain. Göttenborg, 1925.

Les Australiens en Amerique. Paris, 1925.

Le groupe oceanien. Paris, 1927.

ROCHA, D. A. *Carta al Excmo. Señor Don Baltasar de la Cueva.* Lima, 1675.

ROCK, FRITZ. *Ein mythisch-religioses Motiv der alten Mayakunst.* Proceed Twenty-first Intern. Congress of Americanists. Göttenborg, 1924.

ROGERS, W. *Nieuwe reize naa de Zuidsee.* Amsterdam, 1715.

SAFFORD, WILLIAM E. *An Aztec Narcotic.* Washington, 1915.

Food Plants and Textiles of Ancient America. Washington, 1917.

Chenopodium Nuttalliæ, a Food Plant of the Aztecs. Washington.

The Isolation of Ancient America as Established by the Cultivated Plants and the Languages of its Aborigines. Rio de Janeiro, 1924.

Foods Discovered with America. Garrison, N. Y., 1925.

SAHAGUN, FRAY BERN. DE O. S. F. *Historia general de las cosas de Nueva España.* Mexico, 1829.

SALAZAR Y OLARTE, J. DE. *Historia de la conquista de México.* Cordoba, 1743.

SAUR, A. *Statte-Buch.* Frankfort, 1658.

SAVILLE, MARSHALL H. *The Manabi Culture.* Contrib. Mus. Amer. Indian, Heye Foundation. New York.

Turquoise Mosiac Art in Ancient Mexico. Contribution from Mus. Amer. Indian, Heye Found. New York, 1922.

Mayan Sculpture from Guatemala. Indian Notes, Mus. Amer. Indian, Heye Found. New York, April, 1924.

The Wood-Carver's Art in Ancient Mexico. Contributions from Mus. of Amer. Indian, Heye Found. New York, 1925.

SCHELLBACH, DON LOUIS III. *Nevada's Ancient Civilization.* March, 1926.

SCHULLER, RUDOLPH. *The Native Country of the Maya-K'ice Indians.* Amer. Anthropologist. April-June, 1927.

SELER, EDOUARD. *Die mexikanischen Bilderhandscriften.* Berlin, 1893.

Peruanische Alterthumer. Berlin, 1893.

SHETRONE, H. C. *Exploration of the Hopewell Group of Mounds.* Columbus, Ohio, State Archeol. and Hist. Soc. 1926.

SIMOENS DA SILVA, ANTONIO CARLOS. *L'os des Incas dans la prehistorie du Brasil.* Rio de Janeiro, 1926.

O continente Americano propulsor de paz. Rio de Janeiro, 1926.

SOLIS, A. DE. *Istoria della conquista del Messico.* Venice, 1733.

SOLIS ALCALA, EMILIO AND SOLIS MENDIBURU, ERMILIO. *Los ahau-katunes del manuscripto-de Mani.* Merida, Yucatan, 1925.

SOTOMAYOR, DAMASO. *La conquista de México efectuada por Hernan Cortes segun el códice jeroglífico Troano-Americano.* Edición especial. Mexico, 1897.

El siglo jeroglífico Azteca en sus 52 calendarios. Mexico, 1897.

SPENCE, LEWIS. *The Popul Vuh.*

A Dictionary of Mythology.

Atlantis in America. New York, 1925.

The Problem of Atlantis. New York, 1924.

The Myths of Mexico and Peru. London, 1920.

Mythologies of Ancient Mexico and Peru.
The Civilization of Ancient Mexico. New York,
1912.

SPINDEN, HERBERT J. *The Reduction of Maya dates.* Papers
of Peabody Mus. of Amer. Arch. and Ethnol.
Cambridge, 1924.

SQUIER, E. G. *Nicaragua, Its People, Scenery, Monuments,
etc.* New York, 1860.

STAHL, F. A. *In the Land of the Incas.* Mountain View, Cal.
1920.

STARR, F. *Indians of Southern Mexico.* Chicago, 1899.

STOCKLEIN, JOS. Soc. J. *Der Neuw Welt-Bott.* Augsburg,
1726.

STRUBE, LEÓN. *Arte rupestre en Sudamérica . . . los
petroglifos de la Provincia de Coquimbo.* Chile, 1926.

STUBEL, A. UND M. UHLE. *Die Ruinstatte von Tiahuanaco.*
Breslau, 1892.

SUNDSTROM, S. *Diss. du statu regiminis Americanorum ante
adventum Christianorum.* Upsalae, 1716.

SUSTO, JUAN ANTONIO. *Pánama en el archivo general de
Indias.* Panama, 1927.

SVEDELIUS, J. M. ET G. SVEDELIUS. *De effectu detecæ Amer-
icæ in Europam.* 1802.

TAPIA, ZENTENO, C. DE. *Arte novissima de la lengua Mexicana.* Mexico, 1733.

Tarich Ul-Hind Ul-Gharbi. (A new history of the West Indies)
Stamboul, 1729.

TEEPLE, JOHN E. *Maya Inscriptions.* Amer. Anthropologist. January-March, 1925.

Maya Inscriptions; the Venus Calendar, etc. Ibid.
April-June, 1926.

THOMAS, C. *A Study of the Manuscript Troano.* Washington, 1882.

THOMPSON, J. ERIC. *The Meaning of the Mayan Months.*
Man. London, 1925.

The Correlation of the Mayan and European Calendars. Field Mus. Nat. Hist. Anthropol. Series. Chicago, 1927.

The Civilization of the Mayas. Field Mus. Nat. Hist. Chicago, 1927

TIRION, J. *Nieuwe en beknopte handatlas.* Amsterdam, 1769.

Tonalamati, Das, der Aubin'schen Sammlung. Altmexicanische Bilderhandschrift. Berlin, 1900.

TORO, ALFONSO. *Compendio de historia de México, Historia antigua desde los tiempos mas remotos hasta antes de la llegada de los Españoles.* Mexico, 1926.

TORRES BOLLO, DIEGO DE. *Relation breve. Procuratore del la Prov. del Peru, circa il frutto chesi raccoglie con gli Indiani di quel regno.* Rome, 1603.

TOWNSEND, MARTIN BINGHAM. *Prehistoric Structures of Yucatan.* Troy, N. Y., 1900.

TOZZER, A. M. *Time and American Archeology.* Natural History. New York. May-June, 1927.
Chronological Aspects of American Archeology. Proc. Mass. Hist. Soc. Boston, April, 1926.

TRIANA, MIGUEL. *Petroglifos de la mesa central de Colombia.* Bogota, 1924.

Tribes and Temples. A record of the expedition to middle America conducted by the Tulane University of Louisiana in 1925. New Orleans, 1926.

UHLE, MAX. *Los elementos constitutivos de las civilizaciones Andinas.* Quito, 1926.

UHLE, *Zur Chronologie der alten Culturen von Ica;* Journal de la Societe des Americanistes de Paris, 1913.

ULLOA, A. DE Y JORGE JUAN. *Relación histórica del viaje a la América Meridional.* Madrid, 1748.
Histoire des Yncas du Perou. Amsterdam, 1752.

ULLOA, ALF. *Commentarii della guerra che il duca d'Alva ha fatto contra Guglielmo . . . 1568.* Venice, 1570·

ULLOA, ANT. DE. *Noticias Americanas.* Madrid, 1772.

VAN DEN BERGH, HENRY. *The Incas and Their Industries* London, New York, 1921.

Vocabulario Castellano-Zapoteco. Mexico, 1893.

WAFER, LIONEL. *A New Voyage and Description of the Isthmus of America.* London, 1699.

WAITZ, TH. *Anthropologie der Natur-Volker.* Leipzig, 1860.

WATERMAN, T. T. *The Architecture of the American Indian.* Amer. Anthropologist. April-June, 1927.

WILLARD, T. A. *The City of the Sacred Well.* New York, 1926.

WILSON, ROBERT W. *Astronomical Notes on the Maya Codices.* Papers of Peabody Mus. of Arch. and Ethnol. Cambridge, 1924.

WISSLER, CLARK. *The Relation of Nature to Man in Aboriginal America.* New York, 1926.

WHYMPER, EDW. *Travels amongst the Great Andes.* New York, 1892.

INDEX

INDEX